# ICCGI 2016

The Eleventh International Multi-Conference on Computing in the Global Information Technology

November 13 - 17, 2016

Barcelona, Spain

**ICCGI 2016 Editors**

Carla Merkle Westphall, University of Santa Catarina, Brazil

Kendall Nygard, North Dakota State University, USA

Elena Ravve, Ort-Braude College - Karmiel, Israel

**Printed from e-media with permission by:**

Curran Associates, Inc.
57 Morehouse Lane
Red Hook, NY 12571

**Some format issues inherent in the e-media version may also appear in this print version.**



Printed by Curran Associates, Inc. (2016)

International Academy, Research, and Industry Association (IARIA)
412 Derby Way
Wilmington, DE 19810

Phone: (408) 893-6407
Fax: (408) 527-6351

petre@iaria.org

**Additional copies of this publication are available from:**

Curran Associates, Inc.
57 Morehouse Lane
Red Hook, NY 12571 USA
Phone: 845-758-0400
Fax: 845-758-2633
Email: curran@proceedings.com
Web: www.proceedings.com

**Table of Contents**

# ICCGI 2016

## Foreword

The Eleventh International Multi-Conference on Computing in the Global Information Technology (ICCGI 2016), held between November 13-17, 2016 - Barcelona, Spain, continued a series of international events covering a large spectrum of topics related to global knowledge concerning computation, technologies, mechanisms, cognitive patterns, thinking, communications, user-centric approaches, nanotechnologies, and advanced networking and systems. The conference topics focus on challenging aspects in the next generation of information technology and communications related to the computing paradigms (mobile computing, database computing, GRID computing, multi-agent computing, autonomic computing, evolutionary computation) and communication and networking and telecommunications technologies (mobility, networking, bio-technologies, autonomous systems, image processing, Internet and web technologies), towards secure, self-defendable, autonomous, privacy-safe, and context-aware scalable systems.

This conference intended to expose the scientists to the latest developments covering a variety of complementary topics, aiming to enhance one's understanding of the overall picture of computing in the global information technology.

The integration and adoption of IPv6, also known as the Next Generation of the Internet Protocol, is happening throughout the World at this very moment. To maintain global competitiveness, governments are mandating, encouraging or actively supporting the adoption of IPv6 to prepare their respective economies for the future communication infrastructures. Business organizations are increasingly mindful of the IPv4 address space depletion and see within IPv6 a way to solve pressing technical problems while IPv6 technology continues to evolve beyond IPv4 capabilities. Communications equipment manufacturers and applications developers are actively integrating IPv6 in their products based on market demands.

IPv6 continues to represent a fertile area of technology innovation and investigation. IPv6 is opening the way to new successful research projects. Leading edge Internet Service Providers are guiding the way to a new kind of Internet where any-to-any reachability is not a vivid dream but a notion of reality in production IPv6 networks that have been commercially deployed. National Research and Educational Networks together with internationally known hardware vendors, Service Providers and commercial enterprises have generated a great amount of expertise in designing, deploying and operating IPv6 networks and services. This knowledge can be leveraged to accelerate the deployment of the protocol worldwide.

We take here the opportunity to warmly thank all the members of the ICCGI 2016 Technical Program Committee, as well as the numerous reviewers. The creation of such a high quality conference program would not have been possible without their involvement. We also kindly thank all the authors who dedicated much of their time and efforts to contribute to ICCGI 2016. We truly believe that, thanks to all these efforts, the final conference program consisted of top quality contributions.

Also, this event could not have been a reality without the support of many individuals, organizations, and sponsors. We are grateful to the members of the ICCGI 2016 organizing committee for their help in handling the logistics and for their work to make this professional meeting a success.

We hope that ICCGI 2016 was a successful international forum for the exchange of ideas and results between academia and industry and for the promotion of progress in the area of computing in the global information technology.

We are convinced that the participants found the event useful and communications very open. We also hope the attendees enjoyed the charm of Barcelona, Spain.

**ICCGI 2016 Chairs:**

**ICCGI Advisory Committee**

Constantin Paleologu, University Politehnica of Bucharest, Romania
Tibor Gyires, Illinois State University, USA
Luc Vouligny, Institut de Recherche d'Hydro-Québec - Varennes, Canada
John Terzakis, Intel, USA
Yasushi Kambayashi, Nippon Institute of Technology, Japan
Mirela Danubianu, "Stefan cel Mare" University of Suceava, Romania
Teemu Kanstrén, VTT Technical Research Centre of Finland, Finland
Mansour Zand, University of Nebraska, USA
Arno Leist, Massey University, New Zealand
Dominic Girardi, RISC Software GmbH, Austria

**ICCGI Special Area Chairs**

**Knowledge/Cognition**
Constandinos Mavromoustakis, University of Nicosia, Cyprus
Tadeusz Pankowski, Poznan University of Technology, Poland

**e-Learning/Mobility**
José Rouillard, Université Lille Nord, France

**Industrial Systems**
Beata Czarnacka-Chrobot, Warsaw School of Economics, Poland
Bernhard Freudenthaler, Software Competence Center Hagenberg GmbH, Austria

**ICCGI Publicity Chair**

Marek Opuszko, Friedrich-Schiller-University of Jena, Germany

# ICCGI 2016

## Committee

### ICCGI Advisory Committee

Constantin Paleologu, University Politehnica of Bucharest, Romania
Tibor Gyires, Illinois State University, USA
Luc Vouligny, Institut de Recherche d'Hydro-Québec - Varennes, Canada
John Terzakis, Intel, USA
Yasushi Kambayashi, Nippon Institute of Technology, Japan
Mirela Danubianu, "Stefan cel Mare" University of Suceava, Romania
Teemu Kanstrén, VTT Technical Research Centre of Finland, Finland
Mansour Zand, University of Nebraska, USA
Arno Leist, Massey University, New Zealand
Dominic Girardi, RISC Software GmbH, Austria

### ICCGI Special Area Chairs

**Knowledge/Cognition**
Constandinos Mavromoustakis, University of Nicosia, Cyprus
Tadeusz Pankowski, Poznan University of Technology, Poland

**e-Learning/Mobility**
José Rouillard, Université Lille Nord, France

**Industrial Systems**
Beata Czarnacka-Chrobot, Warsaw School of Economics, Poland
Bernhard Freudenthaler, Software Competence Center Hagenberg GmbH, Austria

### ICCGI Publicity Chair

Marek Opuszko, Friedrich-Schiller-University of Jena, Germany

### ICCGI 2016 Technical Program Committee

Pablo Adasme, Universidad de Santiago de Chile, Chile
El-Houssaine Aghezzaf, Gent University, Belgium
Johan Akerberg, ABB Corporate Research, Sweden
Nadine Akkari, King Abdulaziz University, Kingdom of Saudi Arabia
Konstantin Aksyonov, Ural Federal University, Russia
Areej Al-Wabil, King Saud University - Riyadh, Saudi Arabia
Cesar Alberto Collazos, Universidad del Cauca, Colombia
Cristina Alcaraz, University of Malaga, Spain

Jose M. Alcaraz Calero, University of the West of Scotland, UK
Panos Alexopoulos, iSOCO S.A. - Madrid, Spain
Ali Alharbi, The University of Newcastle, Australia
Fernando Almeida, University of Porto, Portugal
Hala Mohammed Alshamlan, King Saud University, Saudi Arabia
Mohammad Alshamri, King Khalid University, Saudi Arabia
José Enrique Armendáriz-Iñigo, Universidad Pública de Navarra, Spain
Stanislaw Ambroszkiewicz, Institute of Computer Science Polish Academy of Sciences, Poland
Christos Anagnostopoulos, Ionian University, Greece
Plamen Angelov, Lancaster University, UK
Anna Antonova, Ural Federal University, Russia
Josep Arnal Garcia, Universidad de Alicante, Span
Ezendu Ariwa, London Metropolitan University, UK
Kamran Arshad, University of Greenwich, UK
Mustafa Atay, Winston-Salem State University, USA
Ali Meftah Bakeer, University of Gloucestershire, UK
Ali Barati, Dezful Branch - Islamic Azad University, Iran
Iman Barjasteh, Michigan State University, USA
Reza Barkhi, Virginia Tech - Blacksburg, USA
Carlos Becker Westphall, Universidade Federal de Santa Catarina, Brazil
Hatem Ben Sta, University of Tunis, Tunisia
Jorge Bernardino, Institute Polytechnic of Coimbra - ISEC, Portugal
Robert Bestak, Czech Technical University in Prague, Czech Republic
Ateet Bhalla, Independent Consultant, India
Fernando Bobillo, University of Zaragoza, Spain
Mihai Boicu, George Mason University - Fairfax, USA
Eugen Borcoci, University 'Politehnica' of Bucharest, Romania
Claudio Borean, Telecom Italia, Italy
Djamila Boukredera, University of Bejaia, Algeria
Jean-Louis Boulanger, Independent Safety Assessor, France
José Braga de Vasconcelos, Universidade Atlântica, Portugal
Daniela Briola, University of Genoa, Italy
Francesco Buccafurri, University "Mediterranea" of Reggio Calabri, Italy
Luigi Buglione, Engineering.IT SpA, Italy
Xiaoqiang Cai, The Chinese University of Hong Kong, Hong Kong
Ani Calinescu, Oxford University, UK
George Caridakis, University of the Aegean / National Technical University of Athens, Greece
Laura Carnevali, University of Florence, Italy
Cheng-Yuan Chang, National United University, Taiwan
Maiga Chang, Athabasca University, Canada
Ankit Chaudhary, MUM, USA
Savvas A. Chatzichristofis, Democritus University of Thrace, Greece
Chi-Hua Chen, National Chiao Tung University - Taiwan, R.O.C.
Tzung-Shi Chen, National University of Tainan, Taiwan
Wen-Shiung Chen (陳文雄), National Chi Nan University, Taiwan
Zhixiong Chen, School of Liberal Arts, Mercy College - Dobbs Ferry, USA
Albert M. K. Cheng, University of Houston, USA
Amar Ramdane Cherif, University of Versailles, France

Jana Varnušková, University of West Bohemia, Pilsen, Czech Republic
Hani Hamdan, CentraleSupélec (École Centrale de Paris and École Supérieure d'Électricité), France
Seung-Hoon Han, Chonnam National University, South Korea
Petr Hanácek, Brno University of Technology, Czech Republic
Fei Hao, Shanxi Agricultural University, China
Sven Hartmann, TU-Clausthal, Germany
Mohammad Mehedi Hassan, King Saud University, Kingdom of Saudi Arabia
Bing He, Cisco System, Inc., USA
Wladyslaw Homenda, Warsaw University of Technology, Poland
Samuelson Hong, Management School - Hangzhou Dianzi University, China
Jun Hu, Eindhoven University of Technology, The Netherlands
Yo-Ping Huang, National Taipei University of Technology, Taiwan
Tee Sim Hui, Multimedia University, Malaysia
Rosziati Ibrahim, Universiti Tun Hussein Onn Malaysia (UTHM), Malaysia
Larisa Ismailova, National Research Nuclear University "MEPhI" - Moscow, Russia
Kyoko Iwasawa, Takushoku University - Tokyo Japan
Helge Janicke, De Montfort University, UK
Mehrshid Javanbakht, Azad University - Tehran, Iran
Wassim Jaziri, Taibah University, KSA
Guorui Jiang, Beijing University of Technology, China
Maria João Ferreira, Universidade Portucalense, Portugal
Paul Johannesson, Royal Institute of Technology - Stockholm, Sweden
Matjaz B. Juric, University of Ljubljana, Slovenia
Imed Kacem, Université de Lorraine, France
Hermann Kaindl, TU-Wien, Austria
György Kálmán, ABB Corporate Research, Norway
Yasushi Kambayashi, Nippon Institute of Technology, Japan
Georgios Kambourakis, University of the Aegean - Samos, Greece
Keiichi Kaneko, Tokyo University of Agriculture and Technology, Japan
Dimitris Kanellopoulos, University of Patras, Greece
Dimitris Karagiannis, University of Vienna, Austria
Randi Karlsen, University of Tromsø, Norway
Andrzej Kasprzak, Politechnika Wrocławska, Poland
Peter Kieseberg, SBA Research, Austria
Byoung Uk Kim, US Air Force Research Laboratory, USA
Marite Kirikova, Riga Technical University, Latvia
Georgios Kioumourtzis, Center for Security Studies, Greece
Wojciech Kmiecik, Wroclaw University of Technology, Poland
Mehmet Koc, Bilecik Seyh Edebali University, Turkey
Leszek Koszalka , Wroclaw University of Technology, Poland
Janet L. Kourik, Webster University - St Louis, USA
Piotr A. Kowalski, SRI Polish Academy of Sciences and Cracow University of Technology, Poland
Dieter Kranzlmüller, Ludwig-Maximilians University of Munich, Germany
Bartosz Krawczyk, Wroclaw University of Technology, Poland
Jakub Kroustek, Brno University of Technology, Czech Republic
Panos Kudumakis, Queen Mary University of London, UK
Mariusz Łapczyński, Cracow University of Economics, Poland
Robert Law, Glasgow Caledonian University, UK

Hichem Omrani, CEPS/INSTEAD, Luxembourg
Chung-Ming Ou, Kainan University, Taiwan
Constantin Paleologu, University Politehnica of Bucharest, Romania
Thanasis Papaioannou, Center for Research and Technology Hellas (CERTH), Greece
Marcin Paprzycki, Systems Research Institute / Polish Academy of Sciences - Warsaw, Poland
Tadeusz Pankowski, Poznan University of Technology, Poland
Mukaddim Pathan, Telstra Corporation Limited, Australia
Al-Sakib Khan Pathan, UAP and SEU, Bangladesh/ Islamic University in Madinah, KSA
Kunal Patel, Ingenuity Systems, USA
Jose J. Pazos Arias, Universidad Vigo, Spain
Bernhard Peischl, Technische Universität Graz, Austria
José Pelegrí Sebastiá, Universitat Politècnica de València, Spain
Marek Penhaker, VSB - Technical University of Ostrava, Czech Republic
Andrea Perego, European Commission - Joint Research Centre, Italy
Fernando Pereñíguez García, Universidad Católica San Antonio Murcia, Spain
Zeeshan Pervez, University of the West of the Scotland, UK
Dana Petcu, Western University of Timisoara, Romania
Willy Picard, Poznan University of Economics, Poland
Selwyn Piramuthu, University of Florida, USA
Iwona Pozniak-Koszalka, Wroclaw University of Technology, Poland
Paula Queluz, Instituto Superior Técnico - University of Lisbon / Instituto de Telecomunicações, Lisbon, Portugal
Kornelije Rabuzin, University of Zagreb - Varazdin, Croatia
Karthik Rajasekar, Oak Ridge National Laboratory, USA
Stefan Rass, Universitaet Klagenfurt, Austria
Elena Ravve, Ort Braude College, Israel
Danda B. Rawat, Georgia Southern University, USA
Ulrich Reimer, University of Applied Sciences St. Gallen, Switzerland
Marek Reformat, University of Alberta - Edmonton, Canada
Luis Paulo Reis, University of Minho/LIACC, Portugal
Eric Renault, Télécom SudParis, France
Feliz Ribeiro Gouveia, Universidade Fernando Pessoa, Portugal
Nasser-Eddine Rikli, King Saud University, Saudi Arabia
Michele Risi, University of Salerno, Italy
Agos Rosa, LaSEEB, Portugal
José Rouillard, Université Lille Nord de France
Pawel Rózycki, University of IT and Management (UITM), Poland
Serap Sahin, Izmir Institute of Technology, Turkey
Ozgur Koray Sahingoz, Turkish Air Force Academy, Turkey
Manuel Filipe Santos, Universidade do Minho - Guimarães, Portugal
Ana Šaša, University of Ljubljana, Slovenija
Peter Schartner, Klagenfurt University, Austria
Florence Sèdes, Toulouse 3 University, France
Isabel Seruca, Universidade Portucalense, Porto, Portugal
Marc Sevaux, Université de Bretagne-Sud, France
Qiao Shaojie, Southwest Jiaotong University, China
Ashok Sharma, TechMahindra, India
Patrick Siarry, Université Paris 12 (LiSSi) - Creteil, France

**Copyright Information**

# Why are Users Switching Among Different Types of Social Media?

An empirical study from China

Xiongfei Cao
School of Management
USTC
Hefei, China
caoxf312@126.com

*Abstract*—**This paper aims to address what unique factors entice bloggers to switch to microblogging, and how they impact bloggers' switching intention. Using the PPM framework as a general guideline, low social presence is posited to form blog's push effects, while network size, and relative ease of use are posited to shape microblogging's pull effects. Furthermore, by integrating status quo bias (SQB) theory and the dedication-constraint dual model, this paper assumes that affective commitment, switching costs, and habit are important sources of inertia. Inertia is presumed to play a key role in mooring effects: it not only negatively influences switching intention, but it also attenuates the pull and push factors' main effects. An empirical study of users who use blog and microblogging services concurrently provides general support for our hypotheses. Theoretical contributions of this paper are discussed.**

***Keywords-IT switching; SQB theory; inertia; push–pull–mooring framework***

## I. INTRODUCTION

Rapid evolution across the spectrum of social media has stimulated unprecedented technology adoption pattern. On one hand, people may quickly converge on newly emerging technologies. Within 10 months after it was released in February 2004, Facebook had achieved one million active users, and this data had increased to 250 million by mid-2009. On the other hand, concurrent with the emergence of new technologies, people often leave previously popular applications en masse. For instance, with the growing popularity of sites, such as Facebook and Twitter, blogs are slowly losing their foothold, especially among younger generation. Given the large number of bloggers who lost interest and have given up on regular updates, Microsoft's Windows Live Space shut down in 2011 [1]. Similarity, Facebook has also been experiencing shrinking user base in its post-IPO era. A Global Social Media Impact Study reports that Facebook users are migrating to novel platforms, such as Instagram and WhatsApp [2]. As competing social media choices emerge in the digital market, users can easily switch to alternative services without a financial loss. The success of online communities depends on a critical mass of active users, while user migration and the subsequent change in the market share of social media is a strategic issue [3]. Investigating IT switching phenomenon is important because it is closely related to the survival of technologies.

## II. RESEARCH MODEL

Existing IT research based on the push–pull–mooring (PPM) framework is insufficient to understand IT switching phenomenon [4][5]. First, most studies are concerned only with user switching within the same service, rather than across different services. Second, few researches have proposed theoretical explanation for mooring effects; the exact mechanism by which the mooring effects hamper switching decisions has also not been investigated so far. Third, most studies adopt single, general constructs (e.g., dissatisfaction and alternative attractiveness) to represent the push and pull effects, and they also fail to identify the factors unique to a particular research context.

To fill these gaps, this paper investigates why users switch among different types of social media. Specifically, we aim to address what unique factors entice bloggers to switch to microblogging, and how they impact bloggers' switching intention. Using the PPM framework as a general guideline, low social presence is posited to form the push effect of incumbent social media, whereas larger referent network size and relative ease of use work together to shape the pull effects of fashionable social media. For the mooring effects, we identify an encompassing set of antecedents (affective commitment, switching costs, and habit) to inertia. Inertia is predicted to attenuate the main effects of pull and push factors. In addition, the effects of affective commitment, switching costs, and habit on switching intention are proposed to mediate fully through inertia.

## III. SAMPLE AND RESULTS

To test the model, empirical data are collected from users who concurrently use blog and microblogging. The target population for this study comprises bloggers who are also using microblogging. We obtained samples from Sina blog, a mainstream blog service in China. At the height of Sina blog in 2007, its traffic hit 3.5 million visitors a day. Thus, this sample reasonably represented a major portion of the blog population. More importantly, Sina corporation's other social media product, Sina Weibo, is the most popular microblogging service in China. As of September 2014, Sina Weibo has 167 million monthly active users. Given that Sina Weibo is widely and pervasively adopted, this approach is effective in accessing people who concurrently use blog and microblogging services and are consequently prone to switching behavior.

Given that the user's list of blog and microblogging services is not accessible, we adopted the snowball sampling technique by spreading survey invitations with the URL of the questionnaire to Sina bloggers. This technique is appropriate when a study is concerned with a small and specialized population of people who are knowledgeable about the topic. The invitation informed that only people who are using both services were eligible for the survey. A total of 239 valid responses were obtained.

Our study has several important findings. First, our results suggest that low social presence pushes incumbent social media users away, whereas relative ease of use pulls them to fashionable social media. However, referent network size has no significant impact on user switching intentions. Although unexpected, this result is not surprising. The coexistence of a variety of social media platforms suggests that each type of social media has a specific user group, and a winner-take-all outcome to occur is impossible. For example, users may keep in touch with specific friends through blogs, and not via the total social circle. In addition, people may intentionally avoid using a popular social media, such as microblogging, which may make them look mediocre. Second, affective commitment, switching costs, and habit are important sources of inertia. However, inertia has a negative influence on user switching intention. Third, inertia exhibits significant negative moderating effects on the impact of push-pull factors (i.e., social presence and relative ease of use) on switching intention. The predictive power of push-pull factors will weaken depending on the strength of user inertia. Finally, the effect of habit on switching intention is fully mediated through inertia, which suggests that incumbent technology habit may not necessarily affect user switching decisions unless inertia is well developed. Contrary to our expectation, inertia only partially mediates the effects of affective commitment and switching costs on switching intention. As the fashion trend of blogs ebbed away, the remaining bloggers have greater loyalty and stickiness. Their affective commitment is enduring over time and stable in the changing environment. The connection between affective commitment and switching intention may happen without an individual being consciously aware of this connection. Meanwhile, given the resource constraints of users and the various social media platforms they can select from, users are likely to calculate the costs versus benefits of the known alternatives to make an optimal decision. Except for the indirect effect through inertia, affective commitment and switching costs could have direct effects on switching intention.

## IV. Theoretical Implications

This study has several key research implications. First, this study is among the first to provide empirical validation of user switching from an incumbent social media to a fashionable one during fashion shifting. Unlike isolated users who make switching decisions individually, we regard social media users as virtual community members who are woven together to seek affiliation and socialization. Thus, specific factors related to the communal nature of social media that affect user switching decisions are identified. Second, by integrating SQB theory and the dedication-constraint dual model, we develop a better theoretical understanding of the mooring effects. Specifically, we expand the antecedents of inertia beyond cognitive determinants to include affective determinants, such as affective commitment, and explore mechanisms by which inertia operates in affecting switching intention. Finally, this study extends the applicability of the PPM framework to the context of user switching across different types of social media.

## V. Conclusion

This study explores the factors that affect user switch from an incumbent social media to a fashionable one, as well as the mechanism behind these factors. Our findings indicate that low social presence pushes incumbent social media users away, whereas relative ease of use pulls them to the fashionable one. Affective commitment, switching costs, and habit are important sources of inertia. In the context of this study, inertia fully mediates the relationship between habit and switching intention, and only partially mediates the effect of affective commitment and switching costs on switching intention. Furthermore, inertia negatively moderates the relationships between social presence, relative ease of use, and switching intention.

To conclude, this study expands our understanding of online service switching mechanism, and identifies key factors in IT switching, such as social presence, affective commitment, and inertia. We believe that these mechanisms and key factors are not necessarily limited to online services, but are largely applicable to other contexts in which people interact with technology. Thus, this study builds a useful foundation for future research.

## References

[1] Li, D., and Walejko, G. Splogs and abandoned blogs: The perils of sampling bloggers and their blogs. Information, Community and Society, 11, 2 (2008), 279-296

[2] Kopytoff, V.G. Blogs wane as the young drift to sites like Twitter. The New York Times, 20 (2011)

[3] Iverson, R.D., and Buttigieg, D.M. Affective, normative and continuance commitment: can the 'right kind ' of commitment be managed? Journal of Management Studies, 36, 3 (1999), 307-333.

[4] Jones, M.A., Mothersbaugh, D.L., and Beatty, S.E. Switching barriers and repurchase intentions in services. Journal of Retailing, 76, 2 (2000), 259-274.

[5] Hsieh, J.-K., Hsieh, Y.-C., Chiu, H.-C., and Feng, Y.-C. Post-adoption switching behavior for online service substitutes: A perspective of the push–pull–mooring framework. Computers in Human Behavior, 28, 5 (2012), 1912-1920.

# 2D-dynamic Representation of DNA Sequences - Computational and Graphical Tool for Similarity Analysis in Bioinformatics

Dorota Bielińska-Wąż

Department of Radiological Informatics and Statistics
Medical University of Gdańsk
Tuwima 15, 80-210 Gdańsk, Poland
Email: djwaz@gumed.edu.pl

Piotr Wąż

Department of Nuclear Medicine
Medical University of Gdańsk
Tuwima 15, 80-210 Gdańsk, Poland
Email: phwaz@gumed.edu.pl

***Abstract*—A new nonstandard method of comparison of deoxyribonucleic acid (DNA) sequences called by us 2D-dynamic Representation of DNA Sequences is presented. This approach is based on a method known in the literature as Nandy plots but in the present method the degeneracy (non-uniqueness) of the Nandy plots has been removed. 2D-dynamic Representation is computationally not demanding and there are no limitations on the lengths of the DNA sequences. Using this method, one can compare DNA sequences both graphically and numerically.**

***Keywords–Bioinformatics; Alignment-free methods; Descriptors.***

## I. Introduction

A variety of problems in bioinformatics is large and new approaches are still constructed. Molecular biology is a young area. Its beginning may be dated to 1953 when Watson and Crick discovered the structure of DNA [1]. In 1995 the genome of bacteria *Haemophilus influenzae* has been sequenced for the first time [2]. The project on human genome *Human Genome Project* has been finished in 2003. According to the data in 2013, the database GenBank contains the nucleotide sequences coming from 260 000 described species [3]. The increase of the amount of information available in databases stimulated the development of bioinformatical methods.

Graphical representations of DNA sequences constitute both numerical and graphical tools for similarity/dissimilarity analysis of DNA sequences. They belong to the class of approaches known in the literature as alignment-free methods. Examples of these kind of methods may be found in [4]–[24] (for reviews see [25] [26]). These methods can be applied for solving a large class of problems in biology and medical sciences that require such an analysis. One of such approaches has been introduced by us and we call it *2D-dynamic representation of DNA sequences* [27]–[31].

## II. Method and Results

2D-dynamic representation of DNA sequences is based on shifts in a two-dimensional space [27]. The DNA sequence is represented by material points with different masses in a two-dimensional space. This method is an improvement of *Nandy plots* [6], in which particular bases are represented by two orthogonal pairs of colinear basis vectors. Such a choice of the vectors leads to the possibility of shifts back and forth along the same trace. The so called repetitive walks lead to degeneracy: different sequences may be represented by the same graphs. In order to remove the degeneracy, points with masses which are a multiplicity of the unit mass have been introduced. After a unit shift, a point with unit mass is localized. If the ends of the vectors during the shifts coincide, then the mass of this point increases accordingly. In order to compare the DNA sequences numerically, we have proposed several numerical characteristics (called descriptors in the theory of molecular similarity) of the 2D-dynamic graphs [28]–[30]. We have shown that our numerical approach allows for the classification of the DNA sequences [31]. 2D-dynamic representation of DNA sequences is also a good graphical tool for sequence comparison. Examples of 2D-dynamic graphs of the whole genomes of the Zika virus are shown in Fig. 1 (HQ234500 Nigeria 1968) and in Fig. 2 (KU312312 Suriname 2015). The shapes and the details of the 2D-dynamic graphs give the information about the DNA sequences.

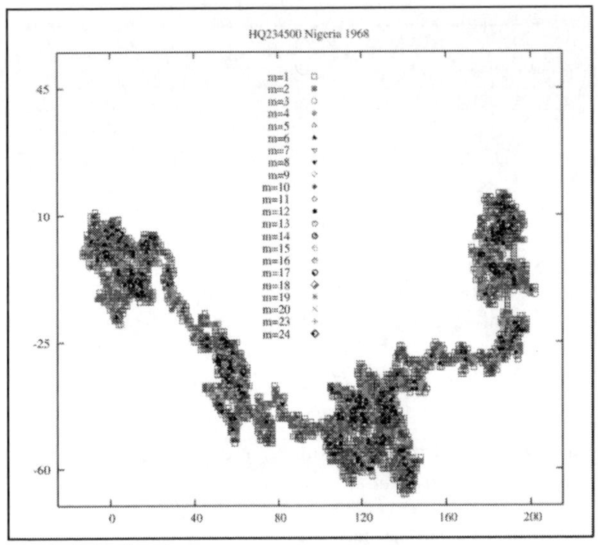


Figure 1. 2D-dynamic graph.

## III. Conclusion

2D-dynamic representation of DNA sequences is both graphical and numerical tool for similarity/dissimilarity analy-

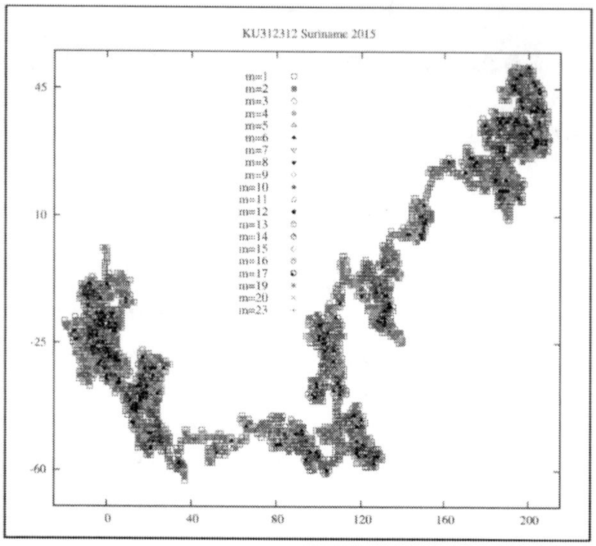


Figure 2. 2D-dynamic graph.

sis of DNA sequences. It can be applied to all problems in biology and medicine, which require such an analysis. An example of an application of 2D-dynamic representation of DNA sequences may be found in our recent work [32]. We have shown that a mutation of the Zika virus genome can be described both graphically, and numerically using for example the so called centers of mass of the 2D-dynamic graphs:

$$\mu_x = \frac{\sum_i m_i x_i}{\sum_i m_i}, \quad \mu_y = \frac{\sum_i m_i y_i}{\sum_i m_i}, \qquad (1)$$

where $x_i$, $y_i$ are the coordinates of the mass $m_i$ in the 2D-dynamic graph. Some other descriptors of the 2D-dynamic graphs will be also applied for characterizing the Zika virus genome in a subsequent article.

## REFERENCES


[1] J. D. Watson and F. H. C.Crick, "Molecular Structure of Nucleic Acids: A Structure for Deoxyribose Nucleic Acid", Nature vol. 171, pp. 737–738, 1953.

[2] R. D. Fleischmann et al., "Whole-genome random sequencing and assembly of Haemophilus influenzae Rd", Science vol. 269, pp. 496–512, 1995.

[3] D. A. Benson et al.,"GenBank", Nucleic Acids Res.vol. 41 (Database issue), pp. D36–D42, 2013.

[4] E. Hamori and J. Ruskin, "H Curves, a novel method of representation of nucleotide series especially suited for long DNA sequences", J. Biol. Chem. vol. 258, pp. 1318–1327, 1983.

[5] M. A. Gates, "Simpler DNA sequence representations", Nature vol. 316, p. 219, 1985.

[6] A. Nandy, "A new graphical representation and analysis of DNA sequence structure. I: Methodology and application to globin genes", Current Science vol. 66, pp. 309–314, 1994.

[7] P. M. Leong and S. Morgenthaler, "Random walk and gap plots of DNA sequences", Comput. Appl. Biosci. vol. 11, pp. 503–507, 1995.

[8] R. Chi and K. Ding, "Novel 4D numerical representation of DNA sequences", Chem. Phys. Lett. vol. 407, pp. 63–67, 2005.

[9] Q. Dai, X. Liu, and T. Wang, "A novel graphical representation of DNA sequences and its application", J. Mol. Graph. Model. vol. 25, pp. 340–344, 2006.

[10] H. González-Díaz et al., "Generalized lattice graphs for 2D-visualization of biological information", J. Theor. Biol. vol. 261, pp. 136–147, 2009.

[11] P. He and J. Wang, "Numerical characterization of DNA primary sequence", Internet Electron. J. Mol. Des. vol. 1, pp. 668–674, 2002.

[12] N. Jafarzadeh and A. Iranmanesh, "C-curve: a novel 3D graphical representation of DNA sequence based on codons", Math Biosci. vol. 241, pp. 217–224, 2013.

[13] B. Liao, Q. Xiang, L. Cai, and Z. Cao, "A new graphical coding of DNA sequence and its similarity calculation", Physica A vol. 392, pp. 4663–4667, 2013.

[14] Y.-Z. Liu and T. Wang, "Related matrices of DNA primary sequences based on triplets of nucleic acid bases", Chem. Phys. Lett. vol. 417, pp. 173–178, 2006.

[15] M. Randić and M. J. Vračko, "On the similarity of DNA primary sequences", J. Chem. Inf. Comput.Sci. vol. 40, pp. 599–606, 2000.

[16] M. Randić, X. Guo, and S. C. Basak, "On the characterization of DNA primary sequences by triplet of nucleic acid bases", J. Chem. Inf. Comput. Sci. vol. 41, pp. 619–626, 2001.

[17] M. Randić and A. T. Balaban, "On a four-dimensional representation of DNA primary sequences", J. Chem. Inf. Comput. Sci. vol. 43, pp. 532–539, 2003.

[18] M. Randić, M. Vračko, N. Lerš, and D. Plavšić, "Analysis of similarity/dissimilarity of DNA sequences based on novel 2-D graphical representation", Chem. Phys. Lett. vol. 371, pp. 202–207, 2003.

[19] X. Yang and T. Wang, "Linear regression model of short k-word: A similarity distance suitable for biological sequences with various lengths", J. Theor. Biol. vol. 337, pp. 61–70, 2013.

[20] Y. Yao and T. Wang, "A class of new 2-D graphical representation of DNA sequences and their application", Chem. Phys. Lett. vol. 398, pp. 318–323, 2004.

[21] Y. Yao, X. Nan, and T. Wang, "Analysis of similarity/dissimilarity of DNA sequences based on a 3-D graphical representation", Chem. Phys. Lett. vol. 411, pp. 248–255, 2005.

[22] J.-F. Yu, J.-H. Wang, and X. Sun, "Analysis of similarities/dissimilarities of DNA sequences based on a novel graphical representation", MATCH Commun. Math. Comput. Chem. vol. 63, pp. 493–512, 2010.

[23] Z. Zhang, T. Song, X. Zeng, Y. Niu, Y. Jiang, L. Pan, and Y. Ye, "ColorSquare: A colorful square visualization of DNA sequences", MATCH Commun. Math. Comput. Chem. vol. 68, pp. 621–637, 2012.

[24] S. Zhang, Y. Zhang, and I. Gutman, "Analysis of DNA sequences based on the fuzzy integral", MATCH Commun. Math. Comput. Chem. vol. 70, pp. 417–430, 2013.

[25] D. Bielińska-Wąż, "Graphical and numerical representations of DNA sequences: Statistical aspects of similarity", J. Math. Chem. vol. 49, pp. 2345–2407, 2011.

[26] M. Randić, M. Novič, and D. Plavšić, "Milestones in Graphical Bioinformatics", Int.J.Quant.Chem.vol. 113, pp. 2413–2446, 2013.

[27] D. Bielińska-Wąż, T. Clark, P. Wąż, W. Nowak, and A. Nandy, "2D-dynamic representation of DNA sequences", Chem. Phys. Lett. vol. 442, pp. 140–144, 2007.

[28] D. Bielińska-Wąż, W. Nowak, P. Wąż, A. Nandy, and T. Clark, "Distribution moments of 2D-graphs as descriptors of DNA sequences", Chem. Phys. Lett. vol. 443, pp. 408–413, 2007.

[29] D. Bielińska-Wąż, P. Wąż, and T. Clark, "Similarity studies of DNA sequences using genetic methods", Chem. Phys. Lett. vol. 445, pp. 68–73, 2007.

[30] D. Bielińska-Wąż, P. Wąż, W. Nowak, A. Nandy, and S. C. Basak, "Similarity and dissimilarity of DNA/RNA sequences", Computation in Modern Science and Engineering vol. 2, Proceedings of the International Conference on Computational Methods in Science and Engineering Corfu, Greece, 25-30 September, 2007, Eds T.E. Simos and G. Maroulis, American Institute of Physics, pp. 28–30, 2007.

[31] P. Wąż and D. Bielińska-Wąż, A. Nandy, "Descriptors of 2D-dynamic graphs as a classification tool of DNA sequences", J. Math. Chem. vol. 52, pp. 132–140, 2013.

[32] A. Nandy, S. Dey, S. C. Basak, D. Bielińska-Wąż, and P. Wąż, "Characterizing the Zika virus genome - A bioinformatics study", Curr. Comput. Aided Drug Des. vol. 12, pp. 87–97, 2016.

# A New Computational Method of Comparison of DNA Sequences

Piotr Wąż

Department of Nuclear Medicine
Medical University of Gdańsk
Tuwima 15, 80-210 Gdańsk, Poland
Email: phwaz@gumed.edu.pl

Dorota Bielińska-Wąż

Department of Radiological Informatics and Statistics
Medical University of Gdańsk
Tuwima 15, 80-210 Gdańsk, Poland
Email: djwaz@gumed.edu.pl

***Abstract*—A new method of comparison of deoxyribonucleic acid (DNA) sequences, 3D-dynamic representation of DNA sequences, is presented. This method allows for both graphical and numerical similarity/dissimilarity analysis of the sequences. This method is a generalization of our previous method called by us 2D-dynamic representation of DNA sequences. The methodology is taken from physics: the DNA sequence is represented by a set of "material points" in a 3D space. Using this nonstandard approach we have obtained high accuracy: a difference in a single base can be recognized. We can indicate which base it is (cytosine, guanine, adenine, or thymine) and its approximate location in the DNA sequence.**

***Keywords–Bioinformatics; Alignment-free methods; Descriptors.***

## I. Introduction

The aim of the presented studies is the creation of new bioinformatical models carrying information about similarity of the DNA sequences. This information is relevant for solving many biomedical problems. The inspiration for these studies has interdisciplinary character.

A sequence is defined as a sequence of symbols. In the case of the DNA, this is a sequence composed of four letters corresponding to four nucleotides: A - adenine, C - cytosine, G - guanine, T - thymine.

The main idea in our work is an application of methodological concepts derived from the classical mechanics to bioinformatics. The application of concepts of classical mechanics to the classification of biochemical objects, in particular to the formulation of new criteria determining the degree of similarity of DNA sequences led to the creation of new methods.

## II. Theory and Results

In this section, we briefly review a new method in bioinformatics which is referred to as *3D-dynamic representation of DNA sequences* [1][2]. The name of this method is related to the descriptors which are analogous as the ones used in the dynamics. The method used to create a 3D-dynamic graph was described in [1]. Two examples of such graphs are shown in Fig. 1.

This method belongs to the group of methods in bioinformatics called *graphical representation methods* (See for reviews [3][4]).

The correctness of these kind of methods is usually shown using standard sets of data: $\beta$-globin and histone H4 coding sequences of different species.

As the descriptors (numerical characteristics) of 3D-dynamic graphs, we have proposed [1] the followings:

- Coordinates of the centers of mass of the graphs $(\mu_x, \mu_y, \mu_z)$,
- Normalized principal moments of inertia of the graphs $(r_1, r_2, r_3)$,
- The values of the cosines of properly defined angles.

The coordinates of the center of mass of the 3D-dynamic graph, in the $\{X, Y, Z\}$ coordinate system are defined as [1]

$$\mu_x = \frac{\sum_i m_i x_i}{\sum_i m_i}, \quad \mu_y = \frac{\sum_i m_i y_i}{\sum_i m_i}, \quad \mu_z = \frac{\sum_i m_i z_i}{\sum_i m_i}, \quad (1)$$

where $x_i$, $y_i$, $z_i$ are the coordinates of the mass $m_i$. Since $m_i = 1$ for all the points, the total mass of the sequence is $N = \sum_i m_i$, where $N$ is the length of the sequence. Then, the coordinates of the center of mass of the 3D-dynamic graph may be expressed as

$$\mu_x = \frac{1}{N}\sum_i x_i, \quad \mu_y = \frac{1}{N}\sum_i y_i, \quad \mu_z = \frac{1}{N}\sum_i z_i. \quad (2)$$

The tensor of the moment of inertia is given by the matrix

$$\hat{I} = \begin{pmatrix} I_{xx} & I_{xy} & I_{xz} \\ I_{yx} & I_{yy} & I_{yz} \\ I_{zx} & I_{zy} & I_{zz} \end{pmatrix}, \quad (3)$$

where

$$I_{xx} = \sum_i^N m_i\left[(y_i')^2 + (z_i')^2\right], \quad I_{yy} = \sum_i^N m_i\left[(x_i')^2 + (z_i')^2\right],$$

$$I_{zz} = \sum_i^N m_i\left[(x_i')^2 + (y_i')^2\right], \quad I_{xy} = I_{yx} = -\sum_i m_i x_i' y_i', \quad (4)$$

$$I_{xz} = I_{zx} = -\sum_i m_i x_i' z_i', \quad I_{yz} = I_{zy} = -\sum_i m_i y_i' z_i'.$$

$x_i'$, $y_i'$, $z_i'$ are the coordinates of $m_i$ in the Cartesian coordinate system for which the origin has been selected at the center of mass.

The eigenvalue problem of the tensor of inertia is defined as

$$\hat{I}\omega_k = I_k \omega_k, \quad k = 1, 2, 3, \quad (5)$$

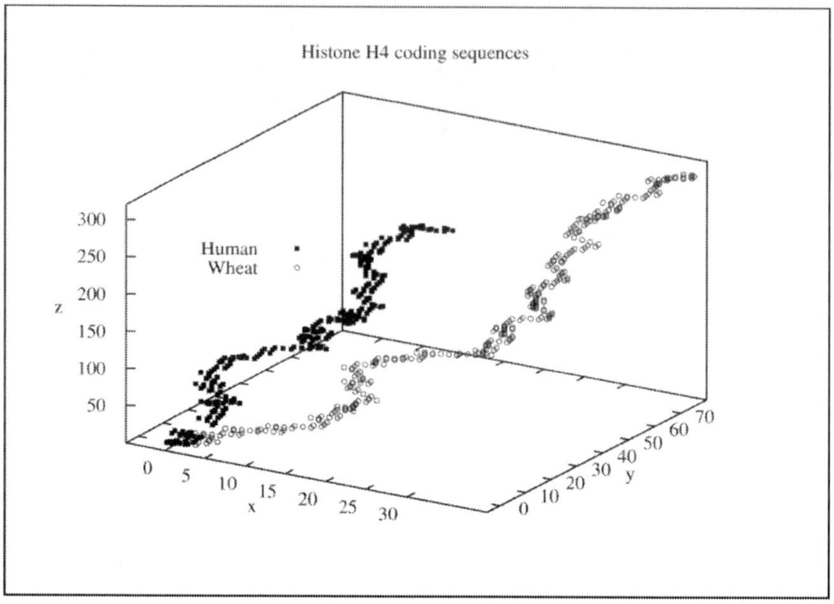


Figure 1. 3D-dynamic graphs.

TABLE I. SIMILARITY/DISSIMILARITY MATRIX BASED ON $D = \frac{\mu_z}{r_3}$ FOR THE SECOND EXON OF $\beta$-GLOBIN GENE OF DIFFERENT SPECIES.

| Species | Human | Goat | Opossum | Gallus | Lemur | Mouse | Rabbit | Rat | Gorilla | Bovine | Chimpanzee |
|---|---|---|---|---|---|---|---|---|---|---|---|
| Human | 0.0000 | 0.9419 | 0.9881 | 0.9952 | 0.9990 | 0.8130 | 0.9992 | 0.9886 | 0.1638 | 0.9971 | 0.0050 |
| Goat | | 0.0000 | 0.7957 | 0.9997 | 0.9826 | 0.6893 | 0.9867 | 0.8044 | 0.9514 | 0.9493 | 0.9416 |
| Opossum | | | 0.0000 | 0.9999 | 0.9147 | 0.9365 | 0.9349 | 0.0422 | 0.9901 | 0.7519 | 0.9881 |
| Gallus | | | | 0.0000 | 1.0000 | 0.9991 | 1.0000 | 0.9999 | 0.9942 | 1.0000 | 0.9952 |
| Lemur | | | | | 0.0000 | 0.9946 | 0.2360 | 0.9110 | 0.9992 | 0.6564 | 0.9990 |
| Mouse | | | | | | 0.0000 | 0.9959 | 0.9392 | 0.8436 | 0.9843 | 0.8120 |
| Rabbit | | | | | | | 0.0000 | 0.9320 | 0.9994 | 0.7375 | 0.9992 |
| Rat | | | | | | | | 0.0000 | 0.9905 | 0.7409 | 0.9886 |
| Gorilla | | | | | | | | | 0.0000 | 0.9975 | 0.1680 |
| Bovine | | | | | | | | | | 0.0000 | 0.9970 |
| Chimpanzee | | | | | | | | | | | 0.0000 |

where $I_k$ are the eigenvalues and $\omega_k$ – the eigenvectors. The eigenvalues are obtained by solving the third-order secular equation

$$\begin{vmatrix} I_{xx} - I & I_{xy} & I_{xz} \\ I_{yx} & I_{yy} - I & I_{yz} \\ I_{zx} & I_{zy} & I_{zz} - I \end{vmatrix} = 0. \quad (6)$$

The eigenvalues $I_1$, $I_2$, $I_3$ are called the principal moments of inertia. As the descriptors we select the square roots of the normalized principal moments of inertia:

$$r_1 = \sqrt{\frac{I_1}{N}}, \quad r_2 = \sqrt{\frac{I_2}{N}}, \quad r_3 = \sqrt{\frac{I_3}{N}}. \quad (7)$$

Using this approach one can calculate similarity values between the DNA sequences. For this purpose, we have introduced the similarity measure [2]

$$S^{ij} = 1 - exp(-|D_i - D_j|), \quad (8)$$

where $i$ and $j$ denote two sequences. The measure is normalized: $0 \leq S \leq 1$. For the descriptors, which are identical in both sequences ($D_i = D_j$) the similarity value $S = 0$.

An example of the calculations using this approach is shown in Table 1. This is the similarity/dissimilarity matrix for the second exon of $\beta$-globin gene of different species [2]. Small values of S correspond to large degree of similarity related to the considered descriptor D. As we can see the largest similarity human-other species is for chimpanzee. Such result is obtained for many descriptors for these data.

## III. Conclusions

- 3D-dynamic representation of DNA sequences facilitates both graphical and numerical comparison of DNA sequences.
- The method is sensitive:
  It can recognize a difference in only one base.
- The new normalized similarity measure is a good tool for similarity analysis of DNA sequences.

## References


[1] P. Wąż and D. Bielińska-Wąż, "3D-dynamic representation of DNA sequences", J. Mol. Model. vol. 20, 2141, 2014.

[2] P. Wąż and D. Bielińska-Wąż, "Non-standard similarity/dissimilarity analysis of DNA sequences", Genomics vol. 104, pp. 464–471, 2014.

[3] A. Nandy, M. Harle, and S. C. Basak, "Mathematical descriptors of DNA sequences: development and applications", Arkivoc ix, pp. 211–238, 2006.

[4] M. Randić, M. Novič, D and Plavšić, "Milestones in Graphical Bioinformatics", Int. J. Quant. Chem. vol. 113, pp. 2413–2446, 2013.

# Parallelization of Loops with Complicated Data Dependency and its Experiment

Kyoko Iwasawa
Computer Science dept.
Takushoku University
Hachioji, Tokyo Japan, 193-0985
E-mail : kiwasawa@cs.takushoku-u.ac.jp

*Abstract*— **This study discusses a loop parallelizing method for compilers in a multi-core architecture that enables to detect fine grain parallelism. Our method involves generating parallelized loops from nested loops carrying complicated data dependencies. These loop transformations are formalized by matrix operations. They enable the original loop indexes to be expressed using new loop indexes so that compiler does not need to make any changes in loop body. Our experiments have determined that bubble sort programs can also be parallelized effectively by using our proposed method.**

***Keywords-fine grain parallelism; parallelization; data dependency ; compiler; double- nested loops;***

## I. Introduction

Multi-core architecture is being widely use; however sometimes multiple central processing unit (CPUs) are not used efficiently for sequential programs. In particular, in some instances, loops with complicated data flow dependency are designed to execute in parallel without any synchronization among compilers (or such types of system software).

To optimize multi-core architecture, developers have been attempting to speed up the execution times of nested loops, which consume a large fraction of execution time, by mean of parallelization.

One of the method to parallelize double-nested loops is the wave-front-line method [1]. This method analyzes not only the inner loop data flow but also the outer loop data flow, in order to identify the line where loop bodies can be executed in parallel. This method uses various synchronization controls (e.g., data passing, lock-unlock, etc.), and the overhead of these synchronization is too high for multi-core and Single Instruction Multiple Data (SIMD) architecture (e.g., packed operation or vector operation).

The characteristic of our study is the restructuring of double-nested loops that may include complicated data dependency constraining loop exchange and splitting. Our method generates a parallel loop by shearing conversion on the double-loop iteration space and then exchanging loops. Our method involves shearing along the inner loop index. This method does not seem to have been discussed previously, in literature and is particularly useful in case of fine grain parallelism. In our study we show how compilers should generate parallelized codes, so that loops with complicated data dependencies can be parallelized and vectorized without any synchronization, this would lead to reduces overheads in multi-core or SIMD architecture.

The rest of this paper is organized as follows: Section II describes parallel conversions. Section III discusses the result of our experiments. Section IV describes the related works and Section V concludes this article.

## II. Parallelizing Conversion

We first discuss the case of the loop which includes separable data dependence between inner and outer loop. Then, we discuss the parallelizing conversion of the more complicated case; this is due to the inseparable data dependence between inner and outer loop, is shown.

### A. *Separable data dependence between inner and outer loop*

In double-nested loop, when both inner and outer loops carry data dependence, individual loop bodies cannot be executed in parallel neither along the inner loop index nor the outer loop index. In the case where inner loop carried data dependencies and outer loops carried data dependencies are independent, it is easier to identify the wave front line, where loop bodies can execute in parallel. Fig. 1 shows the loop iteration space and separable loop carried dependencies. As is clear from Fig. 1 parallelism takes place on a diagonal line.

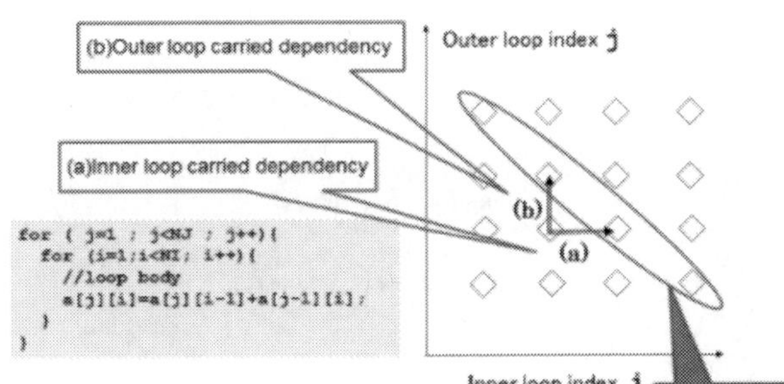


Figure 1 The wave front line on the iteration space

### B. *Inseparable data dependence between inner and outer loop : critical data dependence*

If both inner and outer loops carry critical data dependence, then it bothers neither loop parallelization nor loop exchange. In such a case, loop body on diagonal line cannot execute in parallel.

To detect parallelism, we generate a new inner parallel loop. The loop bodies are on the line where they can be executed independently, using the following

1. (1) Find critical data dependencies and calculate the delay by its loop carried iteration number.
2. (2) Exchange the inner loop and the outer loop
3. (3) Insert the calculating code of the new loop indexes(I, J) from the original loop indexes(i, j)

$$\begin{pmatrix} J \\ I \end{pmatrix} = \begin{pmatrix} 1 & 0 \\ delay & 1 \end{pmatrix} \begin{pmatrix} j \\ i \end{pmatrix} = \begin{pmatrix} j \\ delay * j + i \end{pmatrix}$$

This result in a parallel inner loop is generated without any of the loop body conversion as can be seen in Fig. 2

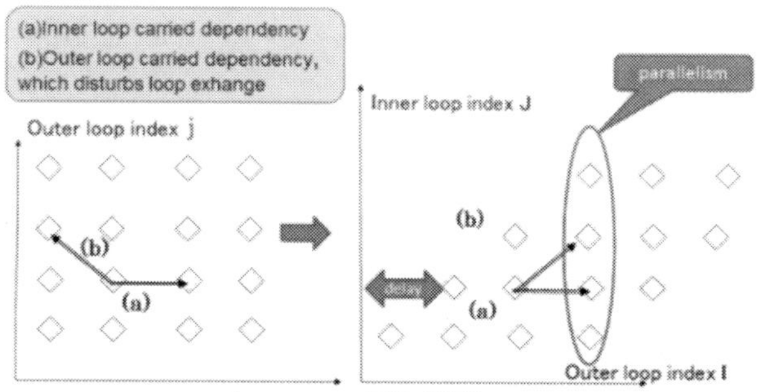


```
for ( j=1 ; j<NJ ; j++){
 for (i=1;i<NI; i++){
  a[i][j]=a[i-1][j]+a[i+1][j-1];
 }
}
```

```
for ( I=1 ; I<NI+delay*NJ ; I++){
 for (J=max(1,(I-NI)/delay+1 ;
          J<min(I/delay+1,NJ) ; J++){
   i=I-delay*J;
   j=J;
   a[i][j]=a[i-1][j]+a[i+1][j-1];
 }
}
```

Figure. 2 Shearing conversion along to inner loop index on the iteration space

## III. Experiment Of Bubble Sort Program

This section discusses the experiment of parallelizing bubble sort program, which is executed serially in general. It accesses one dimensional array in a double-nested loop, therefore there is critical data flow dependency. In addition the wave-front-line (Section II(a)) cannot be detected.

```
(1) Original bubble sort program
void BubbleSort(float A[], int N)  {
 for (int j=0; j<N-1; j++) {
  for (int i=0; i<N-j; i++)
  if (A[i]>[A[i+1])   swap(A[i], A[i+1]);
  }
 }
```

(2) After parallelized bubble sort program delay=2 (distO=1, distI=-2)

```
void BubbleSort(float A[], int N){
 for (int I=0; I<2*(N-1); I++) {
   int initial=max(0 , J-(N-1));
   int last=min(I/2, N-1);
   for (int J=initial;J<=last;J++){  /*  parallel */
     int i=I-2*J;
     if (A[i]>A[i+1])  swap(A[i], A[i+1]);
   }
 }
}
```

Figure. 3 Parallelizing of bubble sort program

The inner loop of Fig. 3(2) can be executed in parallel. Some parameters from the result of data flow analysis are necessary to fill the template (Fig. 2.), and the OpenMP direction is inserted. The converted program was compiled by Intel OpenMP C compiler.

Fig. 4 shows the execution time of Fig. 3(2) program using Intel i7 quad core CPU. When the input data is sufficiently large, it takes half the time on four parallel. The paralle execution time can not be reduced down to a fourth of serial execution time, because outer loop length of parallel program becames two times of the serial program by sheraing conversion.

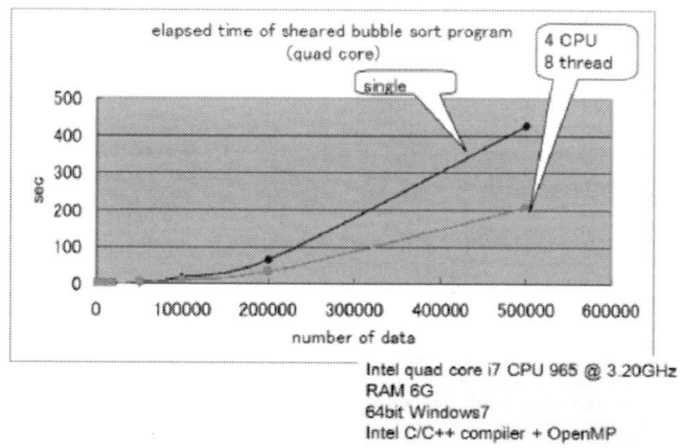


Figure. 4 Execution time of parallelized bubble sort program

## IV. Related Works

There is a lot of previous work. Array data flow analysis has been studied widely [1][2][4][5][7]. Wolf [1] showed loop skewing by wave front line. Kim [2] showed loop parallelization by using wave front method.

Our study is different from them at the following points. One of them is preparing two shearing methods and choosing suitable one. Shearing along the inner loop index has not been studied, but we notice that it has some advantages [6]. This article shows the result of the implementation by automatic translator of these nested loop conversion [6][7].

## V. Conclusion

This study presents a parallelizing method for nested loops for compiler. The compiler makes inner-most parallel and vector loop from nested loop with complicated loop carried data dependency. The new parallel loop enables the expression of original loop indices using new loop indices without requiring the compiler to make any changes in the loop body. The parallelizing translator based on COINS-project [3] has been developing, and it will generate parallelized code from programs with more complicated data dependencies automatically, in the future.

## REFERENCES


[1] Wolfe, M., Loop Skewing: The Wavefront Method Revisited, International Journal of Parallel Programming, Springer Netherlands, pp.279-293, (1986).

[2] Kim, K., and Nicolau, A., Parallelizing tightly nested loops, Proceedings of Parallel Processing Symposium, pp.630-633 (1991).

[3] http://coins-compiler.osdn.jp/international/index.html (2016.9.1)

[4] Dulong,C., Krishnaiyer,R., Kulkarni, D. Lavery, W. Li, J. Ng, and D. Sehr, An Overview of the Intel IA-64 Compiler, (2005).

[5] Vasilache, N., Bastoul, C., and Cohen, A., Polyhedral Code Generation in the Real World, proceedings of 15th International Conference CC2006, pp.185-201, (2006).

[6] Iwasawa, K. and Mycroft, A., Choosing Method of the Most Effective Nested Loop Shearing for Parallelism, Proc. Eighth International Conference on Parallel and Distributed Computing, Applications and Technologies, pp.267-276, (2007).

[7] Chakilam, K. C., Representing and Minimizing Multidimensional Dependencies. M.S.C.S. Thesis, Dept. of Computer Science, The University of Akron, (2009).

# Subjective Assessment for Resolution Improvement on 4K TVs

## - Analysis of Learning-Based Super-Resolution and Non-Linear Signal Processing Techniques -

Hiroki Shoji† Seiichi Gohshi‡
†‡Department of Information Science
Kogakuin University
Tokyo, Japan
e-mail: †em15011@ns.kogakuin.ac.jp, ‡gohshi@cc.kogakuin.ac.jp

***Abstract*—Super-resolution (SR) is a technology to create high-definition images. According to television (TV) manufacturer's advertisements, TVs sold recently in Japan have SR functions. In Japan, when such TVs are sold, SR is aggressively advertised on a large scale; however, in countries other than Japan, SR is not mentioned in similar TV manufacturer's advertisements. In previous research, real-time processing to generate SR images has been found to be difficult. It is necessary to verify whether SR advertised by TV manufacturers exhibits its original performance in a TV that requires a real-time processing. However, an objective assessment of SR on TVs cannot be conducted because images processed in TVs cannot be extracted. Therefore, in our previous work, a subjective assessment of Learning-Based Super-Resolution (LBSR) was conducted, and it was shown that the subjective assessment is effective in performance verification of SR on a TV. Moreover, we conducted a subjective assessment of LBSR and Non-Linear Signal Processing (NLSP) using a 4K TV to evaluate the image quality of each SR image produced via up-conversion from HD video to 4K. In this study, the image quality of each SR when improving resolution of 4K video is evaluated by the subjective assessment. Furthermore, the performance results of both LBSR and NLSP for resolution improvement on a 4K TV are reported.**

***Keywords*—Learning-Based Super-Resolution; Non-Linear Signal Processing; 4K TV; Subjective Assessment; Performance Verification.**

## I. INTRODUCTION

Super-Resolution (SR) is a technology for improving the resolution of images and videos. In recent years, research and development of SR for 4K television (TV) has been increasingly active. Most 4K TVs currently sold have SR functions; SR on a 4K TV is used to up-convert low-resolution content to 4K. SR on 4K TV is used to up-convert low-resolution content to 4K. Broadcasting and Blu-ray content typically use high-definition (HD) resolution and because 4K content has been insufficient until only a few years ago, most content for 4K TV must be up-converted from HDTV content. However, recently, 4K content is increasing and is being streamed over the Internet. Further, test broadcasting for the practical use of 4K broadcasting has been actively conducted. Therefore, we expect 4K content to be increasingly common in the future.

SR can also improve resolution. When 4K content becomes more widespread in the future, SR on 4K TV will be needed for resolution improvement. SR is uniquely developed by TV manufacturers to include resolution improvement functions. Most TV manufacturers focus their development of SR on Learning-Based Super-Resolution (LBSR) [1][2][3].

In Japan, when TVs are sold, SR is aggressively advertised on a large scale. However, in countries other than Japan, SR is not mentioned in similar TV manufacturer's advertisements [4][5][6][7]. It is necessary to verify whether SR advertised by TV manufacturers exhibits the original performance in the TV that requires real-time processing.

Performance of SR is generally measured using Peak Signal-to-Noise Ratio (PSNR). The authors conducted an objective assessment using PSNR about performance of LBSR [8]. In [8], real-time processing of SR has been found to be difficult. However, the performance of SR developed by the TV manufacturers is not published in advertisements. Additionally, the objective assessment of SR on a TV cannot be conducted because images processed in the TV cannot be extracted. Therefore, the authors conducted a subjective assessment to measure performance of SR on a TV [9]. In [9], performance of LBSR and Non-Linear Signal Processing (NLSP) [10] were evaluated when HD video was up-converted to 4K. It is possible to compare performance of each SR by analyzing statistically subjective assessment data. Accordingly, the subjective assessment is effective in performance verification of SR on a TV. In related research, subjective assessments of SR image Reconstruction (SRR) and NLSP have been completed using methods that up-convert (i.e., HD to 4K) and resolution improvement (i.e., 4K to 4K) [11][12]. Further, a subjective assessment of LBSR in up-converting HD to 4K was completed and compared to NLSP; however, LBSR performance for resolution improvement is yet to be evaluated.

Therefore, in this study, we focus on a subjective assessment of resolution improvement. The subjective assessment comprises an experiment for collecting data subjectively assessed by study subjects. Assessment targets of our experiment comprise the following three methods: a 4K original signal; NLSP; and LBSR. The collected assessment data is statistically analyzed and LBSR performance on a 4K TV is quantitatively shown. Significance tests using Analysis of Variance (ANOVA) and a yardstick graph are then performed; a significant difference between each the technique is obtained. Finally, we prove that LBSR is inferior to NLSP and conclude that NLSP is useful as a SR resolution improvement technique for 4K TV.

The paper is structured as follows. In Section II, the subjective assessment experiment is explained. In Section III, experiment results are analyzed by statistical methods are explained. In Section IV, the analyzed results are discussed. Finally, Section V presents a conclusion about this study.

## II. SUBJECTIVE ASSESSMENT EXPERIMENT

In this section, the subjective assessment method and the experiment overview are explained.

### *A. Subjective assessment method*

In [9][11][12], subjective assessments via paired comparisons are conducted. In this study, to quantitatively assess LBSR performance for resolution improvement, Scheffe's paired comparison, ANOVA, and the yardstick graph are adopted. Each of these methods is described in the next section.

### *B. Experimental method*

Assessment targets in this study are OFF (i.e., the original 4K signal), NLSP, and LBSR. The subjective assessment method is Scheffe's paired comparison in which assessment pairs are created and compared to one another when three or more assessment targets are present. A relative comparison in this experiment is a method to assess the other target using a five-step scale (i.e., -2 to 2) when one side of the targets is a criterion (i.e., 0 points). The assessment scale is shown in Table 1, with the five steps defined as Excellent, Good, Fair, Poor, and Bad. As an example, when evaluating NLSP as compared to LBSR, an assessment score of 2 is assigned if NLSP has a higher definition than LBSR, 0 if NLSP is the same as LBSR, and -2 if NLSP has a lower definition than LBSR. Here, high definition is a state in which fine components of a given video are more clearly displayed.

Assessment data obtained via the subjective assessment are then applied to a significance test using ANOVA. Further, experimental results having significant differences are ranked via the yardstick graph.

In the subjective assessment of the video, there is a possibility that the assessment score is changed because of the evaluation order. Therefore, it is conducted our experiments using various combinations to increase the reliability of the assessment data. More specifically, one subject assesses the following six patterns: NLSP and LBSR when the criterion is OFF; OFF and LBSR when the criterion is NLSP; and OFF and NLSP when the criterion is LBSR. Because the subjects are not experts, an oral description regarding the resolution of the video is provided before each experiment, and the subjects understand the differences in resolution via a demonstration. Moreover, in this experiment, because the subjects provide their assessments by replaced the criterion, they often get confused. Therefore, the subjects are instructed to assess only after correctly understanding the given criterion target. Further, the subjects are instructed to ignore the differences in color temperature, color tone, and noise during the reproduction.

TABLE 1. SUBJECTIVE ASSESSMENT SCALE

| Assessment score | Assessment word | Description of assessment words (as compared to a reference) |
|---|---|---|
| 2 | Excellent | Very good resolution |
| 1 | Good | Good resolution |
| 0 | Fair | Degree resolution is the same |
| -1 | Poor | Bad resolution |
| -2 | Bad | Very bad resolution |

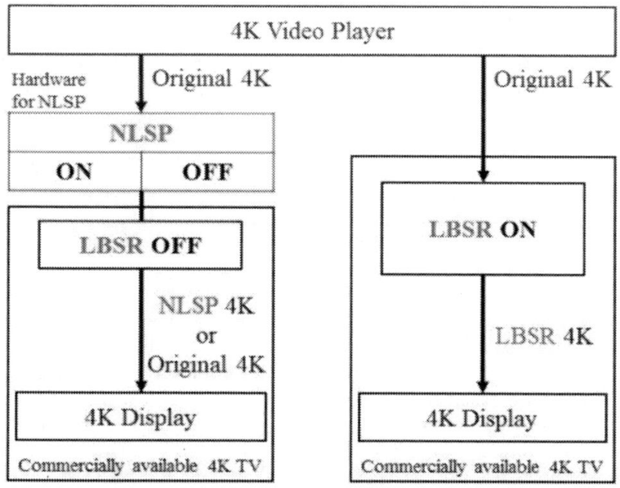


Figure 1. Block diagram of our experimental equipment

Figure 2. NLSP hardware

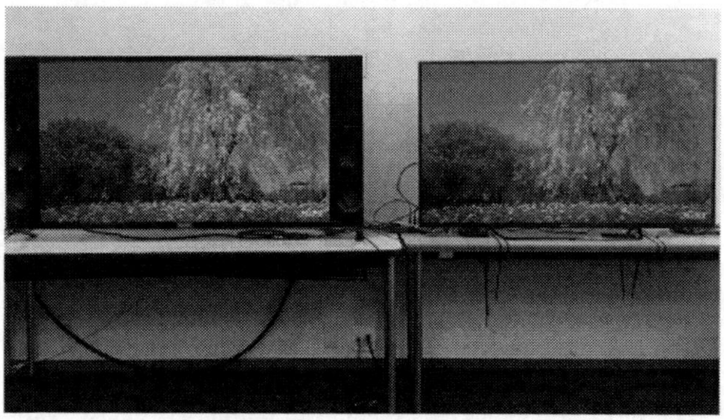

Figure 3. Assessment targets
(Left TV is OFF or NLSP, Right TV is LBSR)

(a) Scene 1 (Bricks)

(b) Scene 2 (Ship1)

(c) Scene 3 (Ship2)

(d) Scene 4 (Bus)

(e) Scene 5 (Cherry Blossoms)

(f) Scene 6 (Ferris wheel)

Figure 4. Experimental 4K videos

### C. *Experimental equipment*

In this section, our experimental equipment is described. Figure 1 shows a block diagram summarizing our experimental equipment. In the figure, the HDTV player is able to reproduce video in an uncompressed form, unlike a conventional DVD player. Although experimental videos were recorded in MPEG-4 format, such videos were never compressed during reproduction while using this player. Details of the experimental videos are described later.

Figure 2 shows the NLSP hardware; here, NLSP and OFF are able to switch a single TV ON and OFF via this hardware. An indicator displaying ON-OFF is present, enabling us to understand whether the subjects have watched either NLSP results or the 4K original signal. Here, ON indicates NLSP, whereas OFF indicates the 4K original signal.

As shown in Figure 3, two 4K TVs are used in this experiment. Here, the manufacturers of the two 4K TV sets are the same, but because the model numbers differ, each 4K TV's color temperature and color tone differs slightly. The liquid crystal panel does not exist exactly the same thing, even if the model number or the product lot are the same. Therefore, using different model numbers is not problem.

### D. *Experimental videos*

The experimental videos were shot using a consumer 4K video camera with fine components to easily confirm differences in resolution but also with coding deterioration of MPEG-4. Here, flickers or deformations of high-frequency components are caused by the coding degradation. In this experiment, videos that included these degradations are assessed. Note that there were no large movements such as panning or tilting in any of the experimental videos. Reproduction time was 10-15 seconds and each video is looped. The input resolution was 4K resolution (i.e., $3840 \times 2160$) and was improved to 4K resolution by each of the resolution enhancement processes. Figure 4 summarizes the videos used in our experiments. Regions indicated by white circles in the figure include a fine pattern of bricks in Scene 1, passengers and details of window frames in Scene 2, the appearance and character of a ship in Scene 3, the characters on a bus in Scene 4, fineness of petals in Scene 5, and fineness of the framework in Scene 6. All such scenes help the subjects to easily confirm the differences in resolution. The subjects performed their assessments while primarily watching these regions.

### E. *Experimental subjects*

Experimental subjects are 30 non-experts, both men and women of 20s with no problems in visual acuity, color vision, and field of view.

### F. *Experimental environment*

As shown in Figure 5, to reproduce the environment in which a consumer selects a TV in a shop, the viewing environment is bright. Although the viewing distance was not fixed, the subjects always assessed the TVs by standing in front of them.

Figure 5. Experimental environment

TABLE 2. CROSS TABLES

(a) Cross Table of Scene 1 (Bricks)

| | OFF | NLSP | LBSR | Xi |
|---|---|---|---|---|
| **OFF** | | 56 | 18 | 74 |
| **NLSP** | -54 | | -22 | -76 |
| **LBSR** | -22 | 30 | | 8 |
| Xj | -76 | 86 | -4 | X… |
| Xj-Xi | -150 | 162 | -12 | 6 |

(b) Cross Table of Scene 2 (Ship1)

| | OFF | NLSP | LBSR | Xi |
|---|---|---|---|---|
| **OFF** | | 55 | 15 | 70 |
| **NLSP** | -56 | | -23 | -79 |
| **LBSR** | -9 | 33 | | 24 |
| Xj | -65 | 88 | -8 | X… |
| Xj-Xi | -135 | 167 | -32 | 15 |

(c) Cross Table of Scene 3 (Ship2)

| | OFF | NLSP | LBSR | Xi |
|---|---|---|---|---|
| **OFF** | | 49 | 11 | 60 |
| **NLSP** | -47 | | -21 | -68 |
| **LBSR** | -12 | 22 | | 10 |
| Xj | -59 | 71 | -10 | X… |
| Xj-Xi | -119 | 139 | -20 | 2 |

## III. ANALYSIS AND RESULTS

In this study, the assessment data obtained in the subjective assessment are analyzed and statistically quantified. Below, the results of our analysis is presented.

### *A. Cross table*

A cross table is used to organize the assessment data. The cross tables shown in Table 2 provide summed values of the assessment data. In Table 2, typical results are shown and other results are similar to these results. Below, the use of a cross table is explained using Scene 1 of Table 2. In the table, OFF, NLSP, and LBSR in the first column show the criterion methods, whereas OFF, NLSP, and LBSR in the first row show the assessment targets. Each value is the sum of the assessment scores of each subject. For example, the score of 56 in row two, column three is the sum of the assessment scores for NLSP when the criterion is OFF. Conversely, the score of -54 in row three, column two is the sum of the assessment scores of OFF when the criterion is NLSP. In general, Xi is the sum of the assessment scores in each row and Xj is the sum of the assessment scores in each column. Further, X… is the sum of Xi and Xj. As an example, -150, 162, and -12 scores in the sixth row (i.e., Xj - Xi) are calculated from the difference of each Xj and Xi; these values are used for ANOVA and the yardstick graph.

### *B. Analysis of variance (ANOVA)*

Table 3 shows our typical results of ANOVA. Using Scene 1 of Table 3, the ANOVA table is explained. In this study, the factors analyzed by ANOVA are the main effect, main effect × individual, combination, order effect, and order effect × individual; these are shown in rows two through six of the ANOVA table. The factor shown represents the cause that affected each assessment score. The seventh row is a residual, and the eighth row is a total. The second column is the sum of squares (S), the third column is the degree of freedom (DoF), and the fourth column is variance (V). The main effect is calculated as follows:

$$S = \frac{1}{2nN} \sum (Xj - Xi)^2 \quad (1)$$

$$DoF = n - 1 \quad (2)$$

$$V = S/DoF \quad (3)$$

In (1) and (2), n is the number of assessment targets and N is the number of subjects. In our experiments, n = 3 and N = 30 are set. Further, the values shown in Table 2 as Xj - Xi values are used. In the fifth column, F represents the variance ratio, which is the quotient obtained by dividing the variance of each factor by the residual. As an example, F (506.41) of the main effect in Scene 1 of Table 2 was calculated by dividing variance (135.80) by residual (0.27); however, an error occurs if F is calculated using this value, because the values in Table 3 are rounded off. In the sixth column, F1% represents the variance ratio (i.e., boundary value) of each factor with a significance level of 1% calculated using the FINV function of Excel. For the significance test of ANOVA, we used the F value of the main effect, noting a significant difference at F > F1%. As an example, in Scene 1 of Table 3, F was 506.41 and F1% was 4.85. Here, because F is larger than F1%, a significant difference exists between the assessment targets with a significance level of 1%. Similar to Scene 1, in Scenes 2 through 6, because F is larger than F1%, the presence of a significant difference has successfully been shown.

TABLE 3. ANALYSIS OF VARIANCE (ANOVA) TABLES.

※DoF: Degree of freedom

(a) ANOVA Table of Scene 1 (Bricks)

| Factor | Sum of squares | DoF | Variance | F | F1% |
|---|---|---|---|---|---|
| Main | 271.60 | 2 | 135.80 | 506.41 | 4.85 |
| Main × Individual | 40.40 | 58 | 0.70 | 2.60 | 1.60 |
| Combination | 1.80 | 1 | 1.80 | 6.71 | 6.93 |
| Order | 0.20 | 1 | 0.20 | 0.75 | 6.93 |
| Order × Individual | 6.13 | 29 | 0.21 | 0.79 | 1.93 |
| Residual | 23.87 | 89 | 0.27 | - | - |
| Total | 344.00 | 180 | 1.91 | - | - |

(b) ANOVA Table of Scene 2 (Ship1)

| Factor | Sum of squares | DoF | Variance | F | F1% |
|---|---|---|---|---|---|
| Main | 261.88 | 2 | 130.94 | 439.85 | 4.85 |
| Main × Individual | 41.79 | 58 | 0.72 | 2.42 | 1.60 |
| Combination | 5.34 | 1 | 5.34 | 17.93 | 6.93 |
| Order | 1.25 | 1 | 1.25 | 4.20 | 6.93 |
| Order × Individual | 4.25 | 29 | 0.15 | 0.49 | 1.93 |
| Residual | 26.49 | 89 | 0.30 | - | - |
| Total | 341.00 | 180 | 1.89 | - | - |

(c) ANOVA Table of Scene 3 (Ship2)

| Factor | Sum of squares | DoF | Variance | F | F1% |
|---|---|---|---|---|---|
| Main | 188.23 | 2 | 94.12 | 251.29 | 4.85 |
| Main × Individual | 57.43 | 58 | 0.99 | 2.64 | 1.60 |
| Combination | 5.00 | 1 | 5.00 | 13.35 | 6.93 |
| Order | 0.02 | 1 | 0.02 | 0.06 | 6.93 |
| Order × Individual | 7.98 | 29 | 0.28 | 0.73 | 1.93 |
| Residual | 33.33 | 89 | 0.37 | - | - |
| Total | 292.00 | 180 | 1.62 | - | - |

TABLE 4. SCALE VALUE TABLES

(a) Scale value of Scene 1 (Bricks)

| Target | OFF | NLSP | LBSR |
|---|---|---|---|
| **Scale value (α)** | -0.83 | 0.90 | -0.07 |

(b) Scale value of Scene 2 (Ship1)

| Target | OFF | NLSP | LBSR |
|---|---|---|---|
| **Scale value (α)** | -0.75 | 0.93 | -0.18 |

(c) Scale value of Scene 3 (Ship2)

| Target | OFF | NLSP | LBSR |
|---|---|---|---|
| **Scale value (α)** | -0.66 | 0.77 | -0.11 |

(d) Scale value of Scene 4 (Bus)

| Target | OFF | NLSP | LBSR |
|---|---|---|---|
| **Scale value (α)** | -0.76 | 0.89 | -0.13 |

(e) Scale value of Scene 5 (Cherry Blossoms)

| Target | OFF | NLSP | LBSR |
|---|---|---|---|
| **Scale value (α)** | -0.85 | 1.01 | -0.16 |

(f) Scale value of Scene 6 (Ferris wheel)

| Target | OFF | NLSP | LBSR |
|---|---|---|---|
| **Scale value (α)** | -0.76 | 0.83 | -0.07 |

## C. *Yardstick*

Given that a significant difference is proved in the main effect via ANOVA, detailed significance tests are conducted between each assessment target via the yardstick graph. Accordingly, existence of significant difference is proved visually.

Here, a scale value is calculated to create the yardstick graph. The scale value in this study quantifies the performance of the resolution enhancement processing of the assessment target, wherein the height of this value represents the height of performance. The scale value is calculated as follows:

$$\alpha = \frac{1}{2nN}(Xj - Xi) \tag{4}$$

Here, n, N, and Xj - Xi are the same as above. Table 4 shows the scale values for each experimental video.

A graph using this scale as its horizontal axis is a yardstick graph. Figure 6 shows yardstick graphs for each experimental video. In the figure, a rhombus indicates OFF, a triangle indicates LBSR, and a square indicates NLSP. Values between the assessment targets represent the distances of the scale value. According to Figure 6, for all experimental videos, scale value ranking was OFF, LBSR, and NLSP in ascending order. Regarding the distance between the assessment targets, differences between NLSP and the other two methods were large, which indicated a particularly good performance of NLSP in resolution enhancement processing. Similarly, it can be confirmed that LBSR was better than OFF.

From the yardstick graph, performance differences are quantitatively showed. To confirm the presence of significant differences in these performance differences, a significance test is conducted using assessment standard value Ya, as calculated below.

$$Y_\alpha = q\sqrt{\frac{V_\varepsilon}{2nN}} \tag{5}$$

Here, q is the q value of the studentized range, Vε is the variance of the residual shown in the ANOVA table, and n and N are the same as above. Table 5 shows assessment standard values Y1% for all experimental videos with significance levels of 1%.

A significant difference is observed in significance level 1% when the distance between the assessment targets was greater than Y1%. In Scene 1 of Figure 6, the distance between NLSP and LBSR (0.97) is bigger than Y1% (0.16). In addition, the distance between LBSR and OFF (0.77) is also

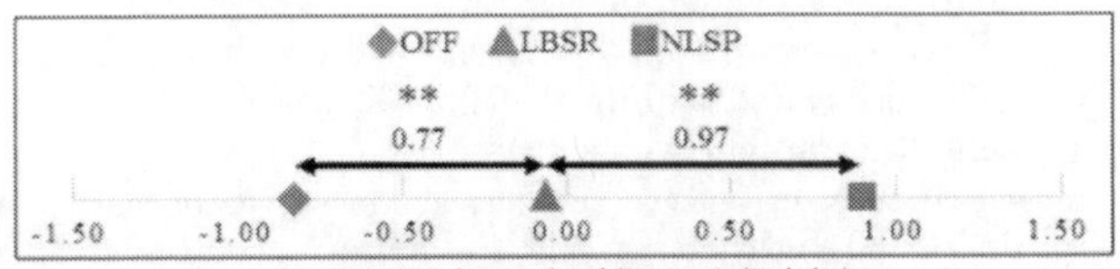


(a) Yardstick graph of Scene 1 (Bricks)

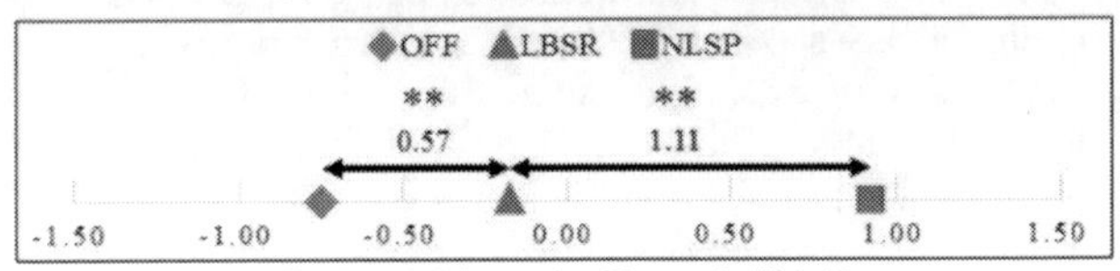


(b) Yardstick graph of Scene 2 (Ship1)

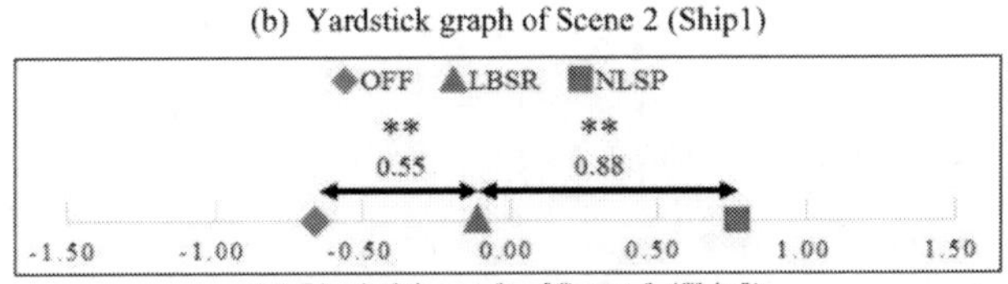


(c) Yardstick graph of Scene 3 (Ship2)

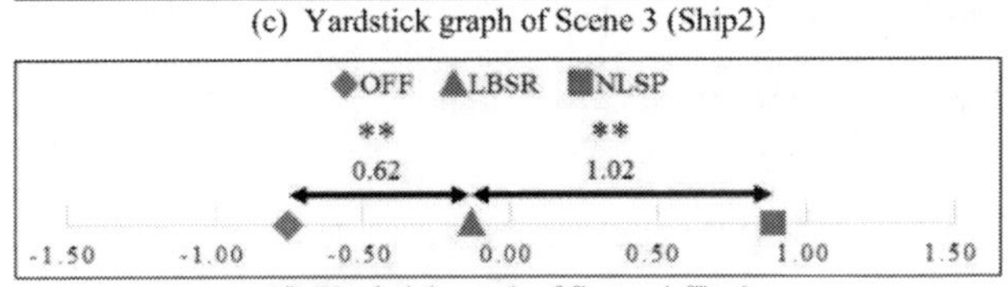


(d) Yardstick graph of Scene 4 (Bus)

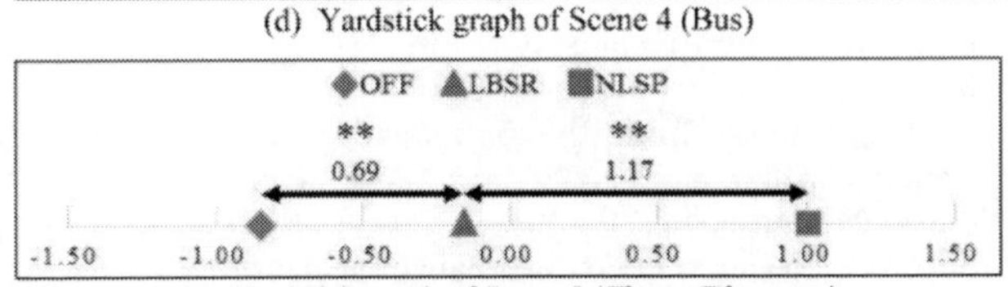


(e) Yardstick graph of Scene 5 (Cherry Blossoms)

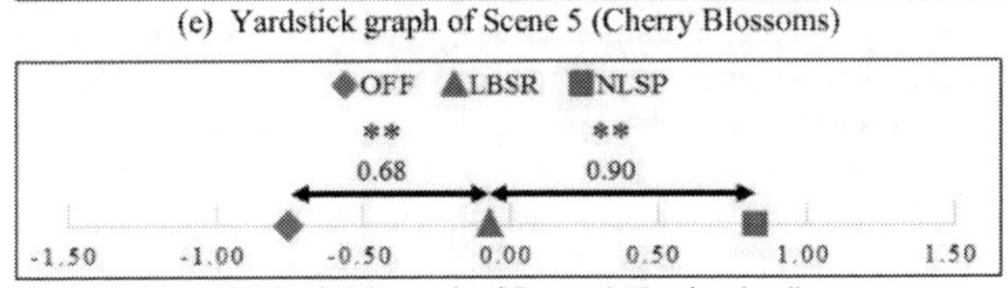


(f) Yardstick graph of Scene 6 (Ferris wheel)

Figure 6. Yardstick graphs

TABLE 5. ASSESSMENT STANDARD VALUES Y1%

| | Y1% |
|---|---|
| Scene 1 | 0.16 |
| Scene 3 | 0.19 |
| Scene 5 | 0.15 |

| | Y1% |
|---|---|
| Scene 2 | 0.17 |
| Scene 4 | 0.16 |
| Scene 6 | 0.17 |

bigger than Y1% (0.16). Therefore, the significant difference is observed in significance level 1%. The two asterisks in each yardstick graph of Figure 6 represent the existence of a significant difference with a significance level of 1%. As a result of the significance tests for all experimental videos, a significant difference is found with a significance level of 1% between NLSP and LBSR, as well as LBSR and OFF. This result shows that resolution enhancement processing of NLSP and LBSR is statistically effective.

## IV. DISCUSSION

Based on the results obtained from our experiments and analysis, it is discussed about the significance of each resolution enhancement method.

LBSR has significant differences in the significance level of 1% as compared with that of the 4K original signal, thus showing the resolution enhancement processing of LBSR to be statistically effective. Further, according to our analysis results of the yardstick graphs, the performance of NLSP is better than LBSR. More specifically, we statistically and quantitatively showed that NLSP is better than LBSR.

In a recent study, using deep convolutional neural networks, more advanced LBSR techniques have been proposed [13] on the premise of applying such techniques to still images. As long as the approach is learning based, processes will require longer processing times, such as for the analysis of an input image, a database search, and block matching. Therefore, LBSR does not meet the real-time requirements for TV. In LBSR on a TV, manufacturers expect that a dedicated large-scale integrated processor could solve the problem of real-time processing; however, there is a limit to what can be solved via hardware. To realize effective real-time processing, it can be considered that there is a possibility that some process has been simplified. On the other hand, NLSP that we have proposed is able to create components are exceeded the Nyquist frequency in real-time. It has been proved in [10]. In addition, NLSP is able to process in real-time even if it is mounted on a conventional simple device because it is very simple signal processing. Therefore, it can be said that a hardware cost is low.

In addition, from the opinions provided by our test subjects, problems in NLSP and LBSR need to be solved. In the videos processed by LBSR, image artifacts are present. Such artifacts are image disturbances such as block noise and aliasing. When conducting subjective assessments, it was necessary to select areas that did not have many artifacts as one's focal point. Therefore, in LBSR, we require processing to reduce aliasing and other such artifacts. In the experimental video of the cherry blossoms with many high-frequency components processed by NLSP, we heard opinions noting that a subject's eyes were tired because of excessive emphasis on the image. Therefore, we conclude it necessary to find optimum processing parameters for each video.

In the future, after resolving the aforementioned problems, we plan to conduct further subjective assessments for various types of images. We also plan to increase the accuracy of our evaluation experiment. In particular, we conclude that videos with a face and text are preferred.

## V. CONCLUSIONS

In this study, we conducted a subjective assessment of NLSP and LBSR on 4K TV. Analyzing the assessment results obtained in our experiments, we quantitatively showed the performance of NLSP and LBSR incorporated into a 4K TV. It was found that NLSP was better than LBSR. Further, it was found that LBSR was statistically more effective as compared with the original 4K signals. Therefore, we conclude that SR for resolution improvement on 4K TVs is indeed effective. In the future, we plan to implement more accurate assessment experiments by increasing the number and variety of assessment videos.

## REFERENCES

[1] http://www.sony.jp/bravia/featured/picture.html [retrieved: Oct, 2016]
[2] http://panasonic.jp/viera/technology/hexa_chroma/remaster.html [retrieved: Oct, 2016]
[3] http://www.lg.com/jp/lgtv/4k-ultrahdtv#colum2 [retrieved: Oct, 2016]
[4] http://www.sony.com/electronics/4k-resolution-4k-upscaling-tvs [retrieved: Oct, 2016]
[5] http://shop.panasonic.com/tvs/4k-tvs [retrieved: Oct, 2016]
[6] http://www.lg.com/us/tvs [retrieved: Oct, 2016]
[7] http://www.samsung.com/us/video/tvs [retrieved: Oct, 2016]
[8] H. Shoji, and S. Gohshi, "Limitations of Learning-Based Super-Resolution," 2015 International Symposium on Intelligent Signal Processing and Communication Systems (ISPACS 2015), pp.646-651, Nov.2015.
[9] H. Shoji, and S. Gohshi, "Performance of Learning-Based Super-Resolution on 4K-TV," The 47th ISCIE International Symposium on Stochastic Systems Theory and Its Applications (SSS'15), pp.79-80, Dec.2015.
[10] S. Gohshi, "Realtime Super Resolution for 4K/8K with Nonlinear Signal Processing," Journal of SMPTE (Society of Motion Pictures and Television Engineers), 124, pp. 51-56, Oct. 2015.
[11] M. Sugie, S. Gohshi, H. Takeshita, and C. Mori, "Subjective Assessment of Super-Resolution 4K Video using Paired Comparison," 2014 International Symposium on Intelligent Signal Processing and Communication Systems (ISPACS 2014), pp.42-47, Dec.2014.
[12] C. Mori, M. Sugie, H. Takeshita, and S. Gohshi, "Subjective Assessment of Super-Resolution: High-Resolution Effect of Nonlinear Signal Processing," 10th Asia-Pacific Symposium on Information and Telecommunication Technologies (APSITT 2015), IEICE & IEEE, pp.46-48, Aug.2015.
[13] C. Dong, C. C. Loy, K. He, and X. Tang, "Image Super-Resolution Using Deep Convolutional Networks," IEEE Transactions on Pattern Analysis and Machine Intelligence, pp.295-307, June.2015.

# Using Clinical Pathway Patterns for Optimizing the Layout of an Emergency Department

Young Hoon Lee and Farhood Rismanchian
Department of Information and Industrial Engineering
Yonsei University
Seoul, South Korea
E-mail addresses: youngh@yonsei.ac.kr, rismanchian.farhood@yonsei.ac.kr

*Abstract*—**During the recent years, demand for healthcare services has dramatically increased. As the demand for healthcare services increases, so does the necessity of constructing new healthcare buildings and redesigning and renovating existing ones. Increasing demands necessitate the use of optimization techniques to improve the overall service efficiency in healthcare settings. However, high complexity of care processes remains the major challenge to accomplish this goal. This study proposes a method based on process mining results to address the high complexity of care processes and to find the optimal layout of the various medical centers in an emergency department. ProM framework is used to discover clinical pathway patterns and relationship between activities. Sequence clustering plug-in is used to remove infrequent events and to derive the process model in the form of Markov chain. The process mining results served as an input for the next phase which consists of the development of the optimization model. Comparison of the current ED design with the one obtained from the proposed method indicated that a carefully designed layout can significantly decrease the distances that patients must travel.**

***Keywords-healthcare processes; process mining; optimization; facility layout problem.***

## I. Introduction

Efficiency improvement is increasingly recognized as a serious concern for health organizations all around the world. Particularly, in developed countries, there has been a remarkable improvement in life quality factors during the last decades. This fact, in addition to development of new treatments, increased average longevity and hence dramatic demands for healthcare services have been observed.

As the demand for healthcare services increases, so do the need for new healthcare buildings as well as the need for redesign and renovating existing ones. Several studies have reported an unprecedented healthcare building boom and proven the importance of creating optimal physical environments to achieve the best possible outcomes for patients, families, and staff [1][2]. Over the last decades, many healthcare managers have referred to the industrial sector and applied techniques and principles that have been developed in industrial processes to improve the performance of healthcare processes. However, high complexity of healthcare processes makes it challenging to apply these techniques in healthcare environments. Over the years, attention has gradually expanded from resource allocation and strategic planning to include operational issues such as resource scheduling and treatment planning [3]. In particular, Discrete Event Simulation (DES) based approach has been extensively used by researchers to address problems generally faced by hospital`s managers. In addition, analytical approaches like queuing based models played a vital role in this area. Facility layout design, in particular, has received considerable critical attention. Studies showed that an efficient layout design can result in a remarkable reduction in the total costs of manufacturing and service industries. Difficulties arise, however, when an attempt is made to apply these approaches to real-world healthcare systems. This is mainly a consequence of high complexity of healthcare systems. As argued by Rebuge et al. [4], healthcare domain is considered to have complex models due to four characteristics: i) health care processes are highly dynamic, ii) health care processes are highly complex, iii) health care processes are increasingly multi-disciplinary, and iv) health care processes are ad hoc. Process mining techniques provide an opportunity to discover what is actually happening in the system. It aims at extracting process knowledge from event logs which may originate from all kind of systems like hospital information systems [5]. Taking benefits of wide range of available event logs in hospitals, these data can be used for improving the efficiency of care processes. In recent years, there has been an increasing growth on the number of papers addressing the applications of process mining in different disciplines and particularly, in healthcare domain. In a study by Mans et al. [5], the gynecological oncology healthcare process within a university hospital has been analyzed. They analyzed the healthcare process from three different perspectives: (1) the control flow perspective, (2) the organizational perspective and (3) the performance perspective. Relevant event logs extracted from the hospital's information system and analyzed using the ProM framework. Rebuge et al. [4] proposed a methodology for the application of process mining techniques that leads to the identification of regular behavior, process variants, and exceptional medical cases. The approach is demonstrated in a case study conducted at a hospital emergency service. Based on process mining outcomes, Zhou et al. [6] proposed a discrete event simulation model to analyze the clinical center. Sensitivity analyses have also been carried out to investigate the care activities with limited resources such as doctors and nurses. Analyzing and evaluating seven different process mining algorithms was done in [7]. Poelmans et al. [8] argued that neither process nor data discovery techniques alone are sufficient for discovering knowledge gaps in particular domains such as healthcare. They showed that the combination of both gives significant synergistic results.

In light of high complexity of healthcare systems, we believe success requires a complete understanding of actual processes. Indeed, practical experiences showed a significant gap between what is prescribed to happen, and what actually happens. The only requirement for applying process mining techniques is availability of event log. Nowadays, clinical data are stored as a hospital information system. A hospital cannot operate without an information system and hence, a very detailed information about the executed activities is readily available. In addition, user-friendly environments of process mining software tools, such as ProM (open-source tool for process mining algorithms) and DISCO (Fluxicon process mining software), enable analysts and designers to provide new insights that facilitate the improvement of existing care processes without a complete understanding of the algorithms and techniques involved.

The aim of this study is to propose a method to help healthcare organizations to analyze complex hospital processes and find the optimal patient-centered layout based on real characteristics of the system in order to increase the efficiency of the care services. In order to do so, process mining techniques were applied to extract process related information, namely process model and pathway patterns, from event log of an ED in Seoul, South Korea. Based on the results obtained from process mining, number, age and acuity level of patients traveling between each two medical functions have been obtained. An architectural layout optimization model is then proposed in order to minimize patients traveling distance and length of stay by sensing sequence of activities. Up to now, far too little attention has been paid to facility layout optimization of hospitals. Moreover, existing studies have been mostly based on subjective judgments of patients` movement and relationship of medical functions. It is worth pointing out that the main advantage of a process mining-based method, however, is that the outcomes are based on real executions of processes rather than relying on subjective observations or opinions. Given the enormous cost of designing and constructing hospital buildings in addition to the significant impact of their layout on productivity and efficiency of hospitals, we believe the design process of hospital buildings is a challenging managerial problem which requires integration of architectural and operational management views.

The remaining part of the paper proceeds as follows: Section 2 describes the process mining-based method to discover the clinical patterns form the clinical records. As the main objective of this study, outcomes from process mining were used in a layout optimization problem in Section 3. Finally, Section 4 concludes the paper.

## II. PATIENT MOVEMENT ANALYSIS

The study uses a process log that consists of the care processes of 11357 patients of the ED of S Hospital in Seoul, South Korea. Treatment activities were collected during a period of 61 days. There are totally 9 activities that a patient might go through during his/her visit to the ED. Table 1 shows the details about the activities. Since patients correspond to cases in the log, 11357 cases, and 52250 events have been observed. We used the ProM framework to perform the study [9]. ProM has been developed to support various process mining algorithms. *Sequence clustering plug-in* has been implemented to support the clustering goal. It allows to cluster patients in dataset and further apply other desire process mining techniques to each cluster [10]. However, in this study, sequence clustering plug-in is used for two reasons. First, it allows the user to apply preprocessing steps to clean the data set and to remove infrequent events. Second, the process model can be obtained in the form of Markov chain, which allows the user to understand the relations between activities.

TABLE I. ACTIVITIES PERFORMED BY PATIENTS

| Index | Activity | Index | Activity |
|---|---|---|---|
| A | Registration | F | CT ( Brain) |
| *B* | Triage | G | CT (Other) |
| *C* | Blood test | J | Hospitalization |
| *D* | Chest PA or AP | I | Departure |
| *E* | Consultation | | |

During our investigations, we realized that those patient pattern behaviors, which occurred less than ten times, can be considered as infrequent sequences and can be eliminated from the dataset. After setting the minimum occurrence of a sequence to 10, information about 424 patients (less than 4 percent) deleted from the dataset (from 11357 instances, 10933 were kept). The resulting data set, consist of 10933 patients with 57 different activity patterns. Fig. 1 and Fig. 2 illustrate sequences and events present in the filtered event log receptively.

Figure 1. Activity patterns present in the filtered log.

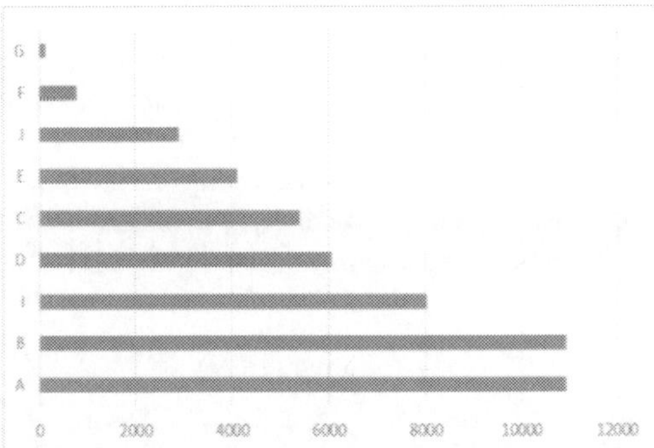


Figure 2. Events present in the filtered log.

In order to obtain the Markov chain for complete log without dividing it into clusters, the number of desired clusters must be selected equal to one. Fig. 3 represents the discovered process model in the form of Markov chain (darker elements are more recurrent than lighter ones).

## III. LAYOUT OPTIMIZATION MODEL

In this section, a mathematical optimization problem has been proposed to find the best layout of ED. Using the activity relations between medical centers inside the ED obtained by process mining techniques, the model attempts to maximize goodness of the functional interactions of the center with other centers.

### A. *Mathematical model and notations*

Let l be the numbers of available locations, and n denotes the number of required medical centers. The problem is to locate n distinct centers N={1,2,3,... ,n} in l distinct available locations L={1,2,3,...l}. Where l is at least equal to the number of required centers n. It must be mentioned that the two cases "l=n" and "l>n" essentially are equivalent since l-n dummy centers can be added. For clarity, we shall use indices q and r for available locations, and i and j for required centers. We denote by $\delta_{qr}$` the inversed normalized distance between positions q and r (closer locations have higher weight). For center i, the feasible (potential) set of locations is denoted by $P_i$. The position of center i is described by the binary variables $x_{iq}$'s such that the value of $x_{iq}$ is 1 if center i is moved to position q and 0 otherwise. Finally, $r_{ij}$ represents the movement relation between centers i and j. The movement relationship between different centers of ED plays a vital role in the optimization process. The outcomes of the process mining are used in this model as inputs of optimization model. Basically, to medical functions with high logical relationship (i.e., large rij) must be located close to each other in order to decrease the patients' moving distances. Having obtained the Markov chain for process model, it is also possible to provide a matrix representation which makes it more tractable for further analysis (Fig. 4).

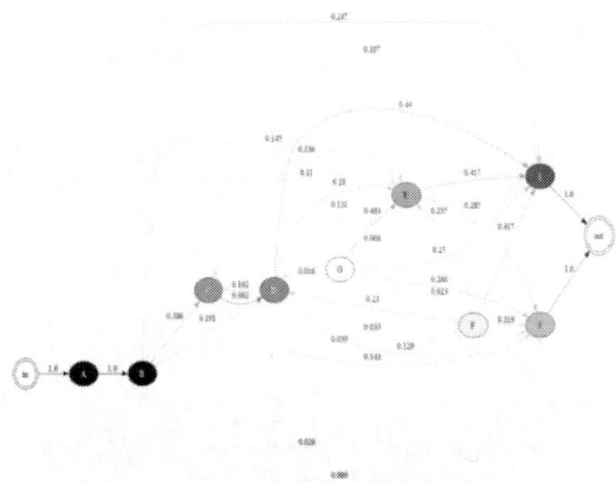

Figure 3. Markov chain model for the complete log.

The objective of the model is to maximize goodness of the functional interactions of the center with other centers.

$$Max\ Z = \sum_i \sum_j \sum_q \sum_r x_{iq} x_{jr} \delta_{qr}^{`} r_{ij}$$

$$\forall\, i:\ \textstyle\sum_{q \in P_i} x_{iq} = 1, \qquad (1)$$

$$\forall\, q \text{ and } q \neq 0:\ \textstyle\sum_{i=1}^{n} x_{iq} \leq 1. \qquad (2)$$

Constraint (1) claims that centers must be assigned to one of its potential positions. Constraint (2) claims that available position can hold at most one center.

### B. *Results and discussion*

Fig. 5 represents the current arrangement of medical centers inside the ED. The problem is to relocate required medical centers to available locations in order to decrease the total distance traveled by patients and hence decrease the length of stay. Our model was implemented in OPL and solved by CPLEX 12. The optimum layout obtained by proposed model (Fig. 6) showed 37.95 percentage of improvement in comparison with current layout regarding total walking distance of patients (changed from 256203 to 158999). The needed CPU time is about 1 min. However, designing hospital units do not happen very often in practice. Therefore, it is acceptable to spend some hours of computational effort.

Having obtained the optimal layout using the proposed method, simulation modeling can be used to assist decision makers to adjust the obtained layout with respect to various considerations. The reasons may include adjusting the layout for qualitative objectives such safety and security. Other reasons may include some quantitative goals which are difficult to express using mathematical formulation. It must be pointed out that the layout obtained from the proposed model is the best layout possible considering distances traveled by patients and should be applied in the early design stage to determine the most efficient layout. The obtained layout may be tuned further according to any aspects that are not included in the formulation presented here.

| | In | A | B | C | D | E | F | G | I | J | out |
|---|---|---|---|---|---|---|---|---|---|---|---|
| In | 0 | 1 | 0 | 0 | 0 | 0 | 0 | 0 | 0 | 0 | 0 |
| A | 0 | 0 | 1 | 0 | 0 | 0 | 0 | 0 | 0 | 0 | 0 |
| B | 0 | 0 | 0 | 0.386 | 0.191 | 0.145 | 0.026 | 0 | 0.247 | 0.006 | 0 |
| C | 0 | 0 | 0 | 0 | 0.602 | 0.110 | 0.039 | 0 | 0.107 | 0.143 | 0 |
| D | 0 | 0 | 0 | 0.102 | 0 | 0.280 | 0.033 | 0.016 | 0.440 | 0.129 | 0 |
| E | 0 | 0 | 0 | 0.136 | 0.131 | 0 | 0.023 | 0.008 | 0.417 | 0.285 | 0 |
| F | 0 | 0 | 0 | 0 | 0.230 | 0.235 | 0 | 0 | 0.417 | 0.119 | 0 |
| G | 0 | 0 | 0 | 0 | 0 | 0.484 | 0 | 0 | 0.250 | 0.266 | 0 |
| I | 0 | 0 | 0 | 0 | 0 | 0 | 0 | 0 | 0 | 0 | 1 |
| J | 0 | 0 | 0 | 0 | 0 | 0 | 0 | 0 | 0 | 0 | 1 |
| out | 0 | 0 | 0 | 0 | 0 | 0 | 0 | 0 | 0 | 0 | 1 |

Figure 4. Matrix representation of the movement relations.

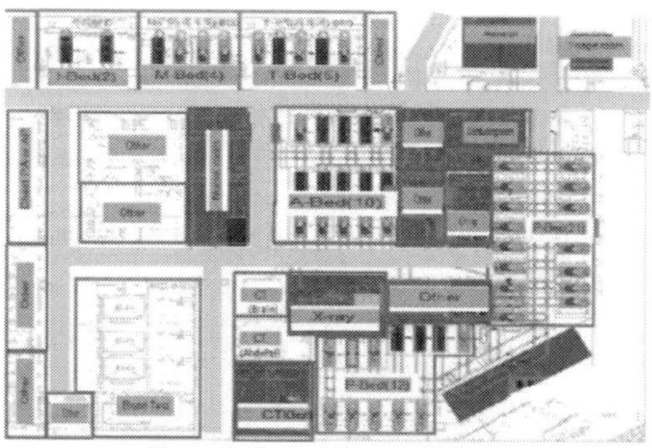

Figure 5. Current layout of ED.

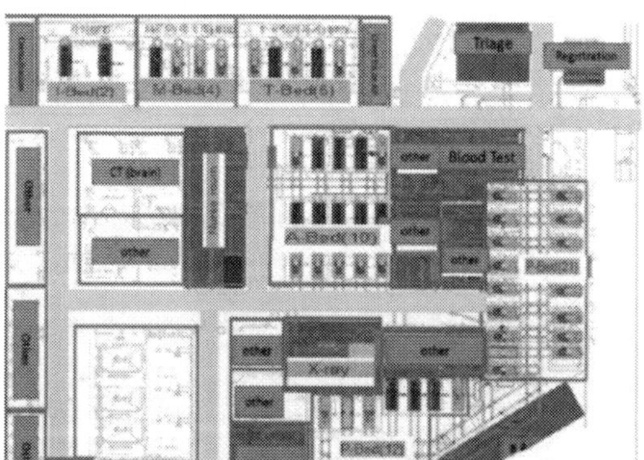


Figure 6. Optimum layout of ED.

## IV. CONCLUSIONS

In this study, a process mining-based method proposed to discover process model and clinical pathway patterns of an ED. Process mining can be used as a reliable tool to enhance care process analysis and to discover the pathway patterns from the clinical records. The process model is then used to find the best layout of medical functions in ED. The objective was to decide upon the location of the various clinical centers so as to reduce the effort spent by the patients while moving from one unit to another. It was found that a carefully designed layout could significantly decrease the distances that patients must travel, as well as related complications. The most important limitation of this study lies in the fact that there are many factors, such as patient and personnel's safety and security that must be taken into account when designing a hospital building. Future studies need to be carried out in order to determine the best layout of hospital buildings by considering multiple layout planning objectives simultaneously.

## ACKNOWLEDGMENT

This work was supported by the National Research Foundation of Korea (NRF) grant funded by the Korean government (MSIP) under Grant No. NRF-2014R1A2A2A03003874.

## REFERENCES

[1] A. Kotzer, S. Zacharakis, M. Raynolds, and F. Buenning, "Evaluation of the built environment: Staff and family datisfation pre- and post-occupancy of the children's hospital," Herd-Health Env. Res. Des. J., vol. 4, pp. 60–78, 2011.

[2] R. Ulrich and X. Zhu, "Medical complications of intra-hospital patient transports: Implications for architectual design and research," Herd-Health Env. Res. Des. J., vol. 1, pp. 31–43, 2007.

[3] A. Rais and A. Viana, "Operations research in healthcare: a survey," Int. Trans. Oper. Res., vol. 18, no. 1, pp. 1–31, Jan. 2011.

[4] Á. Rebuge and D. R. Ferreira, "Business process analysis in healthcare environments: A methodology based on process mining," Inf. Syst., vol. 37, no. 2, pp. 99–116, Apr. 2012.

[5] M. Mans, R.S. Schonenberg, M.H. Song, W. M. P. van der Aalst, and P. J. . Bakker, "Application of process mining in healthcare – A case study in a Dutch hospital," in Biomedical Engineering Systems and Technologies, Springer Berlin Heidelberg, pp. 425–438, 2009.

[6] Z. Zhou, Y. Wang, and L. Li, "Process mining based modeling and analysis of workflows in clinical care - A case study in a chicago outpatient clinic," in Networking, Sensing and Control (ICNSC), 2014 IEEE 11th International Conference on, IEEE, pp. 590–595, 2014.

[7] M. Lang, T. Bürkle, S. Laumann, and H.-U. Prokosch, "Process mining for clinical workflows: challenges and current limitations.," Stud. Health Technol. Inform., vol. 136, pp. 229–34, Jan. 2008.

[8] J. Poelmans, et al., "Combining business process and data discovery techniques for analyzing and improving integrated care pathways," in Advances in Data Mining. Applications and Theoretical Aspects SE - 39, vol. 6171, P. Perner, Ed. Springer Berlin Heidelberg, pp. 505–517, 2010.

[9] B. F. van Dongen, A. K. A. de Medeiros, H. M. W. Verbeek, A. J. M. M. Weijters, and W. M. P. van der Aalst, "The ProM framework: A new era in process mining tool support," in Applications and Theory of Petri Nets 2005 SE - 25, vol. 3536, G. Ciardo and P. Darondeau, Eds. Springer Berlin Heidelberg, pp. 444–454, 2005.

[10] V. Gabriel, "Developing process mining tools: An implementation of sequence clustering for ProM," Lisboa University, 2009.

# Benefits of an Integrated Hierarchical Data Structure for Automotive Demand and Capacity Management

Konrad Pawlikowski
Faculty of Business Economics
Bochum University of Applied Sciences
Bochum, Germany
email: konrad.pawlikowski@hs-bochum.de

Daniel Fruhner
Faculty of Business Studies
Dortmund University of Applied Sciences and Arts
Dortmund, Germany
email: daniel.fruhner@fh-dortmund.de

Katja Klingebiel
Faculty of Business Studies
Dortmund University of Applied Sciences and Arts
Dortmund, Germany
email: katja.klingebiel@fh-dortmund.de

Michael Toth
Faculty of Business Economics
Bochum University of Applied Sciences
Bochum, Germany
email: michael.toth@hs-bochum.de

Axel Wagenitz
Faculty of Business & Social Sciences
Hamburg University of Applied Sciences
Hamburg, Germany
email: axel.wagenitz@haw-hamburg.de

*Abstract*— **The demand and capacity management (DCM) is an essential component of the automotive supply chain management. DCM synchronizes resource requirements with capacities and restrictions of the supply chain and production system. Those requirements result from future or already realized market demands. One major challenge of the DCM is the uncertainty and volatility of the market demands. Other challenges are product variety and supply chain complexity. Here, efficient data management increases transparency and can support the DCM processes effectively. In this context, this contribution analyses the benefits of an integration of distributed product data into a hierarchical tree structure against the background of complexity reduction. The results of this study prove that a hierarchical integrated information model provides an optimized basis for a scenario-based DCM planning process. Data from a German automotive manufacturer served as basis for this evaluation.**

***Keywords- product structure; automotive production; demand and capacity management; optimization; complexity.***

## I. INTRODUCTION

To compete in international markets, automobile manufacturers, i.e., original equipment manufacturers, OEMs, tend to offer their customers buying incentives, a huge variety of models which can be further individualized by several hundred options, i.e., colors, assistance systems, etc. Furthermore, OEMs constantly update their product range in an increasing frequency [1]. Though customers have to deal with the variety of models, they tend to expect that vehicle orders can still be customized shortly before actual production and that the produced car is rapidly delivered on the planned date [2][3].

Here, logistics plays an important role. Nowadays, suppliers do not only produce simple components, but also develop complex modules [4]. The competence of the car manufacturer has shifted to product marketing, the coordination of suppliers, assembly of supplied parts, and the distribution of the end product [5]. Therefore, the integrated management of the automotive production and supply chain is critical for the OEM. The anticipation of the future market demand, the timely derivation of resource and component requirements as well as the integrated and coordinated capacity planning are indispensable prerequisites [6]. Most critical, resource requirements resulting from anticipated or realized market demand need to be synchronized with resource capacities and restrictions of the production and procurement system by an effective demand and capacity management (DCM). DCM processes identify demand- and capacity-asynchronies and implement appropriate countermeasures in a timely manner. DCM acts as an essential interface between market, production and supply chain processes [7][8]. Nevertheless, it is obviously impossible to predict the exact future vehicle orders, as customers can choose from billions of possible configurations for each car type [9][10]. Today, regional and central sales departments of the OEM forecast sales volumes for the models offered in the different sales regions (e.g., number of VW Golf Trendline 2.0

TDI) and sales quotas for the selectable options (e.g., ratio of vehicles with xenon light or navigation system).

Fig. 1 depicts the interdependences of demand and capacity information. The compatibility of options for a respective car is described by a complex set of technical rules, while the relationship between the fully-configured car type and the corresponding parts is described by the bill of material (BOM). Capacity constraints and restrictions exist on sales level, production level and supply chain level. To balance volumes and quotas with constraints and restrictions in order to identify possible bottlenecks, it is necessary to bridge the gap between demand information and capacity information [11][12][13]. Forecast uncertainty, demand volatility, rapid product changes, as well as changes in the supply chain complicate this task significantly.

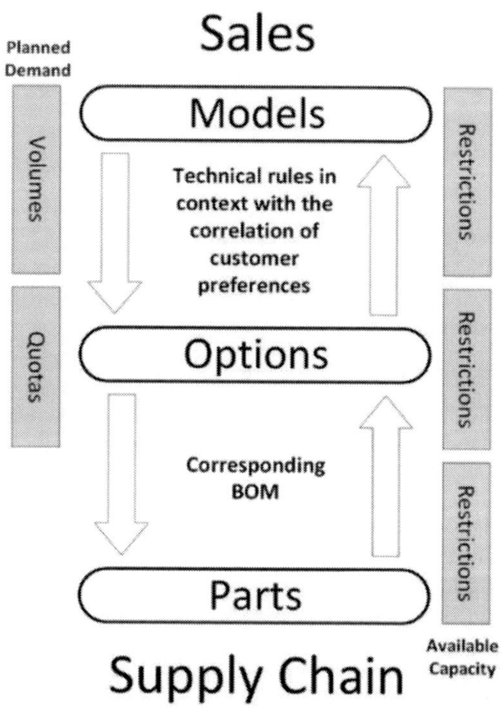


Figure 1. Bridging the gap between demand information and capacity information

Furthermore, the relevant data is typically kept in a highly fragmented information landscape. For example, part demand is typically gradually derived from sales figures in a number of sequential processes taking into account a variety of systems [14][15]. Since automated processes only allow the identification and reporting of formal inconsistencies, typically an experienced human planner has to review the process.

As it is easily understood, an integrated information base could reduce the complexity and increase transparency of the DCM processes immensely. So, highly innovative systems integrate all related data from sales to supply chain into a consistent and integrated information structure, thus providing the essential basis for a continuous DCM process. In this context, this paper analyses the benefits of a hierarchical tree-based data structure for the integration of distributed product data against the background of complexity reduction and transparency increase.

In the next Section, the state of the art of information structures for automotive DCM is presented. Afterwards, an introduction to specific data optimization methods is given in Section 3. Section 4 analyses the complexity reductions gained by these optimization methods. A conclusion including a summary and a perspective on future research and development is given in Section 5.

## II. State of the Art in Automotive DCM Processes

This Section illustrates the state of the art in automotive DCM processes. The DCM process is initiated by the sales department predicting medium-term and future market demands [16]. Here, model volumes and option quotas for hundreds of sales regions worldwide must be planned. These figures are integrated with order volumes and translated into a production program for all sites. The planning complexity of this step is tremendous due to the variety of products. For example, a typical mid-class series (e.g., VW Golf, BMW 1 Series, Audi A3) offers about 30 to 50 different car models (car type of a specific series with typically body type, engine and gear system specification) with about 400 to 800 options. This results in several thousand volumes to be planned for car models in sales regions in a specific time period (e.g., month, week or day depending on planning granularity) and some 10 million option quotas. Furthermore, technical restrictions prohibit options for specific models (e.g., no 17'' tires for convertibles), force specific combinations of options (e.g., LED head light only in combination with LED back lights) or prohibit combinations (e.g., a navigation system rules out all other radios). In addition, sales constraints and customer preferences need to be included. This complex planning can often only be handled by the integration of human experience and intuition (cf. [17]).

Even more so, a huge amount of the resulting resource requirements for production or logistics (supply of parts) are not only depended on single model volumes and quotas for options, but on a particular combination of model, options and sales region. Therefore, some part volumes are hard to predict until the exact configuration of the vehicle, i.e., the order, is known. Nevertheless, as lead times in global supply networks can be long, a certain amount of vehicle parts has to be ordered long before customer orders are known (cf. [16]).

Consequently, the DCM process is challenging and characterized by conflicting goals: because of market dynamics, a huge number of possible vehicle configurations and correlations among vehicle models, options, and parts, the planning itself is already complex [18]. Sales departments are forced to react to volatile markets, increased global competitions, and changing customer requirements: flexibility and reactivity is requested. Production is interested in a stable production program, which guarantees both high capacity utilization and optimal operating results. Material planning wants to fix part requirements as early as possible to avoid bottlenecks proactively as well as to negotiate the flexibility of suppliers appropriately.

This conflict can be named the dilemma of automotive DCM. Typically, it is solved by planning cycles of four to six weeks, which are based on numerous workshops and committee meetings between sales, programming- and material planning [18][19]. The consequence is insufficient flexibility in reaction to market changes. Furthermore, the program is adjusted manually between program approvals and even after program freeze, within the so-called frozen period. However, these adjustments cause a lack of program stability and poor transparency on future demand for parts on supply side. The probability of bottlenecks increases and induces additional internal costs, as well as deterioration of the delivery service to the customer.

There are two theoretical approaches for the integration of these sequential planning processes in an effective holistic DCM process.

The first one is the early inclusion of selected critical resource restrictions into the sales and program planning. The planning variables, i.e., model volumes and option quotas, typically include several million variables. Furthermore, technical rules and BOM rules relate these planning variables to part demands and thus capacity restrictions. For example, a capacity restriction may exist which limits the number of a specific powerful battery. Unfortunately, the selection of this battery may depend on several combinations of options, e.g., the battery is only selected if specific electronical options are chosen. To derive restrictions on model volumes and option quotas all BOM rules and technical rules that relate directly or indirectly to that battery have to be analyzed. In the worst, case this amounts to a significant proportion of the overall number of rules, for a midrange model about 15,000 technical and 600,000 BOM rules. Even more so, partially unmanageable correlations exist between option quotas and model volumes. These result not only from technical restrictions, but also from product strategy, customer preference, and marketing strategies. A customer preference as the choice of navigation system and hands-free module shall be given as an example for such correlations. These two options are independent from the viewpoint of the customer. But historical data has shown that most customers (80%) who choose the navigation system also select the hands-free module; customers who do not select the navigation system rarely choose the hands-free module [20].

As a result, not all restrictions may be deterministically traced back to the decision variables. This is aggravated by ramp-ups and run-outs (continuous change in options, models, etc.), dynamic changes in capacity information, multiple use of parts, parts commonality strategies and other restrictions that may change daily. The complete derivation of restrictions on planning variables harbors an immense complexity and is not deterministically feasible. The selection of historically critical restrictions is not sufficient.

Consequently, the most promising perspective of an effective holistic DCM process is seen in scenario-based real-time planning. Starting from a planning scenario, resources and component requirements are derived and capacity bottlenecks are identified and disclosed.

The basis for this is a consistent and holistic information model, which consists of all planning information for the planning process. The simplest form of the DCM information model is divided into three data partitions: the planning scenarios, the resource information, and the product structures. Resource and part requirements are then derived from planning scenarios by propagation of the product structure from models and options to parts. Typically planned orders are applied here.

To make fast and qualified statements about the feasibility of a scenario, the integrated DCM requires the application of smart quantitative methods to derive future resource requirements from market requirements.

In [17], an evaluation of a number of publications has been performed, that have introduced innovative processes and methods for DCM (e.g., approaches of [11][21][22][23]) and developed an approach that applies planned orders that are applicable for calculation of part demand for the automotive industry.

These algorithms have been implemented and validated at several German OEMs. The respective tool suite is now known under the name of OTD-DCM, where OTD refers to the basic instrument OTD-NET (order-to-delivery and network simulator, cf. [23]). To reduce the amount of data of BOM rules and to optimize their terms, the next Section presents optimization methods that are partially used in this approach.

## III. Hierarchichal Product Structure and Optimization Methods used in the DCM

As described in Section 2, the possible number of BOM rules for a fully specified car amounts to over 600,000. Hence, it is necessary to assure consistency and avoid redundancy in and between all data entities when integrating data into one data structure. Inconsistencies occur for example when subsets of technical rules contradict each other so that orders cannot be specified fully. Hence, it is necessary to adapt planning-relevant information regarding structural requirements and to verify their consistency before they are processed. As a result, the implemented data processing in OTD-DCM has been based on the principle of generating a hierarchically-linked structure of variant clusters (cf. [24]). Here, a variant cluster contains by definition a subset of allowed vehicle variants (typically car models), that have common properties (example: sales region=Germany, body=medium class sedan, engine=150hp diesel, transmission=automatic, and trim=comfort). The first pre-optimization of the product structure is the generation of a hierarchical data tree where tree levels are based on subsequently detailed variant cluster specifications. The tree structure is an intuitively attractive approach because of its proximity to car design principles. Tree levels may be defined based on for example the model type, target country, engine type (see Fig. 2).

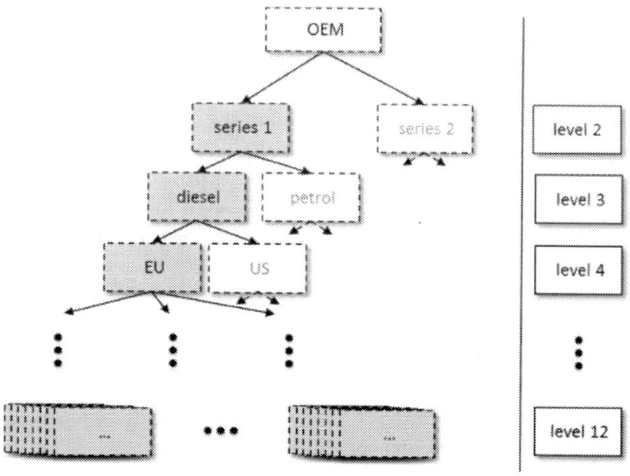


Figure 2. Extract of the generated tree structure

Each level can have one to several nodes, depending on the level and type of car (e.g., gasoline, diesel, electronic for the fuel nodes). As all product information have a specific temporal validity, these dynamics have to be handled within this tree structure [17].

This paper especially focuses on the processing and thus complexity reduction of rules when integrating product data into this hierarchical structure. Technical rules represent the technical feasibility by Boolean expressions, e.g., "if motor = 90 kW then suspension = 6-speed manual gearbox". BOM rules follow the same Boolean schema but link options to part demands, e.g., "if motor = 90 kW and radio = "Radio Basic" then parts 5678973 and 5678974". The mentioned optimization has been subdivided into three optimization steps.

- The first objective has been to identify all forced options, i.e., the options that have necessarily to be chosen for a specific variant cluster (e.g., every car for the German market has necessarily a specific exhaust system). Therefore, principally allowed options for one variant cluster are reduced by non-feasible options. This is done by checking intelligently selected, partly specified theoretical configurations against all applicable technical rules. If a contradiction occurs, the option will be deleted from the set of allowed options. When this process leads to only one possible option from a set of alternative options, this option is set as forced.
  An inner inconsistency is identified if the last identified forced property violates a technical rule. An outer inconsistency is identified if a positive demand quota for an option has been planned, but the option itself is technically not allowed. Another outer inconsistency is identified, if the sum of all planned quotas for all allowed options within a subset of alternative options in a specified time period does not equal 100%.
- The second optimization step reduces the number and the length of rules by application of the Identity Law of the Boolean algebra (cf. [25]). It should be noted that these steps are valid only for one variant cluster and a specified, fixed time period. Therefore, these steps need to be executed for each variant cluster and all relevant time periods. The OTD-DCM implementation is able to shorten rules by merging several BOM or technical rules that belong to more than one resource, i.e., workstations, assembly lines and more [17][26][27]. Next, this second optimization step aims to further reduce the actual length of all rules by Boolean simplification of terms. In contrast to the first step, it is used for each rule separately. If the optimized length of the rule is shorter than the original one, it is replaced by the new representation. Example: The Boolean expression "$\neg(\neg A \wedge B \wedge \neg C)$" will be reduced to "$\neg B \vee A \vee C$".
- The third and last optimization step tries to identify commonalities for nodes in the hierarchical product structure. For example, rules which are valid for each child node of one variant cluster are moved upwards to the parent node and deleted from all children. The preliminary condition for this step is that all derived variant clusters share this rule over the same time period. Example: The forced option "Owner's manual in German language" may be valid for all variant clusters within the sales market = Germany. Hence, it can be transferred upwards to the variant cluster "variants - German" [17].

The analysis of the complexity reductions which these methods provide, will be presented in the next Section.

## IV. ANALYSIS OF COMPLEXITY REDUCTIONS

The evaluation of the previously described optimization steps has been executed on real data for two middle class series from a German OEM. It should be noted that these two car series represent only a small fraction of the OEM portfolio and the analysis is limited here on BOM rules only. In the following the parameter $n(l)$ is defined as the number of tree nodes on a level. A tree node represents a variant cluster as described in the previous Section. The respective sum of BOM rules before optimization are defined as $r^{pre}(l)$ and after optimization as $r^{post}(l)$. The number of average rules per tree node within a level is defined as

$$a^{pre}(l) = r^{pre}(l) / n(l) \quad (1)$$

and

$$a^{post}(l) = r^{post}(l) / n(l). \quad (2)$$

A null-entry rule characterizes a rule without condition, i.e., this rule is valid for the whole variant cluster. Accordingly, the total number of null-entry rules on a specific level $l$ before optimization is defined as $v^{pre}(l)$ and on a specific level $l$ after optimization as $v^{post}(l)$.

The results in Table 1 illustrate, that the lowest level of the hierarchical product structure contains all existing BOM rules $r^{pre}(l)$ before all optimization steps. Levels 1 to 11 do not contain rules because these levels have been added artificially to the product structure in the first pre-optimization step in order to construct the primary tree structure. After optimization, several BOM rules have been hoisted to higher levels resulting in $r^{post}(l)$.

Furthermore, the overall number of rules is reduced from 1,076,428 to 111,070, which amounts to a reduction of 89.7% in relation to the original number.

The reduction as well as the average ratio of rules per node are recognizable by comparing $a^{pre}(l)$ and $a^{post}(l)$. The weighted average considers the number of nodes of the whole tree per level, where the reduction in this case also results in 89.7% coincidentally. This analysis proves the immense complexity reduction by application of the OTD-DCM hierarchical product structure.

TABLE I. INDICATORS WITHOUT OPTIMIZATION (PRE) AND WITH OPTIMIZATION (POST)

| level $l$ | $n(l)$ | $r^{pre}(l)$ | $r^{post}(l)$ | $a^{pre}(l)$ | $a^{post}(l)$ | $v^{pre}(l)$ | $v^{post}(l)$ |
|---|---|---|---|---|---|---|---|
| **1** | 1 | 0 | 38 | 0 | 38 | 0 | 35 |
| **2** | 2 | 0 | 4,389 | 0 | 2,194 | 0 | 2,554 |
| **3** | 3 | 0 | 1,204 | 0 | 401 | 0 | 425 |
| **4** | 3 | 0 | 0 | 0 | 0 | 0 | 0 |
| **5** | 4 | 0 | 1,293 | 0 | 323 | 0 | 498 |
| **6** | 4 | 0 | 0 | 0 | 0 | 0 | 0 |
| **7** | 5 | 0 | 1,047 | 0 | 209 | 0 | 111 |
| **8** | 8 | 0 | 4,101 | 0 | 512 | 0 | 845 |
| **9** | 8 | 0 | 0 | 0 | 0 | 0 | 0 |
| **10** | 8 | 0 | 0 | 0 | 0 | 0 | 0 |
| **11** | 12 | 0 | 1,501 | 0 | 125 | 0 | 416 |
| **12** | 184 | 1,076,428 | 97,497 | 5,850 | 529 | 287,841 | 7,324 |
| | **sum** | **sum** | **sum** | **weighted average** | **weighted average** | **sum** | **sum** |
| | 242 | 1,076,428 | 111,070 | 4,448 | 458 | 287,841 | 12,208 |

Nevertheless, rules at parent nodes are valid for all child nodes. When a specific variant cluster at lowest level is regarded (for example, for generation of fully specified planned orders) it is necessary to take into account all valid rules for this specific node. Thus, rules on the upper levels need to be propagated downwards to all child nodes and have to be considered when calculating the total number (sum) of valid rules for one variant cluster.

TABLE II. PROPAGATED RULES PER VARIANT CLUSTER AT LOWEST LEVEL (LEVEL 12)

| propagated rules - level 12 | pre-optimization | post-optimization |
|---|---|---|
| **sum** | 1,076,428 | 813,823 |
| **average ratio** | 5,850 | 4,423 |
| **median** | 6,734 | 4,725 |
| **minimum** | 3,007 | 2,653 |
| **maximum** | 7,522 | 5,344 |

Table 2 shows that the propagated number of rules on the lowest level. The total number is still significantly smaller than the original number. The reduction of the number of rules is still about 24.4%.

## V. CONCLUSION AND FUTURE WORK

An integral component of the automotive supply chain management is DCM, where resource requirements, resulting from future or already realized market demands, are synchronized with capacities and restrictions of the supply chain and production system. Because it is impossible to predict the exact future vehicle orders, part demand is typically gradually derived from sales figures in a number of sequential processes involving a variety of systems as well as experienced human planners. In this paper, the integration of the respective distributed product data into a hierarchical tree structure has been analyzed against the background of complexity reduction.

It has been demonstrated that by choosing a hierarchical tree structure the total number of BOM rules could be reduced by a factor of 10 (reduction of 89.7%). Furthermore, the number of BOM rules relating to a variant cluster could be reduced by 24.4% in the current case. In summary, the hierarchical integrated information model provides more transparency as redundant and surplus information is dramatically reduced. Thus, it proves to be an optimized basis for a scenario-based DCM planning process for the automotive industry which relies on transparent and consistent data. A sound DCM process will increase program stability and transparency on future part demand. Bottlenecks and the resulting deterioration of delivery service levels will be decreased. Furthermore, all applications using the information model will save computation time and memory space [17].

Since only a small information model of two car series has been considered here, an analysis of a full product spectrum may be necessary to provide greater insights into the effects of the optimization steps. The chosen tree structure is an intuitively attractive approach because of its proximity to car design principles. Nevertheless, when targeting an integrated product structure, product characteristics from other departments like sales, productions and logistics need to be taken into account. Here, a more generalized graph structure instead of the applied tree structure may hold further benefits in terms of complexity reduction. Against this background, generic graph structures will be analyzed in the near future.

## ACKNOWLEDGMENT

Special thanks to the German "Bundesministerium für Forschung und Bildung" (BMBF) for making this study possible by providing funding to the ILogTec project. The funding of BMBF was granted with Funding-ID 03FH008IA5.

## REFERENCES

[1] J. Schuberthan and S. Potrafke, "Die Anforderungen des Kunden…," in F. Gehr and B. Hellingrath, eds. Logistik in der Automobilzulieferindustrie: Innovatives Supply Chain Management für wettbewerbsfähige Zulieferstrukturen. Springer, p. 9, 2007.

[2] D. Alford, P. Sackett, and G. Nelder, "Mass customization - an automotive perspective," International Journal of Production Economics, vol. 65(1), pp. 99-110, 2000.

[3] E.-H. Krog and K. Statkevich, "Kundenorientierung und Integrationsfunktion der Logistik in der Supply Chain der Automobilindustrie,"in H.Baumgarten, ed. Das Beste der Logistik: Innovationen, Strategien, Umsetzungen, Springer, p. 187, 2008.

[4] A. Trojan, "…und die Auswirkungen auf den 1st-Tier-Lieferanten," in F. Gehr and B. Hellingrath, eds. Logistik in der Automobilzulieferindustrie: Innovatives Supply Chain Management für wettbewerbsfähige Zulieferstrukturen. Springer, p. 12, 2007.

[5] S. Meißner, "Logistische Stabilität in der automobilen Variantenfliessfertigung," Lehrstuhl für Fördertechnik Materialfluss Logistik, Technische Universität München, Germany, p. 1, 2009.

[6] R.T. Yu-Lee, "Essentials of Capacity Management," John Wiley and Sons, Inc., p. 3, 2002.

[7] E.-H. Krog, G. Richartz, R. Kanschat and, M. Hemken, "Kooperatives Bedarfs- und kapazitätsmanagement der Automobilhersteller und Systemlieferanten," Logistik Management, vol. 4(3), p. 47, 2002.

[8] D. Arnold, H. Isermann, A. Kuhn, H. Tempelmeier, and K. Furmans, Handbuch Logistik, 3rd ed., Springer, p. 472, 2008.

[9] M. Holweg and F. K. Pil, "The Second Century: Reconnecting Customer and Value Chain through Build-to-Order", MIT Press, p. 165, 2004.

[10] F. Klug, "Logistikmanagement in der Automobilindustrie: Grundlagen der Logistik im Automobilsbau", Springer, Berlin, Germany, p. 49, 2010.

[11] T. Stäblein, "Integrierte Planung des Materialbedarfs bei kundenbeauftragsorintierter Fertigung von komplexen und variantenreichen Serienprodukten," Aachen, Germany, Shaker, 2008.

[12] T. Zernechel, „Gestaltung und Optimierung von Unternehmensnetzwerken: Supply Chain Management in der Automobilindustrie," in F. Garcia, K. Semmler, and J. Walther, ed. Die Automobilindustrie auf dem Weg zur globalen Netzwerkkompetenz: Effiziente und flexible Supply Chains erfolgreich gestalten", Berlin, Germany, Springer, p. 372, 2007.

[13] J. Gebhardt, H. Detmer, and A.L. Madsen, "Predicting Parts Demand in the Automotive Industry — An Application of Probabilistic Graphical Models," Proc. Int. Joint Conf. on Uncertainty in Artificial Intelligence (UAI'03, Acapulco, Mexico), Bayesian Modelling Applications Workshop, Morgan Kaufman, San Mateo, CA, USA, 2003.

[14] H. Meyr, "Supply Chain planning in the German automotive industry," OR Spectrum, vol. 26(4), p. 453, 2004.

[15] T. Stäblein, "Integrierte Planung des Materialbedarfs bei kundenbeauftragsorintierter Fertigung von komplexen und variantenreichen Serienprodukten," Aachen, Germany, Shaker, p. 35, 2008.

[16] T. Zernechel, „Gestaltung und Optimierung von Unternehmensnetzwerken: Supply Chain Management in der Automobilindustrie," in F. Garcia, K. Semmler, and J. Walther, ed. Die Automobilindustrie auf dem Weg zur globalen Netzwerkkompetenz: Effiziente und flexible Supply Chains erfolgreich gestalten", Berlin, Germany, Springer, pp. 367-378, 2007.

[17] A. Wagenitz, K. Liebler, and S. Schürrer, "A Holistic Approach to Demand and Capacity Management in the Automotive Industry," in Proceedings of tge 21st International Conference on Production Research, Stuttgart, Germany, p. 101, 2011.

[18] H. Meyr, "Supply Chain planning in the German automotive industry," OR Spectrum, vol. 26(4), pp. 447-470, 2004.

[19] J. Diercks. *IT verliert Kontrolle über Geschäftsprozesse.* [Online]. Available from: : http://heise.de/-1244454 [last accessed 17 May 2016], 2011.

[20] K. Liebler, "Eine prozess- und IT-gestützte methode für die Produktionsplanung in der Automobilindustrie," Dissertation, Dortmund, Germany, Praxiswissen Publications, p. 105, 2013.

[21] S. Ohl, "Prognose und Planung variantenreicher Produkte am Beispiel der Automobilindustrie," Düsseldorf, Germany, VDI, 2000.

[22] H. Wagner, „Kollaboratives Bedarfs- und Kapazitätsmanagement am Beispiel der Automobilindustrie: Lösungsansatz zur Sicherstellung der Wandlungsfähigkeit," 1st ed., Huss, 2006.

[23] A. Wagenitz, "Modellierungsmethode zur Auftragsabwicklung in der Automobilindustrie," Dissertation, Technische Universität Dortmund, Germany, 2007.

[24] K.-U. Meininger, "Abstraktionsbasierte Bereitstellung bereichsübergreifender Planungsdaten für die Produktionsplanung bei Serienfertigung variantenreicher Erzeugnisse," 1st ed., Idstein, Germany, Schulz-Kirchner, p. 32ff, 1994.

[25] R. L. Goodstein, Boolean Algebra, Mineola, New York, Dover Publications, 2007.

[26] K. Liebler, "Eine prozess- und IT-gestützte Methode für die Produktionsplanung in der Automobilindustrie," Dissertation, Dortmund, Germany, Praxiswissen Publications, p. 101, 2013.

[27] K. Liebler, "Eine prozess- und IT-gestützte Methode für die Produktionsplanung in der Automobilindustrie," Dissertation, Dortmund, Germany, Praxiswissen Publications, p. 110, 2013.

# Taking Advantage of Turkish Characteristic Features to Tackle with Authorship Attribution Problems for Turkish

Neslihan Şirin Saygılı, Tassadit Amghar, Bernard Levrat
Computer Science Laboratory
University of Angers
Angers, France
e-mail: {neslihansirin.saygili,amghar,levrat}@{etud,info}.univ-angers.fr

Tankut Acarman
Computer Engineering Department
Galatasaray University
Istanbul, Turkey
e-mail: tacarman@gsu.edu.tr

*Abstract*—**The rapid increase in the number of the electronic and online texts, such as electronic mails, online newspapers and magazines, blog posts and online forum messages has also accelerated the studies carried out on authorship attribution. Although the studies are not as abundant as in English language, there have been considerable studies on author identification in Turkish in the last fifteen years. This paper includes two parts; first part is a quick review of Turkish authorship attribution studies. The review is focused on the stylometric features that enable authors to be distinguished one from another. In the second part, we analyze the main characteristics of the Turkish language and depict our first experiments on Turkish corpora. In these lasts, we experiment different kind of n-gram and word structure, taking advantages of Turkish characteristic features by the frequent usage of gerunds in Turkish language, and use Support Vector Machines as learning algorithm.**

***Keywords-authorship attribution; Turkish language; stylometry; n-gram; gerunds; Support Vector Machines.***

## I. INTRODUCTION

Authorship attribution studies based on statistical methods have begun in the late 19th century where Mosteller and Wallace's impressive 'Federalist Paper' study [1] renewed interest on this issue. The aim behind automatic authorship attribution task is the identification of the author of a text among several ones using for that different characteristics in which stylistic features predominate, depending on the methodology used for achieving the task.

Over the past two decades three research domains have played an important role in development of authorship attribution methods: information retrieval, machine learning and natural language processing. To consider roughly the contributions of each of these domains we can say that information retrieval provides efficient methods for modeling and processing huge number of documents, machine learning furnishes ways to extracts the most suitable set of features characterizing a great volume of data to be used for a specific task, and natural language processing gives models suited to cope with natural language data. Furthermore, the remarkable increase of available electronic text amount (e.g., emails, blogs, online forum messages, source code, etc.) greatly expanded the range of applications of authorship attribution among which cites criminal law, intelligence and computer forensic [2].

Quantitative authorship detection earlier studies began in the 18th century with works on, plays supposed to be authored by William Shakespeare [3] [4]. Two periods could be distinguished in Authorship attribution methodologies:

The first one is dominated by linguistic, stylometry and computer-assisted studies. Computer-assisted means computer programs only calculate some metrics and human decides the final authorship attribution result. T. Yule proposed a metric called vocabulary richness which points out the probability of any randomly selected pair of words will be identical [5]. Ellegard proposed distinctiveness ratio that indicates how far the author is from the average usage of a word [6]. Later, in 1964, Mosteller and Wallace's work was based on Bayesian statistical analysis [1].

Until 1990, the authorship attribution methodologies were computer-assisted instead of computer-based. Computer-based means computer programs both calculate metrics and decide the final authorship attribution result. After developments of information retrieval, machine learning and natural language processing authorship attribution proceeded to second phase. The second phase consists of computer-based studies rather than computer-assisted studies. Increment of available electronic texts reveals the potential of authorship attribution usages in various applications such as criminal law, intelligence, civil law, computer forensic, and literary research [2]. In addition to this, from machine learning perspective, authorship attribution is regarded as a multiclass single label text categorization task [7].

Before this study, we made a short survey of Turkish authorship attribution studies from the point of stylometry. The main goal in this paper is to enrich stylometric features set used in the works described in the review, and to use them in our first experimental approaches. Regarding to these goals the paper follows the following plan: Section II tries to characterize Turkish language in its major characteristics which, distinguish it from other languages like English or French, Section III is a quick review of stylometric features used in authorship attribution, Section IV depicts the experimental processing. Section V is a conclusion where we give some lights on the continuation of this ongoing research.

## II. TURKISH LANGUAGE

Turkish belongs to the Turkic family of Altaic languages and as such deeply differs from most natural languages on which natural language processing researcher mostly bears on. This is the reason why it is interesting to analyze its main characteristics in the aim of adapting generally used methodology to its idiosyncrasies. First of all, Turkish is an agglutinative language, where functions and derivative of words are mainly indicated by suffixes added to the end of the words where languages like English generally mark the function by the position of the words in the sentences and have comparatively less derivative. To give an idea of this, in corpora words occurrences are formed by productive affixations of multiple suffixes from about 30 K root words.

Oflazer gave wide coverage to the challenges of Turkish regarding with natural language processing in his study [8]. There are a variety of difficult features of Turkish in terms of the natural language processing such as agglutinating morphology, vowel harmony and free constituent order in syntax. Derivational morphemes are frequently used in the Turkish language. Frequent uses of derivational morphemes provide the language productivity. Practically, infinite vocabulary raises interesting issues to be considered in any natural language processing applications. There are some difficulties of Turkish language on the natural language processing applications below.

- Spelling correction: the methods using finite vocabulary are not appropriate for Turkish.
- Tag set design: finite tags set numbers of techniques are not suitable for Turkish.
- Statistical language modeling: there is high rate of unknown words for Turkish.
- Syntactic modeling: Turkish derivational morphemes complicate the modeling.
- Statistical translation: based on morphological structure translation gives better results [8].

A remarkable point is stemming. Texts are expressed as a dimensional space with a number of at least one time occurring words in the different documents. Using derived words increases the size of the dimensional space. Thus, stemming is one of the frequently used methods. Stemming has been applied successfully to many different languages. Nevertheless, this approach is less feasible to an agglutinative language, because agglutinative languages require a more detailed level of morphological analysis. Complex morphological techniques are required that remove suffixes from words according to their internal structure [9]. Another supporting idea is that, stemming in Turkish could not provide the desired result. Turkish has a complex morphological structure, for instance derived words may be incorporated into different classes as morphological and semantic.

## III. MOTIVATION AND REVIEW OF STYLOMETRIC FEATURES

The prevalence of electronic documents initiates a large number of natural language processing studies all around the world. Precisely, there is a variety of English language processing concerning authorship attribution. Unfortunately, the numbers of Turkish authorship attribution studies are less than English studies; Turkish studies have been made for the last fifteen years. Starting this point, our first step is to review Turkish authorship attribution studies. Because these kinds of studies are crucial for Turkish language, which lacks natural language processing compare with English and other commonly treated languages. One of the motivations is to obtain the more important characteristics of Turkish by analyzing these studies.

Stylometry is the application of the study of linguistic style by which a person can make a decision about another person by its writing style. It focuses on readily computable and countable language features, such as sentence length, phrase length, word length, vocabulary frequency, distribution of words of different lengths. Stylometric features can be separated into three main groups in this review; lexical, character based and syntactic features.

Firstly, lexical features can be categorized to token-based, vocabulary richness, vectors of word frequencies and word n-gram model. Token-based features are based on the number of tokens or the length of tokens. Some token-based features are average word length, average sentence length, average number of sentences, and average number of words. Vocabulary richness can be defined as attempts to quantify the diversity of the vocabulary of a text. Vectors of word frequency are described bag-of-words text representations where a text is represented as the bag of its words, each one having a frequency of occurrence disregarding grammar and even word order. N-gram is defined as an adjacent sequence of n items from a given sequence of text or speech, in which the n should be an integer greater than zero. Due to the fact that there is a huge number of lexical features and no restrictions about the field of applications explain why a large number of Turkish authorship attribution methods prefer lexical features. Among 11 studies focused on Turkish, token-based features and frequencies of words have been used six times, the word richness five times and a model of word n-grams three times.

Secondly, a variety of character level measures can be used, such as alphabetic character counts, digit character counts, upper case, lower case character counts, punctuation mark counts, etc. Reference [10] suggested that an author has similar character frequency in her/his all texts. So, this study shows that character frequency based features give successful results in Turkish authorship attribution. Beside, [11] indicates that character level n-grams are suitable models to solve different Turkish text classification problems.

Lastly, the basic idea of the syntactic approach is that the author unwittingly tends to use similar syntax in her/his all articles. A widespread syntactic approach is using Part-of-Speech (POS) tagging. POS tagging is the process of labeling each word in a sentence as corresponding to its adequate part of speech. As is known that Turkish is an agglutinative language, which has a complex morphological structure. This morphological complexity of the Turkish language causes numerous different words appear in surface structures in the text. POS tags of the words can change from each other by using several suffixes. Herewith, it is more difficult to determine the final POS tag of a word using the root than in English language. Nevertheless, POS tagging have been used in four Turkish studies.

This is the first review of Turkish authorship attribution studies and the main point of the study that obtains more successful stylometric features for Turkish language. According to the results of reviewed Turkish author detection studies; word length; character n-gram and word n-gram models are the most successful features.

## IV. NEW CHARACTERISTIC APPROACHES FOR TURKISH

According to the previous section, word length and n-gram models are more important features than other stylometric features for Turkish studies. In addition to this, we assume that highlighting the characteristic features of Turkish will produce favorable results. For that purpose, we conducted two experiments. We have three datasets, which are consisting of Milliyet, Kıbrıs [12], and Radikal newspapers articles. Kıbrıs dataset has 7 authors, 50 articles for each author and average word count per article is 535. Milliyet has 9 authors, 50 articles for each author and average word count per article is 461. Radikal has 7 authors, 250 articles for each author and average word count per article is 836. 80% of each dataset is used as training data and 20% of each dataset is used as test data.

On the implementation side, we used scikit-learn [13], which is a powerful python machine-learning library. Scikit-learn provides skillful text vectorizers, which are utilities to build feature vectors from text documents. A vectorizer converts a collection of text documents to a matrix of intended features; within this context *tf-idf* (product of term frequency and inverse document frequency statistics) vectorizer gives a matrix of *tf-idf* features. All experiments have been done with default parameters of scikit-learn Support Vector Machines (SVM) [14] algorithm. Here an example of linear support vector classification function with default parameters:

LinearSVC(*penalty='l2',loss='squared_hinge',dual=True,tol=0.0001,C=1.0,multi_class='ovr',fit_intercept=True,intercept_scaling=1,class_weight=None,verbose=0,random_state=None,max_iter=1000*)

### A. Different Kinds of Word Structures

The first experiment consists in using different kinds of word structures. Authors often write on various subjects, in this case the word richness could not be distinctive. The authors follow the same syntactic way on their all articles without noticing it. Therefore, finding syntactic features can give more successful results on the author detection process. By this point, we developed the hypothesis that the root of the word would be better than other parts. On the other hand, if the authors use derived words in the same pattern, suffixes are valued in terms of syntactic approach. Turkish has similar features to all other agglutinative languages; such as derivational suffixes usually change the part of speech or the meaning of the word to which they are affixed.

We have designed a process, which is cutting words with a blunt knife; the first 5 letters of the words were marked as the root, the later letters were marked as the suffix part. Then the original versions of the words were marked as full word. Lastly, using the Turkish stemmer of the snowball [15] library was marked as stemmed. Thus, the dataset contains root, suffix, full word and stem.

TABLE I. F1-SCORES OF THE DATASETS VIA SVM ALGORITHM

| *N-gram (1,3)* | *Full word* | *Root* | *Suffix* | *Stemmed* |
|---|---|---|---|---|
| Radikal | 0.9885 | 0.9886 | 0.9792 | 0.9817 |
| Milliyet | 0.9566 | 0.9256 | 0.8768 | 0.8845 |
| Kıbrıs | 0.9621 | 0.9490 | 0.9042 | 0.9174 |

In datasets we used four different forms as mentioned above. SVM algorithm has produced average F1-scores which using *tf-idf* values of word unigram, bigram and trigram as features for each dataset can be seen in Table I. On the other hand, full word is more successful than root form and also full word is more successful than stem in all datasets. There is an important feature of agglutinative languages: derived words can be very different in terms of type and meaning from the root of the word, so the last form of the word has significant role in the Turkish language analysis. So it seems interesting to work with occurrences rather than with stems. Another comment about the results, suffix results are worse than results of other forms for Turkish. However, the gap between suffix and others is highly close. We can say that these results show promise and we could extract a syntactic clue with usage of suffixes.

### B. Gerunds Frequency

The other experiment takes advantages of Turkish characteristic features by using frequencies of gerunds. Gerunds are derived from the verbs but used as nouns in a sentence. Adding derivational suffixes to verbs in Turkish language creates gerunds. According to derivational suffix, the gerunds can be used as nouns, adjectives or adverbs in the sentence.

- **Noun:** Kardeşim oku**ma**yı öğrendi. (My sister learned to **read**.)
- **Adjective:** Gele**cek** yıl işe başlayacak. (She will start to job **next** year.)
- **Adverb:** Yemeğimi biti**rir** bitir**mez** gelirim. (I will come **as soon as I finish** my meal.)

We collected 590 infinitives, 587 participles and 916 verbal adverbs.

On the implementation side, we use the frequencies of the gerunds as features for the SVM algorithm. The program produced 2662 features on Radikal dataset.

TABLE II. F1-SCORES OF GERUNDS AS FEATURED ON RADIKAL VIA SVM ALGORITHM

| *Author Name* | *Precision* | *Recall* | *F1-Score* |
|---|---|---|---|
| AH | 0.87 | 0.67 | 0.76 |
| AO | 0.76 | 0.76 | 0.76 |
| BO | 0.72 | 0.78 | 0.75 |
| EB | 0.66 | 0.70 | 0.68 |
| FT | 0.79 | 0.84 | 0.82 |
| OC | 0.71 | 0.80 | 0.75 |
| TE | 0.83 | 0.76 | 0.79 |
| **Average** | **0.76** | **0.76** | **0.76** |

In according with Table II, the first practice implementation of gerund gives F1-score between 0.68 and 0.82. The first results are compared with reviewed Turkish studies; we can say that these results are promising. Because, the average F1-score is 0.76 and it was resulted from only gerunds frequency. Using Turkish characteristic features brings to a successful conclusion, hence the next step of the experiment will be tried to use other characteristic points of Turkish such as optative mood, synonym and free order.

## V. CONCLUSION

The expeditious increase in the number of electronic text and the development of techniques, such as machine learning and natural language processing tools have enabled the Turkish authorship attribution studies over the last two decades. These important works have been guided to develop the author detection methods that give successful results for the Turkish language. This paper includes two parts; first part is a review of Turkish authorship attribution studies. Focus of the review is the stylometric features that provide distinguishing between authors. This is the first review of Turkish authorship attribution studies, the main point of the study that obtains more successful stylometric features for Turkish language. The result of our review can show that word length, character n-gram and word n-gram models are the most important characteristics for Turkish author detection.

The second part consists of important stylometric features for Turkish and our experiments. The first one of experiments is built with n-gram and word structure by using Support Vector Machines algorithm. The average F1-score of the first experiments are 0.98, 0.90 and 0.92 for Radikal, Milliyet and Kıbrıs datasets respectively. The second experiment consisted of frequencies of gerunds by using SVM. The first practice implementation of gerund gives F1-score between 0.68 and 0.82.

Regarding the first promising results, we will continue experiments on especially n-gram, word structure and Turkish characteristic features such as optative mood, synonym and free order. Thus, we will try to provide successful solutions to the Turkish author detection problems.

## REFERENCES


[1] F. Mosteller and D. Wallace, Inference and disputed authorship: The Federalist. Addison-Wesley , 1964.

[2] E. Stamatatos, "A survey of modern authorship attribution methods", Journal of the American Society for information Science and Technology, vol. 60.3, pp. 538-556, 2009.

[3] T. C. Mendenhall, "The characteristic curves of composition", Science, pp. 237-249, 1887.

[4] E. Malone, A dissertation on part one, two and three of Henry IV tending to show that those plays where not written originally by Shakespeare. Henry Baldwin, 1787.

[5] C. U. Yule, The statistical study of literary vocabulary. Archon Books, 1968.

[6] A. Ellegard, "A Statistical method for determining authorship: the Junius Letters", Gothenburg studies in English vol. 13, pp.1769-1772, 1962.

[7] F. Sebastiani, "Machine learning in automated text categorization", ACM computing surveys (CSUR) vol. 34.1, pp. 1-47, 2002.

[8] K. Oflazer, "Turkish and its Challenges for Natural Language Processing," Language Resources and Evaluation, vol. 48, pp. 639-653, Dec. 2014.

[9] F. C. Ekmekcioglu, M. F. Lynch and P. Willett, "Stemming and N-gram matching for term conflation in Turkish texts", Information Research, 1(1). [Online] Available at: http://informationr.net/ir/2-2/paper13.html, 1996. [Accessed 12 July 2016]

[10] H. Takci and E. Ekinci, "Character Level Authorship Attribution for Turkish Text Documents", The Online Journal of Science and Technology vol. 2.3, pp.12-16, 2012.

[11] F. Turkoglu, B. Diri and M. F. Amasyali, "Author attribution of turkish texts by feature mining", Advanced Intelligent Computing Theories and Applications. With Aspects of Theoretical and Methodological Issues, pp.1086-1093, 2007.

[12] Y. Bay and E. Celebi, "Feature Selection for Enhanced Author Identification of Turkish Text", Information Sciences and Systems 2015, pp. 371-379, 2016.

[13] Scikit-learn Machine Learning in Python, http://scikit-learn.org/stable/ [Accessed 12 July 2016]

[14] C. Cortes and V. Vapnik, "Support-vector networks", Machine Learning, vol. 20, no. 3, pp. 273-297, 1995.

[15] Snowball,http://snowballstem.org/ [Accessed 12 July 2016]

# Microarea Selection Method Based on Service Diffusion Process for Broadband Services

Motoi Iwashita, Akiya Inoue
Dept. of Management Information Science
Chiba Institute of Technology
Chiba, Japan
e-mail: {iwashita.motoi, akiya.inoue}@it-chiba.ac.jp

Takeshi Kurosawa
Dept. of Mathematical Information Science
Tokyo University of Science
Tokyo, Japan
e-mail: tkuro@rs.kagu.tus.ac.jp

Ken Nishimatu
Network Technology Laboratories
NTT
Tokyo, Japan
e-mail: nishimatsu.ken@lab.ntt.co.jp

***Abstract*— Wired/wireless information communication networks have been expanded in order to meet the demand for broadband services as an information and communication technology (ICT) infrastructure. Since the installation of such ICT infrastructures requires a large amount of time and money for expansion, the decision how to select the installation area is a key issue. Low-usage facilities can cause problems for business in terms of investment efficiency. Moreover, it takes time to select areas because of the need to consider how to estimate the potential demand, and how to manage the installation of infrastructures for thousands of municipal areas across the nation. In this paper, we propose an efficient microarea selection method for use during the life cycle of broadband services. The method is constructed with consideration of consumer segmentation, and each type of consumer behaviour as the broadband service propagation model.**

***Keywords-data mining; area marketing; demand forecast; decision support system; algorithm.***

## I. INTRODUCTION

Fibre-to-the-home (FTTH) is an ultra-high-speed, wired, broadband access infrastructure, provided in Japan since 2002. Such an ICT infrastructure provides a variety of technologies and circumstances for corporate activity. Although the FTTH coverage rate for 2014 with respect to the total number of households nationwide was about 98% [1], the customer rate using FTTH in the coverage areas was still only 43%. As for wireless broadband access, long-term evolution (LTE) for high-speed wireless access has been provided since December 2010. The LTE coverage rate for the population was more than 90%, and the customer rate was about 42% in 2014 [2]. The other high-speed wireless access, worldwide interoperability for microwave access (WiMAX), which has been provided since 2009, had a coverage rate of greater than 90%, and the total number of customers was about 7 million in 2014.

Since the infrastructure installation is very expensive, business management is strongly affected when the facility usage is low. Therefore, strategic and economical installation is necessary for ICT infrastructures, such as broadband and wireless access facilities. Such installations strongly depend on how we estimate the potential demand in different areas; therefore, an efficient estimation method is urgently required.

The goal of providing an area with ICT services is to determine the investment order of areas, as ICT infrastructure installation per area is both more effective and less expensive than on-demand installation. If we can come up with an efficient method, it will have a lasting impact on enterprise business.

In this paper, we propose a microarea selection method that is simple to use compared with trade analysis [3]. Our target is ICT infrastructure installation during the life cycle which covers both early and late stages of broadband services. The proposed method is based on consumer segmentation, on each type of consumer behaviour as in the broadband service propagation model, and is verified with the service penetration of WiMAX services. Section II introduces related works. The trend of demand of WiMAX in Japan is described in Section III. Section IV is devoted to the hypothesis of the service diffusion and its model. Section V describes an efficient method for the selection of microareas. Simulation results and discussions are presented in Section VI. Section VII concludes this paper.

## II. RELATED WORKS

Determining the target area for marketing, such as which area to focus on in terms of sales activities, and which area to install the facility in, is based on trade analysis. In fact, the setting up of a convenience store is decided by demographic data and field surveys. The geographic information system (GIS) [4] is an effective tool for area-related decision making. An empirical study using GIS for trade analysis has been previously [5] reported. These approaches are effective for deciding whether a store should be set up in a given area.

For the application of these methods to ICT infrastructure installation, it is necessary to spend a large amount of time selecting areas, because the installation has little effect from the viewpoint of network externality [6] if it is carried out in one area rather than in several areas simultaneously nationwide.

In order to select the areas, we need to first consider the potential demand. Previous research [7]-[9] has focused on a macrodemand forecast to provide facility installation principles, not to specify installation areas. There has been one study on microarea forecasting [10]. It describes only the guidelines for microarea forecasting by using multiple regression analysis.

In order to proceed with microarea marketing, we focused on the diffusion mechanism of the ICT infrastructure. It seems to be diffused in accordance with service reputation in areas where ICT infrastructure has been provided as a trial. Therefore, who pushes forward service diffusion is an important question. An innovative early adopter in the technology lifecycle is characterized as an information source affecting acquaintances from the viewpoint of innovative diffusion [11]. The innovative early adopter is generally reckoned as a person who gets stimulated with many contacts through his/her mobility. It is difficult to identify each person in an area from the viewpoint of the technology life cycle (e.g., who is an early adopter).

Concerning the diffusion of the broadband infrastructure facilities at the moment, the framework of microarea marketing is based on commuting flows in terms of considering human behaviour [12]. Such a flow-based microarea selection method has been developed and compared to the population-based method, which is a simple application of the population order [13]. However, the application of this method is limited to only the early stage of area penetration. Therefore, it is necessary to construct a microarea selection method that is applicable throughout the life cycle (from early to late stage) of broadband services.

## III. TREND OF DEMANDS FOR WIMAX IN JAPAN

WiMAX is a wireless broadband access service that has been in place in Japan since 2009. The total demand is increasing, with about 20 billion customers existing in 2015 as shown in Fig. 1. The demand increases at a consistent rate until 2014, and then increases sharply from 2014 to 2015. This is because service by mobile virtual network operator (MVNO) was introduced in mid 2013. MVNO is defined as a network service operator that does not have a network facility itself, but rather borrows the facility from a real network operator. Therefore, newcomers to MVNO have features for value-added services, such as character brand gadgets, rich content of video, and so on. Customers have many options of network operators through SIM-free terminals. MVNO[*1] represents the demand excluding real mobile network operators, while MVNO[*2] represents the demand including the results of real mobile network operators as MVNO. These results show that the effect by MVNO[*1] is small for the total demand, while the total demand is almost the same with MVNO[*2]. Considering these results, customers who have already been WiMAX users do not change their service to MVNO, this is because the total demand is almost the same as those of MVNO[*2]. Therefore, new customers tend to choose their MVNO in terms of pricing compared to 2013.

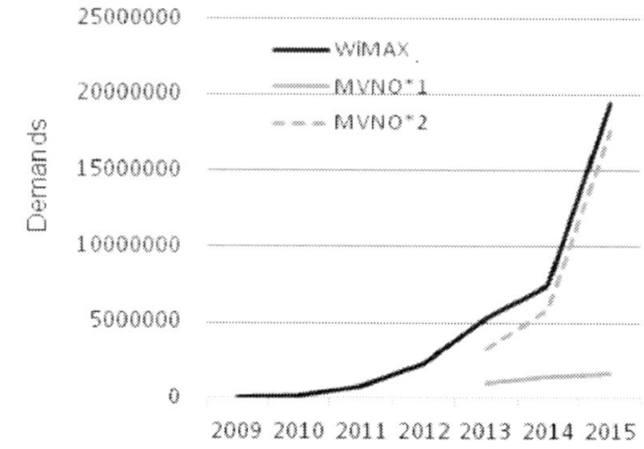


Figure 1. Demand for WiMAX in Japan.

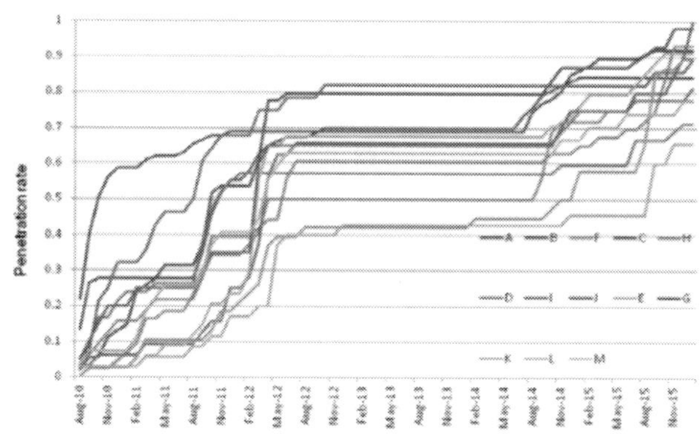


Figure 2. Trend of number of microareas for WiMAX.

Fig. 2 shows the trend of penetration microareas for WiMAX since August 2010. The microarea is defined as the municipal area in this study. The vertical axis is the penetration rate of WiMAX services, meaning the ratio of the number of microareas for a WiMAX facility installed against the total number of microareas in the prefecture. Thirteen prefectures were taken and defined as A to M. The graph shows that many microareas were selected, and that the facilities were installed from 2010 to 2012. This time interval corresponds to the early stage of WiMAX diffusion. The demand grew inside the areas from 2012 to 2014 this is because the number of installed microareas did not change. Since late 2014, the number of installed microareas has increased. This situation corresponds to the appearance of MVNO, and this means that the customers who are interested in the price of services are major factors.

## IV. Hypothesis of Service Diffusion and Its Model

We made a hypothesis of service diffusion in early stage on the basis of personal behaviour [13]. Since face-to-face communication with friends/acquaintances is the key of broadband service diffusion, it is absolutely necessary to introduce the concept of innovation diffusion [11]. There are five types of consumers, namely the innovator, early adopter, early majority, late majority, and the laggard. In particular, an early adopter who is trend-conscious, and collects information and makes decisions by himself/herself plays an important role. It is widely known that an early adopter has a considerable influence on general consumers as an opinion leader. This implies that he/she sends interesting information to his/her acquaintances. If an individual (especially early majority) has many contacts with early adopters, the possibility that he/she will demand the service is high [14], as shown in Fig. 3 (a). Since face-to-face communication is effective in the diffusion of broadband services, the mobility of an early adopter will probably induce broadband service diffusion through contacts with many individuals. Therefore, we assumed a commuting flow that includes early adopters in the service diffusion process, as shown in Fig. 3 (b).

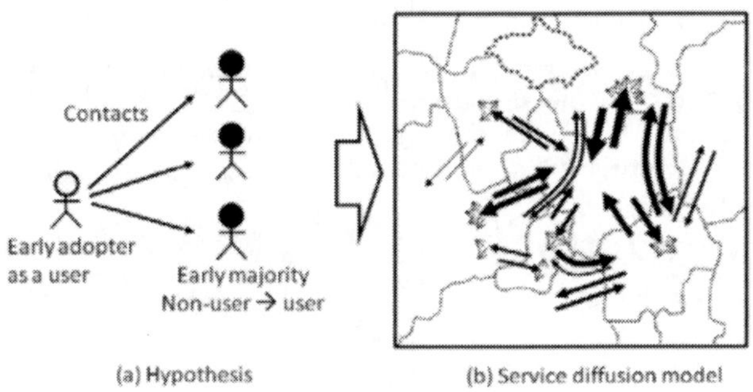


Figure 3. Mechanism of service diffusion in early stage.

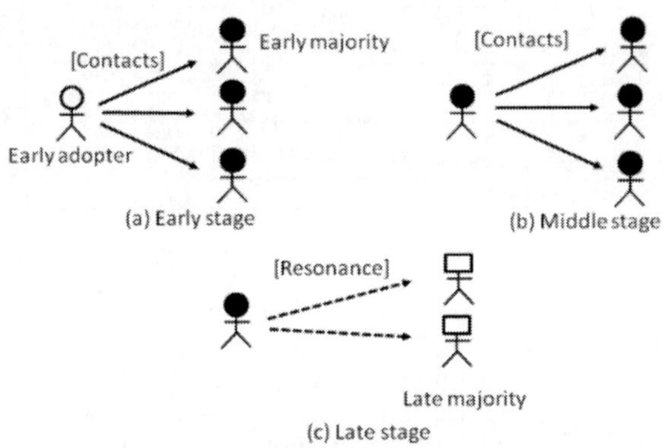


Figure 4. Relationship between service diffusion and customer segmentation.

Next, we explain the mechanism from early to late stage according to the trend as shown in Fig. 2. The early stage of service diffusion corresponds to the time interval between 2010 and 2012. The penetration rate grew with a steep slope, for which the mechanism has already been explained in the previous study. The middle stage of service diffusion corresponds to the time interval between 2012 and 2014. In that stage, there were no increases of the number of installed microareas. This means that the early majority affected by early adopters made contact with others of the early majority in the same microarea, as shown in Fig. 4 (b). As a result, the demand increased inside a microarea of the middle stage. The penetration rate increased in all areas during the late stage of service diffusion after 2014. The new type of services provided by MVNO started in that stage, where there is potential demand from the late majority. The late majority tends to be skeptical of the service, price-oriented and follow the early majority after the service has sufficiently penetrated the field. Therefore, the late majority is not affected by contact with the early majority, but rather by resonance [15] with early majority, as shown in Fig. 4(c).

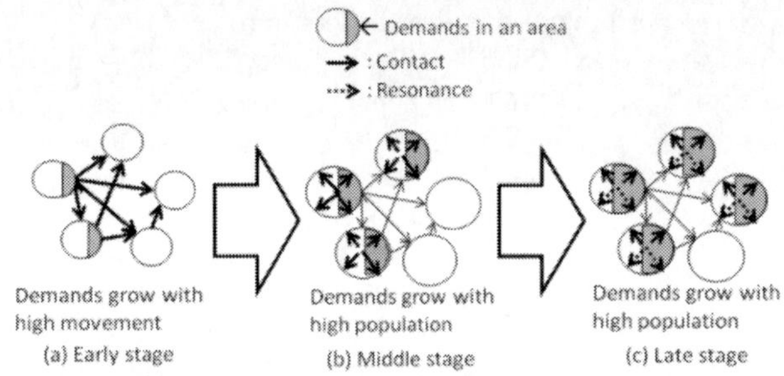


Figure 5. Mechanism of potential demand diffusion.

The next step was to obtain the mechanism of potential demand diffusion as shown in Fig. 5. Our hypothesis at the early stage for service diffusion is that the demand grows with high movement among microareas (Fig.5 (a)). Therefore, the microarea is selected by in- and outflows of commuters in a microarea. Since the possibility of growing potential demand exists inside a microarea during the middle and late stages, the effect of population in microareas becomes great when compared with that of movement among microareas (Fig. 5(b)).

## V. Microarea Selection Algorithms

The population-based algorithm is defined as the method that selects areas by the application of the population order; therefore, areas with a large population tend to be selected. The flow-based algorithm is defined as a method that selects areas on the basis of the inflows and outflows among areas. To analyse inflows and outflows among areas, we introduced the representation of a graph model with an area as a node, and the commuting flow among areas as a link. In particular, a link has an arrow to consider the direction of commuting flows; therefore, areas with a large inflow/outflow tend to be selected. According to the mechanism described in the previous section, the mixed algorithm is constructed so that the flow-based algorithm is used in the low penetration rate while the population-based algorithm is used in the high penetration rate.

Let $G = (N, L)$ be a graph, where $N$ denotes a finite set of nodes ($i \in N$) and $L$ represents a set of links ($l_{ij} \in L$).

For any $l_{ij}$, there exists a function $f: L \rightarrow N_0$ (non-negative integer) such that $f(l_{ij}) = z_{ij}$ for $l_{ij} \in L$. For any $n_i$, there exists a function $g: N \rightarrow M_0$ (non-negative integer) such that $g(n_i) = u_i$ for $n_i \in N$.

The procedure for the mixed algorithm is as follows;

- Step 1: Let $c = 1$ be a counter with an initial value '1', and $n(k)$ be a $k$-th element of the array where $k$ = 1, 2, ⋯. Let "$p$" as the number of selected areas by WiMAX evolution under the penetration rate (40%), Set $N_t \leftarrow N$.
  Sort links according to flow values $f(l_{ij})$ in $N_0$ in the descending order: assign threshold values $\alpha$ and $\beta$.
  Sort nodes according to population values $g(n_i)$ in $M_0$ in the descending order.
- Step 2: If $p \geq c$, then the following steps are performed (flow-based algorithm):
  - Step 2-1: Define a set $K$ ($\subset L$) = arg max $f(l_{ij})$, and denote $f(l^*_{ij}) = z_d \in N_0$ for $l^*_{ij} \in K$.
  - Step 2-2: If there is a node '$m$' $\in N_t$ whose *in-degree* exceeds $\alpha$, then select node '$m$', and set $n(c) \leftarrow m$, $c \leftarrow c+1$, and replace $N_t$ with $N_t \backslash \{n(c)\}$ and replace $L$ with $L \backslash K$.
  - Step 2-3: If there is a node '$m$' $\in N_t$ whose *out-degree* exceeds $\beta$, then select node '$m$', and set $n(c) \leftarrow m$, $c \leftarrow c+1$, and replace $N_t$ with $N_t \backslash \{n(c)\}$ and replace $L$ with $L \backslash K$.
- Step 3: If $|N| \geq c$, then the following steps are performed (population-based algorithm):
  - Step 3-1: If there is a node 'm' $\in N_t$ whose $g(n) = \max g(n_i)$, then select node 'm', and set $n(c) \leftarrow m$, $c \leftarrow c+1$, and replace $N_t$ with $N_t \backslash \{n(c)\}$.

## VI. SIMULATION RESULTS

### A. Classification of prefectures

The 33 prefectures are considered as representative of prefectures in terms of size. Since employee fluidity (as commuting flows) depends on the area selected especially in the early stage [13], the attributes of prefectures are considered to be 'number of employees in own microarea', 'inflow of employees among microareas', and 'outflow of employees among microareas'. We classified the prefectures into the following five categories in terms of employee fluidity according to the correspondence analysis shown in Fig. 6. The vertical axis represents the occurrence ratio of the in- or outflow among the microareas in the prefecture. The horizontal axis represents the staying ratio of employees in their own microareas.

- Group 1: areas with large inflow; Aichi (A)
- Group 2: areas with large in- and outflows; Ibaraki (B) and Shiga (F)
- Group 3: areas with large outflow; Saitama (C) and Nara (H)
- Group 4: areas with little in- and outflows; Niigata (D), Okayama (I) and Hiroshima (J)
- Group 5: balanced areas of average in- and out-flow; Kagawa (E), Ishikawa (G), Yamagata (K), Tokushima (L) and Fukui (M)

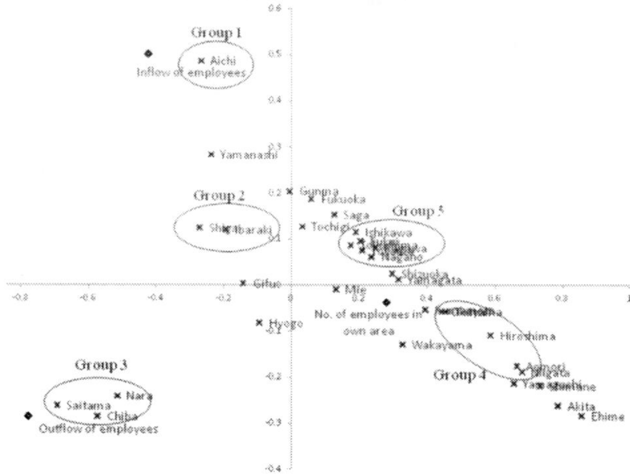


Figure 6. Correspondence analysis of employee fluidity.

### B. Comparison with algorithms

In this section, we compare and evaluate the population-based, flow-based and mixed algorithms. To determine the difference in results depending on region, thirteen prefectures were considered among five groups (A to M).

TABLE I. COMPARATIVE RESULTS

| Prefecture (Area no.) | Group | Population -based algorithm | Flow-based algorithm | Mixed algorithm |
|---|---|---|---|---|
| A (83) | 1 | 0.94 | 0.92 | 0.94 |
| B (54) | 2 | 0.79 | 0.79 | 0.79 |
| F (32) | 2 | 0.80 | 0.80 | 0.80 |
| C (87) | 3 | 0.93 | 0.91 | 0.93 |
| H (42) | 3 | 0.97 | 0.93 | 0.97 |
| D (43) | 4 | 0.82 | 0.82 | 0.82 |
| I (32) | 4 | 0.92 | 0.88 | 0.92 |
| J (28) | 4 | 0.91 | 0.86 | 0.91 |
| E (34) | 5 | 0.81 | 0.89 | 0.81 |
| G (20) | 5 | 0.81 | 0.81 | 0.81 |
| K (38) | 5 | 0.81 | 0.87 | 0.81 |
| L (35) | 5 | 0.87 | 0.91 | 0.87 |
| M (27) | 5 | 0.86 | 0.90 | 0.86 |

Table 1 shows the concordance ratio comparison among the three algorithms. The penetration rate is calculated as the ratio of the number of areas, where WiMAX has been introduced by the provider (WiMAX evolution), to the number for all areas in the given prefecture. The Table 1 results are when the penetration rate was 80% in each prefecture. $\alpha = \beta = 1$ are taken in the flow-base algorithm because of the optimization analysis in the early stage [13]. The concordance ratio (CR) of the number of selected areas between WiMAX evolution and each algorithm is defined by the following equation.

CR = (Number of selected areas matching WiMAX evolution areas /Number of WiMAX evolution areas). (1)

The underlined values indicate the highest CR at each prefecture. Although the CR by flow-based algorithm is sometimes the highest, the CR by population-based algorithm is always the highest for Groups 1 to 4. Employee fluidity well explains the behaviour in the early stage as applying the flow-based algorithm, while the resonant effect well explains the demand increase by population in the late stage as applying the population-based algorithm. Therefore, the mixed algorithm is for use in accordance with the penetration rate for Groups 1, 2, 3 and 4 during the life cycle of the services. However, the CR by flow-based algorithm is always superior to that by population-based algorithm for Group 5. It is better to use the flow-based algorithm for the whole penetration rate.

### *C. Consideration for microarea characteristics*

In this subsection, we consider the differences between Group 5 and the other groups in order to apply the proposed algorithm. The differences of population between areas are focused and analysed. Figs. 7 and 8 show the relationship between population in a microarea, and ranking of microareas for four prefectures (B, C, J and K). The target microareas exclude the microareas which were selected by WiMAX evolution when the penetration rate was lower than 40% in each prefecture.

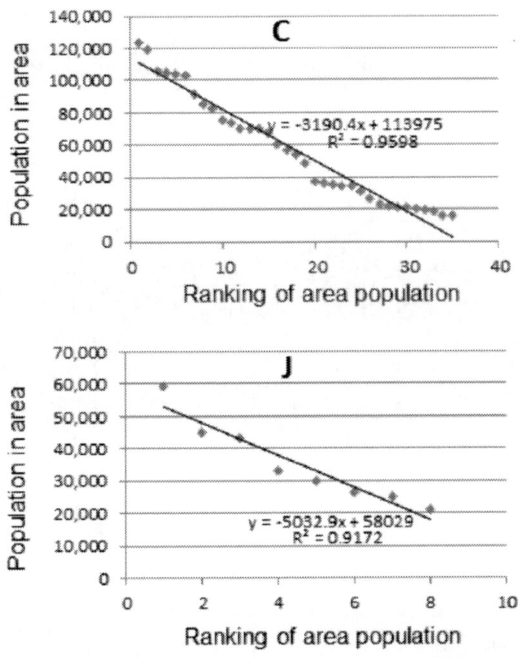


Figure 7. Relationship between population in area and its ranking (C and J).

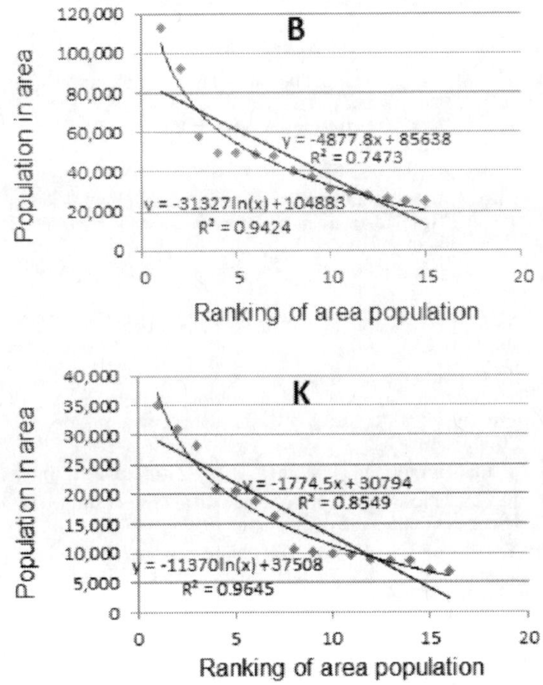


Figure 8. Relationship between population in area and its ranking (B and K).

The results showed that the approximation by regression line fits into the scatter diagram in C (Group 3) and J (Group 4) in Fig. 7, while it does not fit in B (Group 2) and K (Group 5) in Fig. 8. Instead, the diagram fits into logarithmic regression curves in B and K. It is understandable that the population difference is small for low-ranking microareas in B and K, and the effect of fluidity is greater than that of population-based algorithm. The results are significant for Group 5, while the same results (CRs between three algorithms) are obtained for Group 2.

## VII. CONCLUSIONS

It is tremendously important to select an area in which an ICT infrastructure is introduced in order to ensure quick and economic development of an advanced information society. Area selection strongly depends on the potential demand, and one of the main features of the ICT infrastructure is network externality; therefore, a huge amount of time and labour is required to select specified areas from among a large number of candidate areas.

In this paper, we proposed an efficient area selection method based on a service diffusion model. We evaluated the method using real field data from 13 prefectures, and we obtained the application of flow-based and population-based algorithms during the life cycle of the services.

Our future work will analyse the more detailed features of area category, in addition to evaluate the proposed method for the rest of prefectures. Furthermore, we intend to apply the method to other information network infrastructures, such as FTTH, LTE, and energy management services.

## REFERENCES


[1] The Ministry of International Affairs and Communications of Japan, *Broadband Service Coverage Rate With Respect to the Total Number of Households*. [Online]. Available from: http://www.soumu.go.jp/soutsu/tohoku/hodo/h2501-03/images/0110b1006.pdf (accessed 3 September 206).

[2] The Ministry of International Affairs and Communications of Japan, "Information and Communications in Japan," 2014 White Paper, p. 174, 2014.

[3] K. Yonetaka, Fact of areamarketing. Tokyo: Nikkei Pub. Inc., 2008.

[4] Y. Murayama and R. Shibazaki, GIS theory. Tokyo: Asakura Pub. Co. Ltd., 2008.

[5] T. Sakai, et al., "Use of Web-GIS area marketing and its application to the local region," Bulletin of Global Environment Research, Rissho Univ., vol. 6, pp. 125-130, 2004.

[6] T. Ida, Boradband economics. Tokyo: Nikkei Pub. Inc., 2007.

[7] R. L. Goodrich, Applied statistical forecasting. Belmont: Business Forecast Systems Inc., 1992.

[8] T. Abe and T. Ueda, "Telephone revenue forecasting using state space model," Trans. on IEICE, vol. J68-A, no. 5, pp. 437-443, 1985.

[9] H. Kawano, T. Takanaka, Y. Hiruta, and S. Shinomiya, "Study on teletraffic method for macro analysis and its evaluation," Trans. on IEICE, vol. J82-B, no. 6, pp. 1107-1114, 1999.

[10] M. Iwashita, K. Nishimatsu, T. Kurosawa, and S. Shimogawa, "Broadband analysis for network building," Rev. Socionetwork Strat., vol. 4, pp. 17-28, 2010.

[11] E. Rogers, Diffusion of innovation, 5th ed. New York: Free Press, 2003.

[12] M. Iwashita, "A consideration of an area classification method for ICT service diffusion," Knowledge-Based and Intelligent Information and Enginieering Systems, LNAI, 6883, pp. 256-264, 2011.

[13] M. Iwashita, A. Inoue, T. Kurosawa, and K. Nishimatsu, "Efficient microarea selection algorithm for infrastructure installation of boradband services," Internationa Journal of Systems, Control and Communications, Inderscience publishers (to appear).

[14] S. Shimogawa and M. Iwashita, "Method for analyzing sociodynamics of telecommunication-based services," Proc. of 9th IEEE/ACIS International Conference on Computer and Information Science, pp. 99-104, 2010.

[15] Y. Ohsawa, M. Matsumura, and K. Takahashi, "Resonance without Response: The Way of Topic Growth in Communication," Chance Discoveries in Real World Decision Making, Studies in Computational Intelligence, Vol. 30, pp. 155-165, 2006.

# Adapting LEACH Algorithm for Underwater Wireless Sensor Networks

Djamel Mansouri, Malika Ioualalen
MOVEP Laboratory
USTHB
Algeria
e-mail: {dmansouri, mioualalen}@usthb.dz

*Abstract*— **The design of routing protocols for both terrestrial and underwater wireless sensor networks (WSNs and UWSNs) presents several challenges. These challenges are mainly due to the specific characteristics (limited battery, limited processing power and limited storage) of this type of networks. However, saving energy consumption is a real challenge that should be considered. Clustering technique is one of the methods used to cut down on energy consumption in WSNs and UWSNs. It consists of dividing a network into subsets called clusters, where each cluster is formed of cluster head and nodes. Low Energy Algorithm Adaptive Clustering Hierarchy (LEACH) is the most popular protocol for clustering in WSNs. Using TDMA based MAC protocol, LEACH allows significant energy conservation by balancing energy consumption of network nodes. In this paper, we propose an approach based on LEACH algorithm for routing in Underwater Wireless Sensor Networks. The proposed approach profits of the advantages offered by LEACH algorithm for WSNs in terms of energy conservation. Simulation results show that the proposed approach can reduce the total energy consumption and prolong the network lifetime compared to the direct transmission.**

***Keywords-Underwater Wireless Sensor Networks; Acoustic Communication; Clustering Algorithm; LEACH Algorithm; Energy Consumption.***

## I. INTRODUCTION

Oceans and seas comprise over 70% of the earth's surface. However, Underwater Wireless Sensor Networks (UWSNs) are deployed through different applications such as oceanographic data collection, pollution monitoring, undersea exploration, disaster prevention, assisted navigation, tactical surveillance and mine reconnaissance [1].

UWSNs are formed of miniaturized self-alimented entities called sensor nodes, which are interconnected using wireless acoustic links. In UWSNs, communications are established by acoustic waves, which allow a very well propagation through water and require much less power compared to the radio signal, which delivers very poor performance in underwater areas since it provides transmission ranges of only a few meters. A challenge in underwater acoustic communication is limited bandwidth caused by high absorption factor and attenuation, long propagation time, and the fading of the resulting signal, which should attract much interest. Another challenge is the sensor node failure due to environmental conditions.

One major problem related to the UWSNs is the energy conservation which the network lifetime depends on. Since UWSNs are deployed in harsh environment, it is often impossible to recharge or replace battery nodes after their exhaustion. However, the issue of energy conservation for these networks is to develop routing techniques which take into account the different problems of underwater communications such as: limited bandwidth, throughput, long propagation delay (high latency), high bit error rates and signal attenuation. Therefore, regarding the characteristics of underwater communications, UWSNs have recently motivated a growing interest in studying architectures and networking protocols.

In this paper, we propose an approach based on Low Energy Algorithm Adaptive Clustering Hierarchy (LEACH) [2] for Underwater Wireless Sensor Networks. The proposed approach is an adaptation of LEACH algorithm which is one of the most well-known energy efficient clustering algorithms used in terrestrial Wireless Sensor Networks. We implement this proposition on Matlab in order to perform experiments according to many parameters such as the network lifetime.

This paper is structured as follows: A brief introduction on underwater wireless sensor networks and the deal of these networks regarding their constraints and limits, particularly, in acoustic communications are given in Section I. Section II is dedicated to the related works that treat security issue and routing protocols used in UWSNs. In Section III, we present the proposed approach. In Section VI, we present simulation results. Finally, we summarize the main contribution of this study and we give indications on future works in Section V.

## II. RELATED WORKS

In recent years Underwater Sensor Networks have attracted a significant interest of the scientific community. Thus, different works that address design issues related to the characteristics of these networks were introduced in the literature [3][4][5]. The energy resource limitation is an important issue that must be taken into consideration in order to maximize the network lifetime. Generally, routing collected data in the network affects directly the energy consumption. Another aspect related to the energy consumption and smooth functioning of UWSNs is the safety and security of these networks. Therefore, routing protocols must be designed from the beginning with the aim of efficient management of energy resources. Also the proposed security solutions must consider the energy conservation. In this section, we present some works which address the security of acoustic communications and some proposed routing protocols used in UWSNs.

In [6], the authors introduced a novel approach to secure both unicast and multicast communications in underwater acoustic sensor networks. This approach provides confidentiality and message integrity.

Ming et al. [7] proposed a CLUster-based Secure Synchronization (CLUSS) protocol. It is based on the time synchronization for secure clusters formation. CLUSS is executed in three phases: the first phase consists of the authentication process, where each sensor nodes is authenticated to the cluster head which it belongs and the cluster heads are authenticated to beacons. In this phase, the identified malicious nodes will be removed from the network. The inter-cluster synchronization phase corresponds to the synchronization between cluster heads and beacons. The intra-cluster synchronization phase is where ordinary nodes synchronize themselves with cluster heads. The performance evaluation demonstrates that CLUSS can reduce the number of transmitted packets. Thus, it allows saving energy consumption in the network.

A Cluster based Key management Protocol (CKP) was proposed in [8]. CKP is a new key management protocol for clustering hierarchical networks, used to secure communication inside and outside a cluster. CKP operates in four phase: Key generation and distribution phase, Cluster setup phase, Data gathering phase, Data forwarding phase. Simulation results show that the CKP is energy and storage efficient.

In [9], the authors proposed a k-means based clustering and energy aware routing algorithm, named KEAR for underwater wireless sensor networks that aim to maximize the networks lifetime. The proposed algorithm is based on two phases: cluster head (CH) election and data transmission. In the CH election phase, the election of the new cluster heads is done locally in each cluster based on the residual energy of each node. In the data transmission phase, sensing and data transmission from each sensor node to their cluster head is performed, where the cluster heads in turn aggregate and send the sensed data to the base station.

Carmen et al. [10] proposed a distributed energy aware routing protocol called Distributed Underwater Clustering Scheme (DUCS), which is based on clustering techniques and supports energy consumption. In DUCS, firstly, the network is divided into clusters, where each cluster head is selected through a randomized rotation among different nodes in order to allow equitable energy dissipation between nodes in the network. Secondly, to reduce the amount of transmitted data to the base station, the cluster heads aggregate the collected data by the member nodes that belong to their own cluster, and send an aggregated packet to the sink. While this algorithm is efficient, it presents some limitations regarding the nodes mobility, which is not considered. However, it can affect the structure of clusters. Also, exchanged data between CHs can be interrupted in the case where ocean currents move the cluster heads [11].

Seah et al. [12] introduced a hierarchical clustering routing protocol architecture called Multipath Virtual Sink (MVS). In MVS, CHs use many local aggregation points which are connected to local sinks. Using a high-speed communication channels, local sinks are linked to each other through multiple paths.

In [13], the authors proposed a distributed Minimum-Cost Clustering Protocol (MCCP), where clusters are selected by considering the total energy consumption of the cluster, the residual energy of the cluster head and cluster members and the distance between the cluster head and the underwater sink. Firstly, all sensor nodes are candidate to be cluster heads (CHs) and cluster members. In order to form a cluster, each candidate constructs its neighbor set and uncovers neighbor set. Secondly, the average cost of that particular cluster is calculated, and the one with the minimum average cost is selected as a cluster head. We note that the cost of a cluster represents both energy consumptions: to send the packet from a member to the CH and from CH to the base station. Finally, an "INVITE" message is sent by selected CH, to all the other cluster nodes to become its cluster's member, otherwise, it sends a "JOIN" message to the specific cluster head. We note that MCCP protocol improves the energy efficiency and prolong the lifetime of the network.

## III. PROPOSED APPROACH

The hierarchical routing based on clustering is a very efficient technique used to resolve the problem of energy consumption in both WSNs and UWSNs. Thus, the goal of clustering is to extend the lifetime of a network by providing a good load balancing. In the following, we present proposed approach, which consists in integrating into the LEACH algorithm, the energy model used in submarine networks for data transmission. Firstly, we introduce LEACH algorithm, which is a hierarchical routing protocol most widely used in wireless sensor networks (WSN). Secondly, we present the energy models used for data transmission in both WSNs and UWSNs. Finally, we substitute the energy model associated to LEACH algorithm and used in terrestrial sensor networks, by the energy model dedicated to the acoustic communications and through numerical results obtained by simulations, we show the behavior of this algorithm in term of energy conservation.

### *A. LEACH Functioning*

LEACH is a dynamic clustering algorithm which uses a randomized periodical rotation of cluster heads among the nodes in order to distribute equitably the energy load between sensor nodes in the network. Thus, all nodes have the same probability to be elected cluster head. However, the CH election is updated in each iteration. LEACH is divided into rounds. Each round consists of two phases: Set-up phase, where cluster heads are elected and clusters are formed; Steady-state phase, where the data are transferred to the sink node.

In set-up phase, the electing process is started by considering a percentage "P", which is the desired percentage of cluster heads for a given round. Each node "i" chooses a random number between 0 and 1. If the number is less than a threshold T(i), the node declares a cluster head for the current round. The CHs inform their neighbors of their election and each remaining node decides to choose the closest CH.

In steady-state phase, the CHs receive sensed data from cluster members, and transfer the aggregated data to the BS. Thus, using the Time Division Multiple Access protocol (TDMA, which, is used to ensure transmission packages within collision and less costly in energy) [2], each node send its collected data to CH at once per frame allocated to it. After this transmission, the nodes cut off its transmission and goes to sleep mode until next allocated transmission slot.

*1. Detailed principle*

Let P be the average desired percentage of clusters in our network at an instant "t". LEACH is composed of cycles made of $\frac{1}{p}$ rounds.

Each round "r" is organized as follows:

1) Each node "i":
   - computes the threshold T(i) such as:

$$T(i) = \begin{cases} \frac{p}{1-P*\left(r mod \frac{1}{p}\right)} & \text{if i has not been CH yet} \\ 0 & \text{if i has already been CH} \end{cases}$$

   - chooses a pseudo-random number $0 \leq x_i \leq 1$.
   - If $x_i \leq T(i)$ then "i" designates itself as a CH for the current round. T(i) is computed in such as every node becomes CH once in every cycle of $\frac{1}{p}$ rounds we have T(i) = 1, when $r = \frac{1}{p} - 1$.
2) The self-designed CH informs the other nodes by broadcasting an advertisement message with the same transmitting power (using carrier sense multiple access, CSMA MAC).
3) Based on the received signal strength of the advertisement message, the rest of nodes choose its CH for the current round. Thus, they send a message back to inform the considered CH (using the same protocol as in the last step, CSMA MAC).
4) CHs set up a "transmission schedule" based on Time Division Multiple Access) to the nodes that joined their clusters. They inform each node at what time they transmit its data.
5) CHs keep listening for the results. Normal sensors get measures from their environment and send their data. When it is not their turn to send, they stay in sleep mode to save energy (Collisions between the transmissions of the nodes from different clusters are limited thanks to the use of code division multiple access (CDMA) protocol).
6) CHs aggregate, and possibly compress the received data and send it to the base station in a single transmission. This transmission may be direct, or multi-hopped, if it is relayed by other CHs.
7) Steps 5 and 6 are repeated until the last round.

LEACH can be extended such as LEACH-C introduced in [14]. Thus, in LEACH-C, the location information and the residual energy value of the nodes are considered as additional parameters for the computation of the T(i).

Since each node decides whether to designate itself as a CH or not, without considering the behavior of surrounding nodes. Therefore, for a given round, a number of CHs can be very different from the selected percentage "P". Also, all the elected CHs may be located in the same region of the network, leaving "uncovered" areas. For this reason, In that case, one can only hope that the spatial repartition will be better during the next round.

*B. Energy model*

A sensor consumes energy to perform three actions: acquisition, communication and data processing. The energy consumed to perform data acquisition and processing operations is not very significant compared to the energy used for communications. However, communications consume much more energy than other tasks. They cover communications in transmission and reception.

The radio model of energy consumption in terrestrial sensor networks associated to LEACH algorithm and proposed by Heinzelman et al. in [2] is defined as follows: The energy to emit ETx (k, d) and receive ERx (k) data are given by:

- To emit k-bit through a distance "d", the transmitter consumes:
  - ✓ ETx(k, d) = ETxelec(k) + ETxamp(k, d)
  - ✓ $ETx(k, d) = (E_{elec} * k) + (E_{amp} * k * d^2)$
- To receive k-bit message, the receiver consumes:
  - ✓ ERx(k) = ERxelec(k)
  - ✓ ERx(k) = k * Eelec

$E_{elec}$ and $E_{amp}$ represent respectively the energy of electronic transmission and amplification.

Usually, acoustic communications are used in UWSNs. We use the same energy model as introduced in [15], which was proposed for underwater acoustic networks. According to this model, to achieve a power level $P_0$ at a receiver at a distance "d", the transmitter power Etx(d) is :

$$Etx(d) = P_0\, d^2\, (10^{\alpha(f)/10})^d \quad (1)$$

where $\infty(f)$, is the absorption coefficient depending on the frequency range under given water temperature and salinity. $\infty(f)$ is measured in dB/m and is used for frequencies above a few hundred KHz can be expressed empirically using Thorp's formula introduced in [16].

$$\alpha(f) = 0.11 * \frac{10^{-3} * f^2}{1+f^2} + 44 * \frac{10^{-2} * f^2}{4100+f^2} + 2.75x10^{-2} * f^2 + 3 * 10^{-6} \quad (2)$$

where "f" is the carrier frequency for transmission in KHz. The reception power is assumed to $1/3^{th}$ of the transmission power.

After having presented the functioning of LEACH and its conventional energy model used in WSNs, we adapt the use of LEACH in UWSNs by associating the energy model (see the formula 1) dedicated to acoustic communications and the technical analysis of the proposed approach is presented in the next section.

## IV EXPERIMENTAL RESULTS

In order to evaluate proposed approach and show the interest of using LEACH algorithm in underwater sensor networks, we have done simulation by considering an underwater sensor network based on a static 2D architecture type, where the underwater sensor nodes are deployed and anchored to the bottom of the ocean. Underwater sensors may be organized in a cluster-based architecture, and be interconnected to one or more head sensors (underwater gateways) by means of wireless acoustic communication.

The head sensors are network devices that transmit data from the bottom of the ocean network to a surface station [17] (see Fig. 1). Firstly, we implemented LEACH algorithm with the energy model (presented in formula 1) used to transmit data in UWSNs. Simulations are done using Matlab, by considering parameters given in Table 1 and the following assumptions:

- Sensor nodes and the underwater sink are stationary.
- All sensors nodes are homogeneous and have the same initial energy.
- The underwater sink has no limitation in terms of energy, processing and memory.
- The sensors performed periodical measurements at fixed intervals.

Secondly, by considering the lifetime and residual energy, we compare the proposed approach (data is transmitted to the underwater sink via elected cluster head sensors) to the direct communication approach (each underwater sensor transmits directly its data to the underwater sink).

TABLE I. SIMULATION PARAMETERS

| *Parameter* | *Value* |
|---|---|
| Field Dimension x, y, maximum (Network size) | 50m, 50m |
| Number of Nodes | 100 |
| Optimal Election Probability of Cluster Heads (percentage of desired clusters) | 5 |
| Power level $P_0$ at a receiver | $0,1 * 10^{-7}$ |
| Initial Energy | 5J |
| Frequency of carrier acoustic signal | 25KHZ |
| Rounds (Time) | 200 |

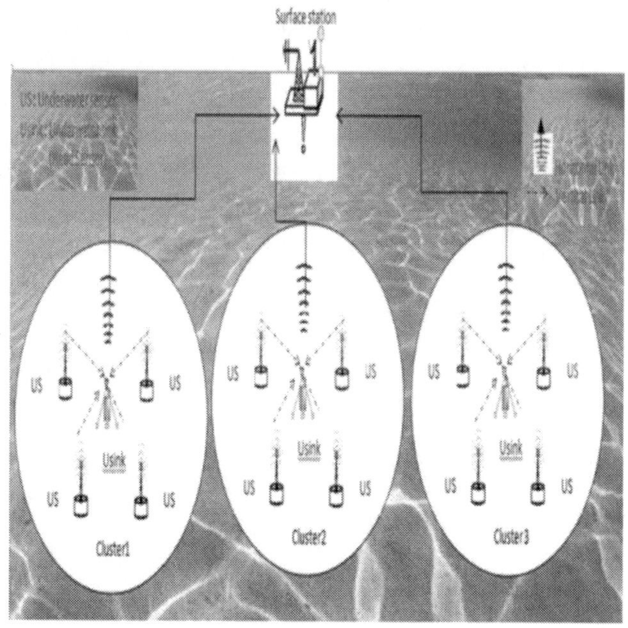


Figure 1. Network Model

Fig. 2 shows the residual energy in the network. We note that using direct communication, the residual energy in the network decreases quickly and reaches 0 values at rounds 175. Compared to LEACH algorithm, the residual energy decreases progressively and it equal to 150 J at rounds 200. However, due to the clustering approach applied on the network, LEACH algorithm retains more energy comparing to the direct communication.

Regarding the histogram in Fig. 3, we note that after 50 rounds, using direct communication algorithm, the first 21 nodes are dead, while, compared to the LEACH algorithm, there is no dead node. After 100 rounds, in direct communication algorithm, we observed that 61 nodes are dead, while in LEACH algorithm the number of dead nodes is 37. Also, after 150 rounds, we note that the number of dead nodes is very important in direct communication compared to LEACH algorithm. At the end of the simulation, all nodes are dead in direct communication, while 21 nodes remain alive in LEACH algorithm. Therefore, in this set of simulations, we note that LEACH is about 21% more efficient in terms of network lifetime compared to the direct communication.

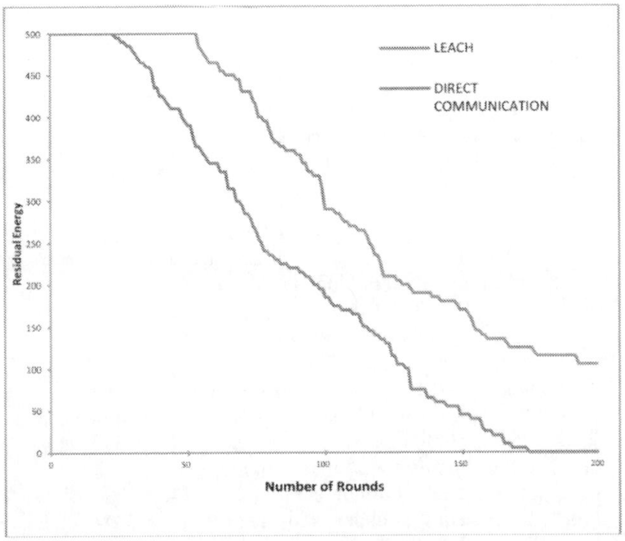


Figure 2. Residual energy vs. Number of rounds

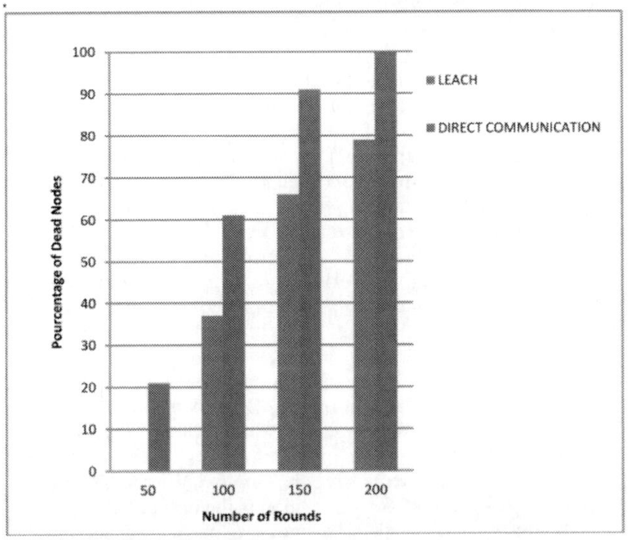


Figure 3. Percentage of dead nodes

## V. CONCLUSION

In both underwater and terrestrial sensor networks, each node is powered by a limited energy source. However, energy conservation is an important issue that must be taken into consideration in order to build mechanisms that allow users to extend the lifetime of the entire networks. LEACH algorithm is one of the most well-known energy efficient clustering algorithms for WSNs. In order to profit of advantages provided by LEACH algorithm in WSNs, we propose in this paper an adaptation of LEACH algorithm for underwater acoustic sensor networks. Our proposition considers the residual energy in the cluster head selection and uses an energy consumption model dedicated to acoustic communications. The experimental results show that compared to the direct communication proposed approach can effectively reduce the energy consumption and extend the networks lifetime. As a future works, we will compare proposed approach to other clustering protocol used in underwater sensor networks and improve it by considering, other parameters such as data rate, throughput, and propagation delay.

## REFERENCES

[1] M. Mohsin, S. Adil. A, M. M. Asif, F. Emad and Q. Saad "A Survey on Current Underwater Acoustic Sensor Network Applications", International Journal of Computer Theory and Engineering, volume 7, number 1, pages 51--56, 2015, IACSIT Press.

[2] W. R. Heinzelman, A. Chandrakasan, and H. Balakrishnan, "Energy-Efficient Communication Protocol for Wireless Microsensor Networks", Proceedings of the IEEE Hawaii international conference on system sciences, pages. 10-xx, 2000.

[3] I. F. Akyildiz, D. Pompili and T. Melodia,"Underwater acoustic sensor networks: research challenges", Ad hoc networks journal, volume 3, number 3 , pages 257--279, 2005.

[4] J. Heidemann, M. Stojanovic, and M. Zorzi, "Underwater sensor networks: applications, advances and challenges", Phil. Trans. R. Soc. A journal, volume 370, number 958, pages 158–175, 2012.

[5] C. Peach and A. Yarali, "An Overview of Underwater Sensor Networks", CWMC 2013 The Ninth International Conference on Wireless and Mobile Communications, pages. 31--36, 2013.

[6] G. Dini and A. Lo Duca, "A secure communication suite for underwater acoustic sensor networks", Sensors, volume 12, number 11, pages 15133--15158, 2012.

[7] X. Ming, L. Guangzhong, Z. Daqi and W. Huafeng, "A Cluster-Based Secure Synchronization Protocol for Underwater Wireless Sensor Networks", International Journal of Distributed Sensor Networks, vol. 2014, pages 1--13, Apr 2014.

[8] S. Verma, et al. "A Cluster based Key Management Scheme for Underwater Wireless Sensor Networks", International Journal of Computer Network and Information Security, volume 7, number 9, pages 54, 2015.

[9] S. Souiki, M. Hadjila and M. Feham "Power Aware Cluster Based Routing Algorithm for Underwater Wireless Sensor Network", 9th Conference on Electrical Engineering EMP, Algiers, pages 67--72, 2015.

[10] D. M. Carmen and P. Ruia, "Distributed Clustering Scheme For Underwater Wireless Sensor Networks", IEEE 18th International Symposium on Personal, Indoor and Mobile Radio Communications, pages 1--5, 2007.

[11] K. Rakesh et. al, "A survey on data aggregation and clustering schemes in underwater sensor networks", International Journal of Grid and Distributed Computing, volume 7, number 6, pages 29--52, 2014.

[12] W. K. G. Seah and T. Hwee-Xian, "Multipath virtual sink architecture for underwater sensor networks", IEEE OCEANS 2006-Asia Pacific, pages 1--6, 2007.

[13] P. Wang, C. Li, and J. Zheng, "Distributed minimum-cost clustering protocol for underwater sensor networks (UWSNs)", IEEE International Conference on Communications, pages 3510--3515, 2007.

[14] W. R. Heinzelman, A. Chandrakasan, and H, Balakrishnan "An application-specific protocol architecture for wireless sensor networks", IEEE Transaction on Wireless Communications, volume 1 number 4, pages 660--670, 2002.

[15] E. Sozer, M. Stojanovic, and J. Proakis, "Underwater acoustic networks", IEEE journal of oceanic engineering, volume 25, number 1, pages 72--83, 2000.

[16] H.W. Thorp, "Analytic description of the low-frequency attenuation coefficient", The Journal of the Acoustical Society of America, volume 42, number 1, pages 270--270, year 1967, Acoustical Society of America.

[17] D.Pompili, T. Melodia and L. F. Akyildiz, "Deployment analysis in underwater acoustic wireless sensor networks", Proceedings of the 1st ACM international workshop on Underwater networks, pages 48--55, 2006.Type Style and Fonts.

# A Secure Messaging and File Transfer Application

Sandhya Armoogum
Dept. Industrial Systems & Engineering
University of Technology, Mauritius (UTM)
La Tour Koenig, Mauritius
asandya@umail.utm.ac.mu

Sanjeet Kumar Mudhoo
Dept. Industrial Systems & Engineering
University of Technology, Mauritius (UTM)
La Tour Koenig, Mauritius
ravi.mudhoo@hotmail.com

*Abstract*— **Instant Messaging (IM) is becoming more and more popular and ubiquitous as it is accessible via mobile devices. However, many existing IM applications do not provide much security. This is a serious limitations of IM systems especially when IM is being used in the workplace as a communications tool. In this paper, we present the different security vulnerabilities associated with communication using IM, as well as the security provided in some IM applications. Finally, we describe the design and implementation of a simple secure lightweight application for secure messaging and file transfer.**

***Keywords- Privacy; Instant Messaging; Encryption; Security; Secure Communication.***

## I. INTRODUCTION

Instant Messaging (IM) is a type of communication service over the Internet that enables individuals to exchange text messages, share files (images, videos and documents) and track availability of a list of users in real-time. IM is popularly used for communications at large. Almost everybody nowadays is familiar with such messaging system as Skype, Instagram, Google Hangouts, Facebook Messenger, WhatsApp and Viber. However, IM services over the last few years have evolved from a casual communication tool to an indispensable and unified communication tool in the workplace, designed to enable rapid response text-based conversation, encourage enterprise collaboration through file sharing and even video conferencing. In a survey conducted in February 2016 by BetterCloud involving 801 respondents[1], it is reported that just 13% of respondents are not using real-time instant messaging for work purposes; 56% of respondents believe that real-time messaging will displace email as their organization's primary workplace communication and collaboration tool; 83% of respondents agree that IM improves communication in the workplace; and more employees report an increase in productivity rather than decrease (only 24% of respondents believe that IM is a distraction and decreases productivity). Currently, IM is not only being used by Startups but also by small and medium organizations, as well as large enterprises. In a survey conducted by SoftwareAdvice [18], 75% of employees using IM reported decreased call and email volume, while 66% of employees reported that the quick resolution of simple questions helped increase productivity.

Similarly, in [2][3], the authors support that IM is an effective communication tool that can enhance the quality of work-related communication and relationship, and thus enhance the organisational agility. Indeed, IM provides an efficient way of communicating and resolving issues quickly, increasing collaboration on projects and reducing the need for meetings, reducing interruption, improving customer service, which help enhance productivity, as well as fostering good relationships. IM can be particularly helpful in communication between geographically separated co-worker or students engaged in distance learning.

As IM gains popularity, particularly for businesses it has also increasingly become the target of attacks [4]. The need for security in such systems becomes important. One such security requirement is confidentiality/privacy, which is becoming very challenging in the face of widespread Internet surveillance. Using simple and free sniffing software, anyone can easily capture data being transmitted in a network.

According to the Electronic Frontier Foundation (EFF), there has been ample evidence that authoritarian governments around the world are relying on technology to facilitate human rights abuses such as listening to voice calls, read emails and text messages [5]. In [6], the author claims that our privacy is slowing eroding and that in the future it would be very difficult to remain anonymous and not have a digital trail. With the advent of "Big Data", sophisticated and inexpensive data mining tools reveal increasing amounts of personal information. Nevertheless, it is believed that making surveillance expensive by employing good security techniques, such as strong encryption is the best defence.

In this paper, we present a secure messaging and file transfer application, which allows a user to communicate securely with another user or group of users. The paper is organized as follows. Existing IM applications and their security are described in Section 2. Section 3, presents the proposed secure messaging and file transfer application. In Section 4, the proposed system is evaluated. Finally, we draw conclusions in the Section 5.

## II. EXISTING MESSAGING SYSTEM & SECURITY

When using IM, the user feels like he/she is directly connected to the recipient, but most IM systems are designed and deployed with a client-server architecture. The user installs a client software of the IM application and creates an account. Most IM systems implement some form of authentication to identify the user and hence does not provide anonymous communication. When a user sends a message to another user, the IM client encapsulates the message into a packet and send it to the IM server, which looks at the recipient and send the packet to the destination if the receiver is online [7]. If the recipient is not online, the undelivered message is held in the server until it can be delivered. Fig. 1 below shows the client-server IM infrastructure and communication process.

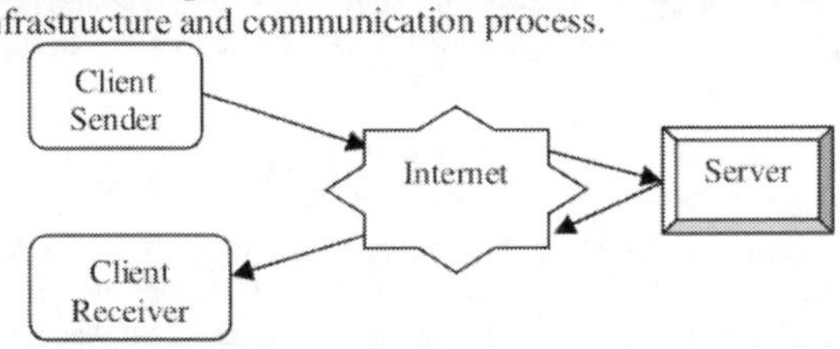


Figure 1. Instant Messaging Infrastructure and Communication Process.

The IM system has several security vulnerabilities. Considering the Microsoft STRIDE Threat Modeling Methodology, IM systems are particularly vulnerable to **S**poofing, **T**ampering of messages, **R**epudiation attacks, **I**nformation disclosure due to eavesdropping and **D**enial of Service attacks. Security mechanisms are required to secure IM systems. Typically, if messages are sent in clear text, the messages can be read; message contents, sender or receiver information can be modified while the message is in transit or while it is stored on the server. Similarly, the IM server can be victim to Denial of Service attack (DoS) and be unavailable for a certain period of time. On the 31st December 2015, WhatsApp was reported to be down temporarily due to the heavy traffic load (which mimics a Distributed Denial of Service (DDoS)) it experienced [8].

In November 2014, the EEF started the Secure Messaging Scorecard where they evaluate the security of the popular messaging system used [9]. The criteria that were used to assess the security of the messaging system were as follows: (i) encryption of data along transmission links with a key not accessible to the provider, (ii) ability to verify the correspondent's identity, (iii) forward secrecy, (iv) whether the code is open to independent review, (v) whether the crypto design is well documented, and (vi) if the messaging tool has been open to independent security audit. Figs. 2-7 depict the resulting scorecard of the following popular messaging tool: Google Hangouts, Facebook chat, Skype, Viber, WhatsApp, and Yahoo Messenger [9].

| | Encrypted in transit? | Encrypted so the provider can't read it? | Can you verify contacts' identities? | Are past comms secure if your keys are stolen? | Is code open to review? | Is security design documented? | Has there been any recent code audit? |
|---|---|---|---|---|---|---|---|
| Google Hangouts | ✓ | ⊘ | ⊘ | ⊘ | ⊘ | ⊘ | ✓ |

Figure 2. Hangouts Scorecard [9].

| | Encrypted in transit? | Encrypted so the provider can't read it? | Can you verify contacts' identities? | Are past comms secure if your keys are stolen? | Is code open to review? | Is security design documented? | Has there been any recent code audit? |
|---|---|---|---|---|---|---|---|
| Facebook chat | ✓ | ⊘ | ⊘ | ⊘ | ⊘ | ⊘ | ✓ |

Figure 3. Facebook Chat [9].

| | Encrypted in transit? | Encrypted so the provider can't read it? | Can you verify contacts' identities? | Are past comms secure if your keys are stolen? | Is code open to review? | Is security design documented? | Has there been any recent code audit? |
|---|---|---|---|---|---|---|---|
| Skype | ✓ | ⊘ | ⊘ | ⊘ | ⊘ | ⊘ | ⊘ |

Figure 4. Skype Scorecard [9].

| | Encrypted in transit? | Encrypted so the provider can't read it? | Can you verify contacts' identities? | Are past comms secure if your keys are stolen? | Is code open to review? | Is security design documented? | Has there been any recent code audit? |
|---|---|---|---|---|---|---|---|
| Viber | ✓ | ⊘ | ⊘ | ⊘ | ⊘ | ⊘ | ✓ |

Figure 5. Viber Scorecard [9].

| | Encrypted in transit? | Encrypted so the provider can't read it? | Can you verify contacts' identities? | Are past comms secure if your keys are stolen? | Is code open to review? | Is security design documented? | Has there been any recent code audit? |
|---|---|---|---|---|---|---|---|
| WhatsApp | ✓ | ✓ | ✓ | ✓ | ⊘ | ✓ | ✓ |

Figure 6. WhatsApp Scorecard [9].

| | Encrypted in transit? | Encrypted so the provider can't read it? | Can you verify contacts' identities? | Are past comms secure if your keys are stolen? | Is code open to review? | Is security design documented? | Has there been any recent code audit? |
|---|---|---|---|---|---|---|---|
| Yahoo! Messenger | ✓ | ⊘ | ⊘ | ⊘ | ⊘ | ⊘ | ⊘ |

Figure 7. Yahoo! Messenger Scorecard [9].

As can be seen from the Scorecards of popular messaging system above, most of the messaging tool do not provide much security except for WhatsApp, which very recently released an update to include encryption of messages for security [10]. WhatsApp now provides end-to-end encryption of messages, calls, videos, images and files.

Skype, a popular communication tool at the workplace, is a telecommunications application software product that provides messaging, video chat and voice calls for computers, tablets, and mobile devices. Skype runs on most of the popular platforms today. Users can send instant messages, exchange files and images, send video messages, and create conference calls with Skype. Skype was purchased by Microsoft corporation in 2011. In 2013, a report by Ars Technica claims that Microsoft can regularly scan message content for signs of fraud, and company managers may log the results indefinitely and this can only happen if Microsoft can access and convert the messages into human-readable form [11].

Documents leaked by Edward Snowden (the whistleblower), showed that the Government Communications Headquarters (GCHQ), which is a British intelligence and security organization, has access to emails and messages that the National Security Agency (NSA) siphons off directly and en masse from Google, Skype and

Facebook; the NSA collects 194m text messages and 5bn location records every day [12]. Just recently, in February 2015, the UK surveillance tribunal ruled that GCHQ acted unlawfully in accessing millions of private communications collected by the NSA up until December 2014 [13].

Facebook employs a technology that scans posts and chats for criminal activity, which clearly means that messages users send are subject to surveillance and is a violation of privacy [14]. This monitoring came to light in 2012, when a man is his thirties was chatting with a 13-year old female minor from South Florida. With Facebook's help, the police were able to arrest the suspected pedophile [15]. It is thus clear that messaging systems need to provide security to achieve confidentiality of communications.

Moreover, anonymity is also another important security requirement of messaging systems. It is usually preferred that someone sniffing data packets on the Internet is not only unable to read the message contents but is also not able to link the messages to the people sending or receiving them. Many users concerned with privacy, such as activists, oppressed people, journalists and whistleblowers, as well as the average person, often make use of an anonymous overlay networks such as the Invisible Internet Project (I2P) and The Onion Routing Network (TOR) for secure communication. Both the I2P and TOR provides anonymous, confidential exchange of messages by the means of cryptography. However, a recent publication by the University of Cambridge, the University of California-Berkeley, and the University College London in February 2016 confirms that users of such anonymous overlay networks are commonly blocked from accessing websites and anonymous users are being treated as second-class Web citizens [16]. Likewise, many organisations attempt to block TOR data packets and the use of the TOR browser, which is commonly used to access the DarkNet, by means of port filtering inside their network to protect themselves from malware, DarkNet access by their employees and other attacks. Still, most commonly used IM systems do not provide anonymous communication feature.

Several secure messaging systems have been proposed and developed in both academia and industry. In [17], the authors present a Systemization Methodology, which divide the security requirements of a secure messaging system into three nearly orthogonal problem areas namely (1) trust establishment, (2) conversation security and (3) transport privacy. The trust establishment relates to the authentication of the communicating parties as well as the distribution of cryptographic keys, whereas conversation security ensures the protection of the exchanged messages & files during conversations. Finally, transport privacy implies the hiding of the communication metadata. In [19], a messaging system called Riposte that allows a large number of clients to anonymously post messages to a shared "bulletin board," is proposed. Riposte mainly provides protection against traffic analysis. In [20], a secure IM system is proposed, which uses identity-based cryptosystems to provide strong authentication and secure communication (confidentiality, integrity and non-repudiation).

Our proposed system, takes a practical approach and adopts well established security mechanisms to provide a simple, lightweight messaging system which provides (i) confidentiality and privacy of messages & files transferred; (ii) a secure channel of communication between two users; (iii) anonymous communication; and (iv) scalability whereby a group of users can chat and share files. In the next Section, we describe the design and implementation of the proposed messaging system.

## III. Design and Implementation of the Secure Messaging and File Transfer Application

Most commercial IM infrastructure allows the transfer of messages via a messaging server as shown in Fig 1 [20]. However, the presence of a third-party server where messages may be temporarily or permanently stored poses several privacy issues. A breach of the IM server may allow attackers to access all messages and files shared. In our proposed system, we do not involve a messaging server, whereby the users chat and exchange files with one another directly as depicted by Fig 8. The disadvantage of adopting this approach however is that communication is only possible when the two communicating parties are online. However, the security benefits are tremendous, as messages and files are not being stored in an intermediate node, and are thus not vulnerable to unauthorized access. Messages exchanged can be cached on the recipient's computer if required by the implementation of a log file. Files, which can be transferred include text documents, PDFs, pictures, audio and video amongst others, is also stored on the recipient's computer. Our proposed system also provides a secure channel for communication between two or more users. A virtual private network (VPN) is a well-established technology that creates a secure and often encrypted connection over a less secure network. A remote-access VPN uses a public telecommunication infrastructure like the internet to provide remote users with a secure channel for communication to another user or network. This is especially important when employees and users are using a public Wi-Fi hotspot or other avenues to use the internet to connect to one another user ubiquitously.

Figure 8. Proposed System layout.

Two users wishing to engage in a secure chat and file transfer, first have to establish a secure VPN network connection. The LogMeIn Hamachi [21], hosted VPN service software, is used to set up the VPN, which allows to set up secure connections between the two users. First LogMeIn Hamachi is installed. When this client software runs, it implements a virtual network adapter, and the computer is assigned an additional IP address that identifies the computer on any virtual network that is joined. The user can then create a virtual network by name and assign it a password; or join an existing virtual network. All users who wishes to communicate can be asked to join the network created. The users have to install the VPN client software and select the network by connecting to it by name, and supplying the password. Similarly, different networks can be created for different groups of communicating friends, collaborating employees etc. The use of a VPN solution to establish the network connections ensures a secure channel for communication, thereby providing both conversation security as well as transport privacy. At all point, the VPN software allows to view which users (users' nicknames displayed) are connected and are online at a particular point in time. This approach to establish a secure connection supports anonymous communication given that the users are not required to identify themselves by means of their email address or telephone numbers. The assigned IP address of the VPN client is thus not linked to a user identifier. Moreover, this approach also supports some level of trust regarding the person(s) with whom the chat or the file transfer is taking place, as the user could only join the network and participate only if the user has been provided with the network name and password. The proposed system implementation provides a user interface, which allows the application user to perform different functionalities such as choosing which user(s) to securely communicate with. Fig. 9 shows the Use Case diagram of the application user.

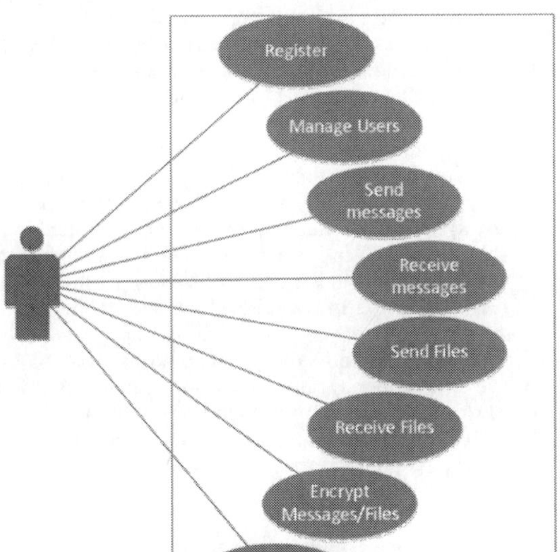


Figure 9. Use Case diagram of a Chat Application User.

Though the VPN connection ensures that messages or files are transferred securely i.e., in encrypted form, the application does not rely on the VPN connection for security but rather implements its own security mechanism for providing confidentiality and privacy of messages and files transferred, as a VPN can be attacked in various ways [22]. Two different approaches are used for providing confidentiality in the proposed system: (1) encryption of messages using public key cryptography, and (2) encryption of files to be transferred using symmetric cryptography.

For every chat instance with a particular user, the application on each users' computer generates a pair of public key cryptography key. The public key is shared with the user with whom communication is intended, while the private key is cached on the users' respective computer. When a user type a message, the message is encrypted using the public key of the recipient and sent to the recipient. The recipient uses his/her private key to decrypt the message as shown in Fig. 10. The use of Public Key Cryptography for encryption and decryption of messages is acceptable despite the fact that Public key encryption is much slower than symmetric cryptography, because the length of each message is usually limited in IM systems. Short Message Service (SMS) messages are limited to 160 characters, while Twitter messages are limited to 140 characters. In the application, the message length was limited to 140 characters.

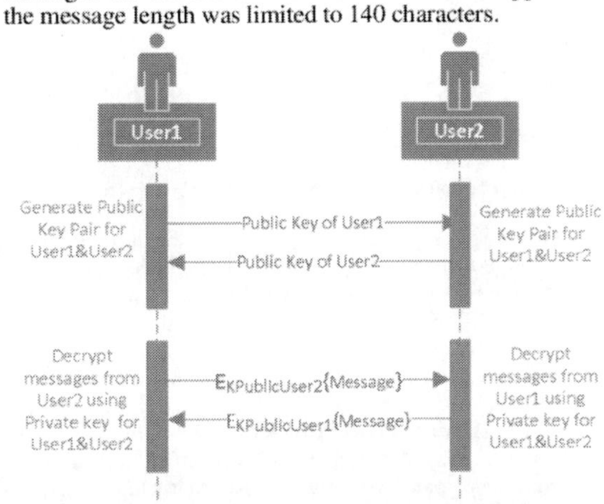


Figure 10. Encryption and Decryption of messages for secure chat.

For securing the files to be transferred between two users, Public Key Cryptography being slow, Symmetric Cryptography is chosen for efficiency, especially considering that the files can be of significant size. Prior to starting a file transfer, the application requests the sender to select a password for locking the file. This password is sent as an encrypted message to the receiver and is thus not at risk of interception. This securely shared password is the basis for deriving the symmetric key, which is to be used for the encryption of the file by the sender, as well as the decryption of the received encrypted file by the receiver. To generate a symmetric key, it is proposed to use a cryptographic hash function to process the password producing a fixed length output (hash code), which can be used as the key. The hash code, i.e., key derived, is strongly dependent on the password; any change in the password results in a different hash code. Fig. 11 depicts the secure processing of files transferred. Files received are automatically decrypted and stored in a download folder associated with the application. For enhanced security, the application is designed to validate the password and ensure that a strong password is selected by the sender for locking the file. A weak password may be easily guessed by an attacker, who may then use the password to derive the encryption key and thus successfully decrypt files being transferred.

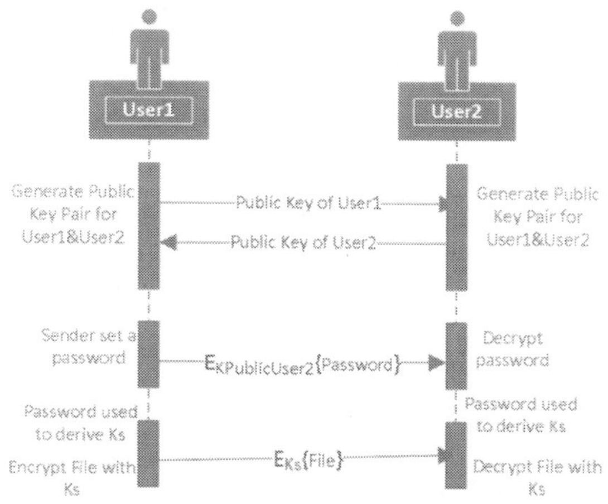


Figure 11. Encryption and Decryption of Files to be transferred securely.

The secure messaging and file transfer application was implemented using Visual Studio. The RSA public key encryption was used for encryption and decryption of the messages. The RSACryptoServiceProvider in .NET was used. When using the default constructor as shown below to create a new instance of the RSA algorithm, a pair of public and private key pair are created by default.

```
RSACryptoServiceProvider rsa = new
        RSACryptoServiceProvider(512);
```

The key pair generated was extracted using the ToXMLString method, which returns an XML representation of the key, which is saved to disk as an XML file. The private key and the public key are captured as follows respectively.

```
rsa.ToXmlString(true)
rsa.ToXmlString(false)
```

The private key is never shared but stored on the key owner's computer, which implies that it safe unless the user's computer is breached. The proposed system can easily be installed and used by any user anywhere, as it does not require users to have digital certificates etc. Fresh keys can be generated for each new chat sessions for each user. This simple, lightweight application is also easily scalable, allowing any number of users to use it to communicate securely and to transfer files.

For the encryption of files, using symmetric encryption, the Rijndael (Advanced Encryption Standard - AES) algorithm was chosen. Instead of using the usual cryptographic hash algorithm for deriving the symmetric key to be used for encrypting files, the Rfc2898DeriveBytes class is used. This class implements a password-based key derivation functionality, PBKDF2, by using a pseudo-random number generator based on the cryptographic hash function HMACSHA1. Moreover, the IM application also has a feature, which allows the user to create chat logs for chat sessions to keep a history of messages exchanged. However, if users prefer not to keep a copy of messages exchanged i.e., if they are using a computer from a library, this feature can be disabled so as to leave no trace of the conversation on that machine.

## IV. Evaluation

The secure chat application is evaluated on the following three criteria: (1) Security and Privacy Properties, (2) Usability Properties, and (3) Ease of Adoption.

The use of the VPN software allows to set a secure underlying network to carry the messages and/or files to be transferred. However, given that the user has no control over the encryption of the messages for transmission over the VPN tunnel, the application does not depend on the VPN network for security. The VPN connection is rather an added benefit, as it provides a means for users to choose who they want to invite in the network for communication. For confidentiality of messages exchanged, the system makes use of the RSA public key cryptography algorithm for encryption. This ensures that the messages sent are private and can only be read by the communicating parties. Attackers sniffing on the network will only capture the encrypted messages, which have been further encrypted by the VPN software. Similarly, the well established and secure AES algorithm is used for the encryption of files to be transferred for confidentiality.

The user interface of the system is simple and intuitive and offers the basic functionality of chat and file transfer. The key generation and sharing is transparently conducted by the system when the user chooses the recipient to whom he/she wants to send a message. The deployment of the proposed system is also simple; it involves the installation and network setup of the VPN, followed by the installation of the secure messaging and file transfer application.

Such a simple and lightweight application can be used for secure messaging by journalists, for collaboration between employees in business organisations, by distance learning/e-learning students for communication and submission of their electronic assignments amongst others.

## V. Conclusion

In this paper, a simple, practical, lightweight and secure messaging application was proposed, which is based on the use of a VPN connection and Cryptography for security. Such an application can be easily deployed and used for secure, anonymous communication between users. Given that this application is designed such that it is not a client server, store and forward system, the network connectivity among different users can be a challenge. An important implication of this design choice is that chat and file transfer is only possible when the recipient is online. However, the absence of a caching server also enhances the security of the system. Furthermore, the proposed system does not rely on the VPN software for security of messages and files during the transfer but rather uses well established cryptographic algorithms for providing confidentiality within the application. The application can easily be used by people looking for anonymity and is easily scalable as keys are dynamically generated when required. Future work on the application involves addressing the out of band transmission of the network name and password for establishing secure and trusted connections with users. Another improvement on the application may be to allow users the choice to authenticate participants or communicate anonymously.

## REFERENCES


[1] Scott Solomon, *Real-Time Messaging: Data Unearths Surprising Findings on Usage, Distraction, and Organizational Impact"* March 3, 2016 available at https://www.bettercloud.com/monitor/real-time-enterprise-messaging-comparison-data/ last accessed 20.09.2016

[2] C. X. J. Ou, R. N. Davison, Y. Liang and X. Zhong, *The Significance of Instant Messaging at Work*, Fifth International Conference on Internet and Web Applications and Services (ICIW), 2010, Barcelona, 2010, pp. 102-109

[3] Hanif Suhairi Abu Bakar, Nor Azmi Hj. Johari, *Instant Messaging: The Next Best Knowledge Sharing Tools in a Workplace After Email* in the Proceedings of the 2nd IEEE International Conference on Computer Science and Information Technology (ICCSIT2009), Beijing, 2009, pp. 268-269.

[4] Neal Leavitt, *Instant Messaging: A New Target for Hackers*, Computer magazine, Published by the IEEE Computer Society, July 2005

[5] *Mass Surveillance Technologies*, available at https://www.eff.org/issues/mass-surveillance-technologies. Last accessed 12.08.2016

[6] Jeffrey MacKie-Mason, *Can We Afford Privacy from Surveillance?* University of Michigan, Copublished by the IEEE Computer and Reliability Societies Sep/Oct 2014.

[7] Craig Sweigart, *Instant Messaging Security*, Global Information Assurance Certification Paper, SANS Institute, 2003

[8] Victoria Woollaston, *WhatsApp apologises as service crashes on New Year's Eve*, available at http://www.dailymail.co.uk/sciencetech/article-3380408/WhatsApp-goes-Users-Europe-report-problems-connecting-chats-messaging-app.html#ixzz4EHfs6Xdg

[9] Electronic Frontiers Foundation, *Which apps and tools actually keep your messages safe?* Web Article, available at https://www.eff.org/node/82654

[10] Bill Budington, *WhatsApp Rolls Out End-To-End Encryption to its Over One Billion Users*, available at https://www.eff.org/deeplinks/2016/04/whatsapp-rolls-out-end-end-encryption-its-1bn-users, April 7, 2016.

[11] Dan Goodin, *Think your Skype messages get end-to-end encryption? Think again*, May 20, 2013, available at http://arstechnica.com/security/2013/05/think-your-skype-messages-get-end-to-end-encryption-think-again/

[12] Carly Nyst, *Today is a great victory against GCHQ, the NSA and the surveillance state* available at https://www.theguardian.com/commentisfree/2015/feb/06/great-victory-against-gchq-nsa-surveillance-state, February 2015

[13] Eric King, *Victory! UK surveillance tribunal finds GCHQ-NSA intelligence sharing unlawful* February 2015, available at https://www.privacyinternational.org/node/485

[14] Joseph Menn, *Social networks scan for sexual predators, with uneven results*, Jul 12, 2012 available at http://www.reuters.com/article/us-usa-internet-predators-idUSBRE86B05G20120712

[15] Jared Howe, *Why Your Facebook Chats are Being Monitored*, January 2016, available at http://blog.privatewifi.com/your-facebook-chats-are-being-monitored-find-out-why-the-social-media-privacy-report/

[16] Sheharbano Khattak, David Fifield, Sadia Afroz, Mobin Javed, Srikanth Sundaresan, Vern Paxson, Steven J. Murdoch and Damon McCoy, *Do You See What I See? Differential Treatment of Anonymous Users*. In the proceedings of the Internet Society Network and Distributed System Security Symposium 2016 (NDSS'16), February 2016, San Diego, CA, USA

[17] Nik Unger, Sergej Dechand, Joseph Bonneau, Sascha Fahl, Henning Perl, Ian Goldberg, Matthew Smith, *SoK: Secure Messaging*, IEEE Symposium on Security and Privacy, 2015.

[18] Daniel Harris, *Boost Productivity With Online Chat Presence Displays*, SoftwareAdvice, available at http://www.softwareadvice.com/resources/boost-productivity-chat-presence/ last accessed 20.09.2016

[19] Henry Corrigan-Gibbs, Dan Boneh, and David Mazières, *Riposte: An Anonymous Messaging System Handling Millions of Users*, in the 2015 IEEE Symposium on Security and Privacy, pp 321-338

[20] Raymond B. Jennings III, Erich M. Nahum, David P. Olshefski, Debanjan Saha, Zon-Yin Shae, and Chris Waters, *A Study of Internet Instant Messaging and Chat Protocols*, in IEEE Network, July/August 2006, pp 6-21

[21] LogMeIn Hamachi, *Create virtual private networks on-demand*, available at https://www.vpn.net/

[22] Spiegel Online, *NSA Documents Attacks on VPN, SSL, TLS, SSH, Tor*, avalaible at http://www.spiegel.de/international/world/nsa-documents-attacks-on-vpn-ssl-tls-ssh-tor-a-1010525.html.. Last accessed 21.09.2016.

# Implementing UNIQUE Integrity Constraint in Graph Databases

Kornelije Rabuzin, Martina Šestak, Mladen Konecki
Faculty of Organization and Informatics, Varaždin
University of Zagreb
Zagreb, Croatia
e-mail: kornelije.rabuzin@foi.hr, msestak2@foi.hr, Mladen.Konecki@foi.hr

***Abstract*—Databases enable users to store and retrieve data. However, uncontrolled data entry often results in having duplicate or incorrect data stored in the database, which makes it inconsistent. To prevent this, it is recommended to specify integrity constraints in the database. In this paper, the current possibilities in the field of integrity constraints, with special emphasis on graph databases as a relatively new category of NoSQL databases, are discussed. After giving an overview of the current situation regarding integrity constraints in mostly used graph database query languages, a successful implementation of UNIQUE integrity constraint in a Neo4j graph database is shown.**

***Keywords-integrity constraints; graph databases; Gremlin; UNIQUE***

## I. INTRODUCTION

Inserting data into a database is an important process that must be properly managed and controlled in order to ensure the validity of the inserted data (no Garbage-In-Garbage-Out situations) and to enforce database integrity, i.e., to maintain the database in a consistent state. The database is considered to be consistent if it satisfies the set of specified integrity constraints [1]. Formally, integrity constraints can be defined as formal representations of invariant conditions for the semantic correctness of database records [2] and as general statements and rules that define the set of consistent database states or changes of states, or both [3].

Thus, integrity constraints contain the semantic information about data stored in the database, i.e., they are properties that must be satisfied for the database and data we want to insert into the database. If these properties are satisfied, then the data is considered to be semantically correct and the operation or transaction is executed successfully. Otherwise, if the integrity constraint is violated, then the transaction is rejected or a specific compensation action is activated, which will reduce the impact of that transaction and repair the current database state.

Once constraints are specified, the database management system (DBMS) has to ensure that all constraints are satisfied and none are broken. Eventually, it is possible that some constraints will be broken during a transaction, but when the transaction ends, all constraints have to be satisfied.

Nowadays, most relational DBMSs provide some kind of support for declarative integrity constraints, which can be grouped into three categories:

- Column constraints, which are specified on table columns (e.g., NOT NULL, UNIQUE, CHECK, PRIMARY KEY, REFERENCES);
- Table constraints, which are used when some constraints cannot be specified as column constraints (e.g., when tables have compound primary keys consisting of multiple columns, then one cannot specify a PRIMARY KEY column constraint on these columns, since the PRIMARY KEY clause can appear only once within the table definition); and
- Database constraints, which are defined for multiple tables or the entire database through assertions, which belong to the database schema and can be created using the CREATE ASSERTION clause.

Triggers represent an interesting alternative for specifying more complex constraints involving several tables, i.e., database constraints. Basically, when an event like INSERT or UPDATE occurs in the database, a function (procedure) is activated and several different statements can be executed as a reaction to the event.

Unfortunately, most DBMSs are quite limited when it comes to expressing more complex conditions and rules to be satisfied, but also the compensating actions responsible for repairing the database state. This disadvantage can be replaced by expressing integrity constraints as triggers and stored procedures. However, note that they are more challenging to manage as data and constraints evolve.

Lately, maintaining database integrity has become very costly and time consuming due to the increasing amount of data stored in databases and the large number of specified integrity constraints, where each requires some time to be validated.

In the last few years, new database solutions have appeared on the database market as an alternative to traditional relational databases. These solutions avoid using the Structured Query Language (SQL) as the only query language for interacting with databases, so they are known under the term Not only SQL (NoSQL) databases. NoSQL databases can be classified in four solution groups: key-value databases, document databases, column-oriented databases, and graph databases.

Unlike relational databases, NoSQL databases are usually schema-less, thus not placing much attention and importance on strictly maintaining database consistency.

As already mentioned, graph databases represent a special category of NoSQL databases. Even though they are a relatively new alternative to relational databases, much effort has been made in their development (both in graph DBMS products implementation and the literature). According to [4], Neo4j, the most widely used graph DBMS, is the 21st most popular DBMS on the database market (including relational and other NoSQL DBMSs) and has constant growth in popularity.

Like every database, graph databases are based on the graph data model, which consists of nodes connected by relationships. Each node and relationship contains (not necessarily) properties, and is given a label. Hence, data is stored as property values of nodes and relationships. In the graph data model, nodes are physically connected to each other via pointers (this property is called index-free adjacency [5], and the graph databases that implement index-free adjacency are said to be using native graph processing), thus enabling complex queries to be executed faster and more effectively than in a relational data model.

The main advantage of graph databases is their ability to model and store complex relationships between real-world entities. Nowadays, there are some situations where it is easier to model a real-world domain as a graph, rather than as a set of tables connected via foreign keys in the relational data model. Querying a graph database is much faster (especially as the database size grows) when nodes are connected physically as compared to relational databases, where many performance-intensive table join operations must be made. Except for the performance improvements, graph databases offer much bigger flexibility in data modelling, since no fixed database schema must be defined when creating a graph database. The lack of a fixed schema makes later changes to the database structure much simpler, since graphs can be easily updated by adding new subgraphs, nodes, relationships, properties or labels.

In this paper, we discuss integrity constraints in graph databases. Section 2 contains an overview of graph databases, related researches on the topic of integrity constraints in graph databases and the current level of support for integrity constraints provided by most commonly used graph DBMSs. In Section 3, the concrete implementation of the UNIQUE integrity constraint in a Neo4j graph database is shown and explained. Finally, in Section 4, we give a short conclusion about the topic of this paper and provide some brief information about our future work.

## II. INTEGRITY CONSTRAINTS IN GRAPH DATABASES

When it comes to data consistency and integrity constraints in graph databases, one can notice that this area is still not developed in detail and provides space for further improvements and research. Some people even say that the reason for this is the flexible and evolving schema supported by graph databases, which makes integrity constraint implementation more difficult.

As discussed in [6], Angles and Gutierrez wrote a research paper in which they identified several examples of important integrity constraints in graph database models, such as schema-instance consistency (the instance should contain only the entities and relations previously defined in the schema), data redundancy (decreases the amount of redundant information stored in the database), identity integrity (each node in the database is a unique real-world entity and can be identified by either a single value or the values of its attributes), referential integrity (requires that only existing entities in the database can be referenced), and functional dependencies (test if one entity determines the value of another database entity).

In [7], Angles also considered some additional integrity constraints such as types checking, verifying uniqueness of properties or relations and graph pattern constraints.

Apart from the Neo4j graph DBMS, which will be used for UNIQUE integrity constraint implementation, there are other graph DBMSs available on the database market. In this paper, an overview of the support level for integrity constraints will be given for the five most popular graph DBMSs. According to [8], when it comes to graph DBMS popularity ranking, Neo4j DBMS is followed by Titan, OrientDB, AllegroGraph and InfiniteGraph. The level of support in Neo4j DBMS will be explained in the following subsections.

Titan is a graph DBMS developed by Aurelius, and its underlying graph data model consists of edge labels, property keys, and vertex labels used inside an implicitly or explicitly defined schema [9]. After giving an overview of its characteristics and features, one can say that the level of support for integrity constraints is pretty mature and developed. Titan offers the possibility of defining unique edge and vertex label names, edge label multiplicity (maximum number of edges that connect two vertices) and even specifying allowed data types and cardinality of property values (one or more values per element for a given property key allowed). OrientDB is a document-graph DBMS, which can be used in schema-full (all database fields are mandatory and must be created), schema-hybrid (some fields are optional and the user can create his own custom fields) and schema-less (all fields are optional to create) modes [10]. OrientDB provides support for defining and specifying even more integrity constraints, such as:

- Defining minimum and maximum property value;
- Defining a property as mandatory (a value for that property must be entered) and readonly (the property value cannot be updated after the record is created in the database);
- Defining that a property value must be unique or cannot be NULL;
- Specifying a regular expression, which the property value must satisfy; and
- Specifying if the list of edges must be ordered.

Unlike Titan and OrientDB, AllegroGraph does not provide support for any kind of user-defined integrity constraints, which means that there are no database control mechanisms to verify the validity of the inserted data. AllegroGraph databases only ensure that each successfully executed database transaction will change the database's consistent internal state [11]. InfiniteGraph is a distributed graph database solution offering strong or eventual database consistency, which only supports property value type checking and referential integrity constraints [12].

As already mentioned, Neo4j is the most commonly used graph DBMS, so its support for integrity constraints will be discussed by giving a practical overview of features provided by query languages used in a Neo4j database: Cypher and Gremlin. In the following subsections, their characteristics and the level of support for integrity constraints will be reviewed.

### A. *Cypher*

Cypher is a declarative, SQL-like query language for describing patterns in graphs using ascii-art symbols. It consists of clauses, keywords and expressions (predicates and functions), some of which have the same name as in SQL. The main goal and purpose of using Cypher is to be able to find a specific graph pattern in a simple and effective way. Writing Cypher queries is easy and intuitive, which is why Cypher is suitable for use by developers, professionals and users with a basic set of database knowledge.

Cypher is the official query language used by Neo4j DBMS. When using Neo4j DBMS, one can define integrity constraints by using the CREATE CONSTRAINT clause and drop them from the database by using the DROP CONSTRAINT clause. At this point of time, Neo4j enables users to define only the unique property constraint, but it only applies to nodes. This constraint is used to ensure that all nodes with the same label have a unique property value. For instance, to create a constraint that ensures that the property Name of nodes labeled Movie has a unique value, the following Cypher query must be executed:

*CREATE CONSTRAINT ON (m:Movie) ASSERT m.Name IS UNIQUE*

Fig. 1 shows the error message displayed to the user when the user tries to insert a movie with duplicate name, which violates the previously specified integrity constraint.

### B. *Gremlin*

Gremlin is a graph traversal language developed by Apache Tinkerpop. Gremlin enables users to specify steps of the entire graph traversal process. When executing Gremlin query, several operations and/or functions are evaluated from left to right as a part of a chain.

At this point of time, Gremlin does not provide support for any kind of integrity constraint, which leaves a lot of space for improvement.

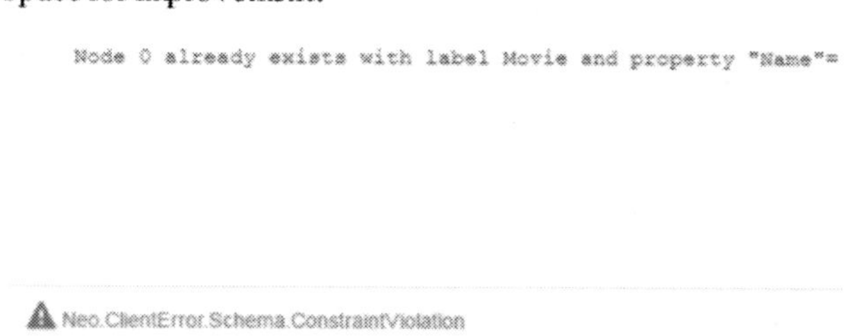


Figure 1. Constraint violation error message

In the next section, it is shown how to implement support for integrity constraints in a Neo4j graph database.

## III. SPECIFYING UNIQUE NODES AND RELATIONSHIPS IN GREMLIN

In the relational data model, the UNIQUE constraint is used when a column value in a table must be unique in order to prevent duplicate values to be entered into a table. The UNIQUE constraint can be specified for one or more columns in a table. For instance, if certain table columns are declared as UNIQUE, it implies that the values entered for these columns can appear only in one table row, i.e., there cannot be any rows containing the same combination of values for these columns.

It is already mentioned that in graph database theory, the UNIQUE constraint is defined as a constraint to be applied on a node/relationship property, therefore having the same meaning as the corresponding constraint in the relational database world. However, to prevent data corruption and redundancy when repeatedly inserting nodes and relationships with the same properties, we propose that the UNIQUE constraint should be and can be defined on nodes and a relationship as a whole, instead of only on some of their properties.

In [6], some implementation challenges regarding different vendors and approaches for the implementation, such as application programming interfaces (APIs), extensions and plugins, have been discussed. The research paper was concluded by choosing the API approach, so a web application has been built by using Spark, a Java web framework, and Apache Tinkerpop, a graph computing framework for graph databases, which contains classes and methods for executing Gremlin queries. The application interacts with a Neo4j graph database through the JAVA API. The purpose of the application is to showcase the usage of the unique node/relationship constraint when creating a node/relationship through executing Gremlin queries. The web application consists of a GUI where a user can create one or two nodes connected via a relationship or query-created nodes and relationships.

The UNIQUE constraint is defined in an additional graph DBMS layer, which behaves as a mediator between the graph database and the application itself. The constraint itself is implemented as a special verification method, which is called when the user wants to create unique nodes and relationships in order to check whether these nodes and relationships already exist in the database.

### A. *Creating one unique node*

When creating one unique node, the user first needs to select a node label from the dropdown list. For instance, to create an author, one needs to select the Author label and set its property values ("firstname" and "lastname"). After that, if the Author node needs to be unique, i.e., in order to ensure that there are no nodes with the same labels and property values in the database, the UNIQUE checkbox must be checked, as shown in Fig. 2.

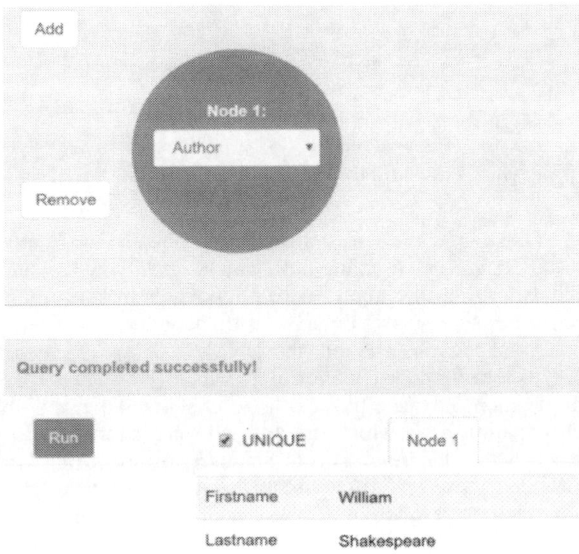


Figure 3. Creating one unique node

When running this query, the entered data is sent as parsed parameters first to the method, which source code is shown in Fig. 3, which checks if an Author node with the received parameters already exists in the database. This method retrieves all nodes (by using the *g.V()* nodes iterator) that are labeled "Author" (by using the *has()* method, which returns true if the values are equal or false if they differ) and have the same property values as the node, which was sent as a parameter to the method. If true, the method returns the existing node. However, if a node with the same label and property values does not exist in the database, it will return a NULL value. Then, a new "Author" node will be created within a Neo4j database transaction by calling the *addVertex()* method and setting the appropriate property values (Fig. 4).

```
if(g.V().has("Label", a.getLabel()).has("Firstname", a.getFirstname())
      .has("Lastname", a.getLastname()).toList().iterator().hasNext())
{
    result = g.V().has("Label", a.getLabel()).has("Firstname", a.getFirstname())
          .has("Lastname", a.getLastname()).toList().iterator().next();
}
```

Figure 2. Checking whether the entered "Author" node exists in the database

```
try (Transaction tx = db.tx()) {
    vertex = db.addVertex(a.getLabel());

    vertex.property("Label", a.getLabel());
    vertex.property("Firstname", a.getFirstname());
    vertex.property("Lastname", a.getLastname());
    tx.commit();
}
```

Figure 4. Creating new "Author" node in the database

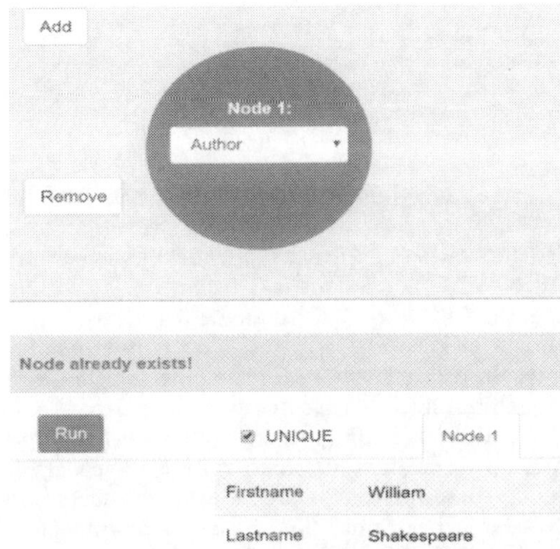


Figure 5. Error message when trying to create duplicate node

If the user tries to create another author named William Shakespeare, no changes are made to the database, i.e., the database does not change its internal state, and the result of this unsuccessful operation is a notification displayed to the user (Fig. 5).

### B. *Creating one unique relationship*

When creating a relationship between two nodes, the user first needs to select the necessary labels from dropdown lists. For instance, if one wants to create a "BORROWED" relationship type between "User" and "Book" nodes, the aforementioned labels must be selected, and their property values defined. After having selected the required node and relationship labels and entered their property values, if the selected relationship needs to be unique, i.e., in order to ensure that there are no relationships of the same type with equal property values in the database, one needs to check the UNIQUE checkbox first (similar to the definition of a unique node).

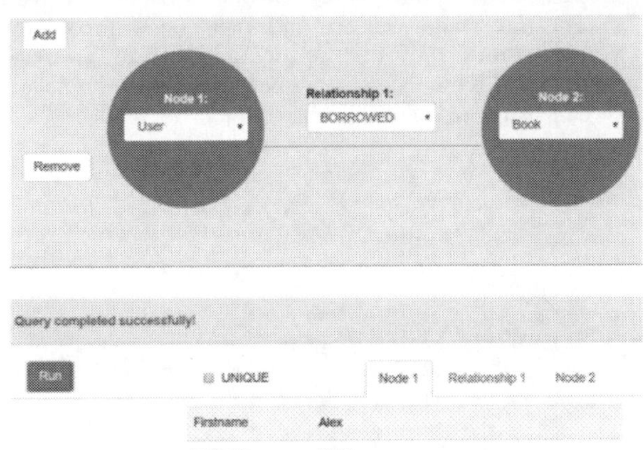


Figure 6. Creating one not unique relationship

```
try (Transaction tx = db.tx()) {
    Vertex node1 =
            Vertex.class.cast(createUser(u, createUnique).get("object"));

    Vertex node2 =
            Vertex.class.cast(createBook(b, createUnique).get("object"));

    edge = node1.addEdge(borrowed.getType(), node2);
    edge.property("DateBorrowed", borrowed.getDateBorrowed());
    tx.commit();
}
```

Figure 7. Creating new "BORROWED" relationship in the database

To show what happens if that checkbox is not checked, a "BORROWED" relationship between the user "Alex Young" and the book "Romeo and Juliet" has been created, as shown in Fig. 6. If a relationship is not specified to be unique, the Gremlin query for creating two nodes and this relationship is directly executed with the received parameters (nodes and relationship property values), which means that there is no verification for whether these objects already exist in the database (there is no call for the verification method). Each time a user runs this query, "Author" and "Book" nodes and a "BORROWED" relationship between them will be created in the database by simply calling the previously explained custom *createUser()* and *createBook()* methods. After creating the nodes, the *addEdge()* Gremlin method is called, which creates a relationship between the two created nodes and sets all necessary relationship property values through the *property()* method. The nodes and the relationship are created within a single database transaction, as shown in Fig. 7.

If a relationship is not specified to be unique, the result is duplicate data in the database, as shown in Fig. 8.

Conversely, as with creating unique nodes, if the UNIQUE checkbox when creating a relationship is checked, then the method that checks if a relationship with same type and properties exists in the database is called and executed. This method, which source code is shown in Fig. 9, performs a graph traversal in order to find the required nodes and relationship within the graph. It first retrieves all nodes labeled "User" with the property values equal to the new node that we want to create, finds the outgoing edges (relationships) labeled "BORROWED" with the same property value as the new relationship by calling the Gremlin *outE()* traversing method, and then finds the incoming vertices (nodes) of that relationship, which are labeled "Book" and have the same property values as the new node by calling the *inV()* method.

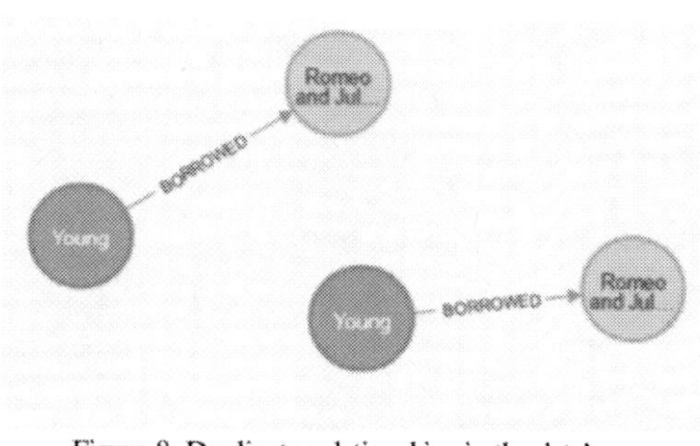


Figure 8. Duplicate relationships in the database

```
User u = User.class.cast(node1);
Book b = Book.class.cast(node2);
BORROWED borrowed = BORROWED.class.cast(rel);

if(g.V().has("Label", u.getLabel()).has("Firstname", u.getFirstname())
        .has("Lastname", u.getLastname())
        .outE().has("DateBorrowed", borrowed.getDateBorrowed())
        .inV().has("Label", b.getLabel()).has("Title", b.getTitle())
        .has("Year", b.getYear()).toList().iterator().hasNext()){
    result = true;
}
```

Figure 9. Checking whether the entered "BOROWED" relationship exists in the database

Thus, if the user tries to create a duplicate "BORROWED" relationship, which already exists in the database, then the appropriate notification message, similar to the message shown in Fig. 4, is displayed.

As already mentioned, the UNIQUE integrity constraint is implemented as a method, which is a part of the application. Its main purpose is to check whether the nodes and relationships, which the user is trying to create, already exist in the database. This is achieved by executing simple Gremlin queries that traverse the graph in order to find the subgraph corresponding to these nodes and relationships. As such, this infers that the implemented UNIQUE constraint does not affect the database performance in any way, since it is implemented through a layered approach as a method within the application. As a result, this constraint and the implemented method increase the complexity of creating nodes and relationships, and, like every other method within an application, it requires additional time to be executed (especially when performing more complex graph traversals). The Gremlin query language is, however, proven to perform well in these situations. Therefore, the cost of time necessary to execute the method is still acceptable when considering the benefits for database consistency.

## IV. CONCLUSIONS AND FUTURE WORK

In this paper, the importance of integrity constraints in the database has been discussed. After giving an overview of the current support for defining integrity constraints provided by the most popular graph DBMSs, it can be said that the level of support is currently minimal and mostly theoretical, thus leaving this issue available for further research and improvements. To showcase the UNIQUE integrity constraint in graph databases, that integrity constraint was implemented as a method within an application, which performs Gremlin queries in a Neo4j database in order to check for existing nodes and relationships. Therefore, the UNIQUE constraint has been successfully implemented as a separate independent layer, which fulfills the required task (preventing duplicate nodes and relationships from being created in the database and enforcing database integrity and consistency), with minimal effect on application performance and absolutely no effect on database performance while executing queries.

In the future, this research is to be extended by implementing more complex integrity constraints, which will be discussed in our future research papers.

## REFERENCES

[1] H. Ibrahim, S. Ceri, P. Fraternali, S. Paraboschi, L. Tanca, U. S. Chakravarthy, et al., "Integrity Constraints Checking in a Distributed Database," in *Soft Computing Applications for Database Technologies*, vol. 19, no. 3, IGI Global, 1AD, pp. 153–169.

[2] H. Decker and D. Martinenghi, "Database Integrity Checking," *Database Technol.*, pp. 961–966, 2009.

[3] E. F. Codd, "Data models in database management," in *ACM SIGMOD Record*, 1980, vol. 11, pp. 112–114.

[4] DB-Engines, "Popularity ranking of database management systems," 2016. [Online]. Available: http://db-engines.com/en/ranking. [Accessed: 17-Sep-2016].

[5] I. Robinson, J. Webber, and E. Eifrem, *Graph Databases: New Opportunities for Connected Data*. " O'Reilly Media, Inc.," 2015.

[6] K. Rabuzin, M. Šestak, and M. Novak (in press), "Integrity constraints in graph databases – implementation challenges," 2016.

[7] R. Angles, "A comparison of current graph database models," in *Data Engineering Workshops (ICDEW), 2012 IEEE 28th International Conference on*, 2012, pp. 171–177.

[8] "DB-Engines Ranking - popularity ranking of graph DBMS." [Online]. Available: http://db-engines.com/en/ranking/graph+dbms. [Accessed: 16-Sep-2016].

[9] Titan:db by Aurelius, "Schema and Data Modeling." [Online]. Available: http://s3.thinkaurelius.com/docs/titan/0.5.1/schema.html. [Accessed: 17-Sep-2016].

[10] OrientDB Manual, "Graph Schema." [Online]. Available: http://orientdb.com/docs/2.1/Graph-Schema.html. [Accessed: 17-Sep-2016].

[11] Franz Inc., "Introduction | AllegroGraph 6.1.1," 2016. [Online]. Available: http://franz.com/agraph/support/documentation/current/agraph-introduction.html. [Accessed: 17-Sep-2016].

[12] R. Angles and C. Gutierrez, "Survey of graph database models," *ACM Comput. Surv.*, vol. 40, no. 1, pp. 1–39, 2008.

# Template Based Automatic Generation of Runsets

Elena V. Ravve
Software Engineering Department
Ort Braude College
Karmiel, Israel
Email: cselena@braude.ac.il

***Abstract*—Layout of modern electronic devices consists of billions of polygons for chemical layers. There exist hundreds of design rules, defining how the polygons may be drowning. Design rule checkers (DRC) guarantee that the chip may be manufactured. Moreover, any manufacturing process allows a finite set of supported legal devices. Layout versus schematic (LVS) comparison determines one-to-one equivalency between a circuit schematic and its layout. The correctness of the DRC and LVS runsets are verified using test cases, which contain shapes, representing failing and passing conditions. Creation and maintenance of the complete set of runsets and the corresponding test cases is complicated and time consuming process that should be automatized. Usually almost all design rules may be divided into a set of categories: width, space/distance, enclosure, extension, coverage, etc. Moreover, the set of legal devices for any process may be divided into a set of technology independent categories: transistors, capacitors, resistors, diodes and so on. In this paper, we use these categories in order to define re-usable patterns. The integrator will use the pre-defined patterns in order to compose the design rule manuscript (DRM) rather than to write it. DRC and LVS runsets are then automatically generated using the DRM. Moreover, we use the patterns in order to automatically create the corresponding test cases.**

***Keywords–Design Rule Manuscript; Design Rule Checker Runset; Layout versus Schematic Runset; Test Cases; Templates; Automatic Generation.***

## I. Introduction

Typical layout of modern electronic devices consists of billions of polygons for different chemical layers. For each such a layer, there exist dozens of design rules (DRs), which define how the polygons may be drowning. Any semiconductor manufacturing process/technology contains a set of physical DRs for geometrical configuration of available layers, wiring, placement and so on.

DRs are series of quantitative limitations, provided by semiconductor manufacturers that enable the designer to verify the correctness of a mask set. DRs have become increasingly more complex with each subsequent generation of semiconductor process. Every chip, which is expected to be manufactured in the given technology, must satisfy the limitations of the DRs. Design rule checking (DRC) runsets are provided by the manufacturer in order to guarantee that the given chip does not give the DR violations.

The document that contains all these rules: Design Rule Manuscript (DRM) has dozens of tables for each layer with free style description of the limitations. The fact leads to various problems, starting from inconsistency in the understanding of the meaning of the rules and going to lots of bugs in coding of the rules in DRC as well as poority of test cases in verification of the DRC runsets. On the other hand, according to our experience of the common work with Tower-Jazz foundry, usually almost all the DRs may be divided into a relatively small set of categories and sub-categories, such as width, space/distance, enclosure, extension, coverage, etc. In this paper, we use these categories in order to derive a set of patterns. These patterns are the basis of an environment that allows the integrator, who writes the DRM, to use the pre-defined patterns in order to compose the DRM rather than to write it. DRC runset is then automatically generated, based on the instantiations of the patterns in the DRM.

DRC runsets are provided in order to guarantee that the given chip does not give the design rule violations. The correctness and completeness of the DRC runsets are verified using test cases, which contain shapes of different chemical layers, representing various failing and passing conditions for each rule of the technology.

Creation, modification and maintenance of the complete set of test cases is complicated and time consuming process that should be automatized. Now, we enrich the derived set of patterns, used for DRC runset generation, by the option to create a set of test cases, which corresponds to the pass condition or to failures of the DRs. When the option of failures or passing is chosen, the particular type of the failure or of the passing is defined as well as the form of the report. In addition, particular subsets of the test cases, generated by the given pattern, may be chosen by the user, etc.

The set of the varied parameters for the test cases generator may be extended upon request. When all parameters are defined, the set of test cases would be created automatically. The complete set of the parametrized patterns may be (but not necessary) organized as a library. For any design rule for a given technology, one chooses the relevant parametrized pattern or set of patterns, provides the specific values of required parameters, and puts the obtained instances into the set of test cases, which corresponds to the technology.

The instantiation and(or) modification process may be automated as well. Using such a method, the complete set of test cases for the full set of DRs for the given technology may be created and easily maintained and(or) modified.

Any semiconductor manufacturing process allows a finite set of legal devices, supported and recognizable in the process. Layout versus schematic (LVS) comparison runsets determine one-to-one equivalency between an integrated circuit schematic and an integrated circuit layout. The correctness and completeness of the LVS runsets are verified using test cases, which contain shapes (with connectivity) representing failing and passing conditions for each legal device of the technology.

In this paper, we briefly explain how our general approach may be extended to the case of automatic generation of LVS runsets and sets of test cases in order to verify them. The proposed innovation is based on the fact that again the set of legal devices for any process or technology may be divided into final set of technology independent categories and sub-categories such that transistors, capacitors, resistors, diodes and so on.

The environment that partially implements the approach is provided. We restricted ourselves to the case of automatic generation of a DRM and a DRC runset, which define and verify limitations, related to width of different layers, as well as the automatic generation of the corresponding set of test cases. The complete tool would produce automatically the DRM, the DRC/LVS runsets and the testcases to test them in a uniform way for all layers and legal devices.

There are several benefits of the presented invention:

- Common methodological basis for different processes, technologies and verification tools;
- Formal approach to DRM composition that allows precise and consistent formulation of physical design rules and description of legal devices for different processes, technologies and verification tools;
- Human independent accumulation of knowledge;
- Significant reduction of human factor and manual writing;
- Total elimination of manual coding and re-use of patterns;
- Better quality and confidence level of the delivered DRM, DRC/LVS runsets and test cases;
- Significant reduction of time and effort to implement DRM, DRC/LVS runsets and test cases;
- Full coverage of all physical design rules and legal devices and the corresponding test cases;
- Integrator does not learn any new programming language;
- Effective, consistent and safe way to change, update and maintain DRM and the corresponding DRC/LVS runsets as well as test cases for all verification tools;
- Detection and correction of mistakes and bug at earliest stages of the flow;
- Effective, consistent and safe way of bug fixes.

The paper is structured in the following way. In Section II, we consider the previous results in the field under investigation. Section III is central in our paper and describes our general approach to solve the problem. In Section IV, we describe in great details a particular implementation of our general approach for creation of a DRC runset for verification of width related DRs. In Section V, we provide the implementation details. Method of automatic generation of test cases for verifying DRC/LVS runsets, using process independent pre-defined generic set of parametrized patterns is described in Section VI. Section VII summarizes the paper.

## II. Review of previous works

These exist a lot of attempts to improve the process of creation of DRC and LVS runsets. They start at least from [1], where a process flow representation was proposed in order to create a single, unified wafer processing representation in order to facilitate the integration of design and manufacturing. Hardware assisted DRC was considered in [2][3][4] but quickly returned back to software based solutions [5]. There exist a lot of patents, which attack the same problem. We take the description of the most relevant patents almost verbatim.

In [6], a method for generating test patterns for testing digital electronic circuits, is defined. It fully specifies some primary inputs, while other primary inputs are specified in accordance with selected series of codes. The test pattern template is then repeatedly converted into a stimulus pattern, using different integers in the selected series of codes, and fault simulation is performed on a circuit under test using each stimulus pattern. A stimulus pattern is then saved for subsequent testing of the circuit under test whenever fault simulation using that stimulus pattern shows that fault coverage has increased.

Another close approach was proposed in [7], which considers automatic generation of DRC runsets, using templates per verification tools. The main idea of the invention is that instead of a user creating runsets in a language of a specific verification tool (also called "native language"), the user expresses the DRC rules in a high level programming language (also called "meta language") that is independent of the native language. The meta language includes, in addition to normal constructs of the high level programming language, a set of keywords that identify DRC rules from an abstract viewpoint, unrelated to any native language.

In [8], an approach to deal with programming language, such as C, C++, Perl or Tcl was proposed. In addition, DRC templates of the type described herein capture the expertise of the template author for use by numerous novice users who do not need to learn the native language of a verification tool. In our approach, we eliminate the need to use any (either experienced or novice) user/programmer in order to write the DRC/LVS runsets. In order to reach the target, we propose to force the DRM composer (who is assumed to remain in the game in any case) to instantiate the relevant pre-defined generic patterns rather than to write the DRM as a free-style document. When these patterns are instantiated and the relevant information is extracted and stored in the suitable way, we use the patterns for DRC runsets generation and similar (new proposed) patterns for LVS runsets generation for any particular verification tool.

In [9], use of patterns for improving design checking was proposed but in another context. Moreover, one aspect of the present invention includes a method for generating functional testcases for multiple boolean algorithms from a single generic testcase template. The method includes the preliminary step of creating a generic testcase template containing user-entered mask levels shapes and grouping the shapes within each mask level of the template. Next, testcase generation code comprising mask build language is developed to copy and rename the mask levels from the template into the desired input levels necessary to test a mask build operation. Finally, testcase generation code is executed to generate a testcase. The testcase generation code can be easily modified as necessary to change the mask levels. Additionally, shape interactions for new mask level builds can be added into the generic testcase template, allowing the patterns to be reused to generate additional testcases, see also [10].

A more general approach to use patterns was proposed in [11]. During the design of semiconductor products which incorporates a user specification and an application set, the application set being a partially manufactured semiconductor platform and its resources, a template engine is disclosed which uses a simplified computer language having a character whereby data used in commands identified by the character need only be input once, either by a user or by files, and that data, after it has been verified to be correct, is automatically allocated to one or more templates used to generate shells for the specification of a final semiconductor product. Data must be correct and compatible with other data before it can be used within the template engine and the generated shells; indeed the template engine cooperates with a plurality of rules and directives to verify the correctness of the data. The template engine may generate one or more of the following shells: an RTL shell, a documentation shell, a timing analysis shell, a synthesis shell, a manufacturing test shell, and/or a floorplan shell.

In [12], an automatic LVS rule file generation apparatus, which includes a definition file generating unit and a rule file generating unit, was proposed. The definition file generating unit generates definition files used for a layout verification based on first data and templates that are used for the layout verification in a layout design of a semiconductor apparatus. The rule file generating unit automatically generates a LVS rule file based on the definition rule files. The templates includes first parameters indicating three-dimensional structures of the semiconductor apparatus. The definition files includes second data with respect to the first parameters. However, unlike our approach, a template for an automatic LVS rule file generation is used for generating a LVS rule file that indicates a rule for a layout verification of a layout design.

In [13], a method for comprehensively verifying design rule checking runsets was proposed. It seems to be the most relevant patent to our test cases generation approach. The patent describes a system and method for automatically creating testcases for design rule checking, which comprises first creating a table with a design rule number, a description, and the values from a design rule manual. Next, any design specific options are derived that affect the flow of the design rule checking, including back end of the line stack options. Then, the design rule values and any design specific options are extracted into testcases. Next, the testcases are organized such that there is one library with a plurality of root cells, further comprising one root cell for checking all rules pertaining to the front end of the line, and another root cell for checking design specific options including back end of the line stack options. Finally, the DRC runset is run against the testcases to determine if the DRC runset provides for design rule checking. However, while the patent deals with the general flow of testcase creation for a particular technology, we propose a general method for instantiations of technology independent generic patterns.

In [14], a system and method for automatically creating testcases for design rule checking was proposed. The method first creates a table with a design rule number, a description, and the values from a design rule manual. The design rule values and any design specific options are extracted into testcases. Finally, the DRC runset is run against the testcases to determine if the DRC runset provides for design rule checking. Other methods for verifying design rule checking were proposed in particular in [15] and [16].

One more techniques for verifying error detection of a design rule checking runset was introduced in [16]. Another method for verifying design rule checking software was proposed in [15]. One more technique for verifying error detection of a design rule checking runset was introduced in [16]. However, all the mentioned methods and approaches do not reach our level of generality. Moreover, they do not use sets of pre-defined patterns in the consistent way.

## III. A SYSTEMATIC APPROACH TO AUTOMATIC GENERATION OF DRC AND LVS RUNSETS AND THE CORRESPONDING TEST CASES

A DR set specifies certain geometric and connectivity restrictions to ensure sufficient margins to account for variability in semiconductor manufacturing processes. DRC is a major step during physical verification signoff on the design. Each process allows a finite list of legal devices, which may be used and recognizable in the process. LVS comparison runsets determine one-to-one equivalency between an integrated circuit schematic and an integrated circuit layout. DRM may contain hundreds of physical design rules and definitions of dozens legal devices.

Like each physical DR must be implemented in DRC runsets, each legal device must be recognized by LVS runsets. Wafer foundry must provide customers with DRC and LVS runsets, implemented in all required verification tools and languages. Creation, modification and maintenance of the complete set of DRC and LVS runsets is a complicated and time consuming process that should be automatized.

The proposed approach is based on the fact that the set of physical design rules for any process or technology usually may be divided into a final set of technology independent categories such that width, space, enclosure and so on. Moreover, the set of legal devices for any process or technology may be divided into a final set of technology independent categories such that transistors, capacitors, resistors, diodes and so on.

We create one set of parametrized patterns for DRC purposes, such that one pattern (or rather sub-set of patterns) corresponds to a DRC category. In addition, we create another set of parametrized patterns for LVS purposes, such that one pattern (or rather sub-set of patterns) corresponds to a LVS category. The parameters of the patterns may contain in particular (but not limited to) involved layout layers, specific design values, connectivity, additional constrains, etc. The set of parameters may be enriched upon request. While earlier proposed methods involve the patterns in pretty late stages of the runsets generation, we propose to force the DRM composer to fulfill the templates, defined by the patterns, (in any relevant way, for example, using GUI) instead of free-style writing of the document.

For any design rule or legal device for a given technology, the DRM composer chooses the relevant parametrized pattern or set of patterns, provides the specific values of required parameters or (preferably) chooses them from a choice list. The obtained information is transformed and stored as a data structure that will be used for different purposes, such that automatic generation of DRM itself as well as DRC and LVS runsets in particular verification tools and so on. All devices of the process are put in the list of legal devices with their description in DRM.

Moreover, any verification tool uses different commands, key words and options for features. When free style is used for DRM writing, different interpretations and further implementations of sentences are allowed that may lead to unexpected results in runs of DRC/LVS runsets. In addition, when different formulations are used for definitions of derived layers as well as special options, hardly detectable effects in DRC/LVS runsets may be produced.

The following flow is proposed. We start first from precise definitions of all derived layers or options, which are expected to be used in physical design rules or descriptions of legal devices. The definitions lead to a final fixed set of key words, which are allowed in physical DRs or descriptions of legal devices. The set contains, for example, entries for definition of such notions as $GATE$, $HOT\ NWELL$, $NTAP$, $BUTTED\ DIFFUSION$ and so on, as well as information, extracted from the technology file, such that names and purposes of layout layers, value of grid and so on. In addition, the set contains key words to choose between minimal, maximal, exact options for the values and so on. The set of key words may be divided into sub-sets, such that only values from a particular sub-set are allowed in certain fields of certain templates.

When the set of allowed key words is fixed and stored as the relevant data structure, the DRM composer may pass to the stage of filling the fields in the pre-defined set of templates for physical design rules or descriptions of legal devices. Any field that is aimed to contain a value from the (sub-)set of key words, either is checked on-the-fly for its correctness or is presented as a choice list.

Only fields for the numerical values (for example, the particular value of the width) will not be so. Moreover, many other checking procedures may be involved at this step. For example, check precision on the given numeric values against grid, etc. The precise information, obtained as the result of the filling of the templates is stored as a relevant data structure and will be re-used for particular patterns for further generation of DRM as well as DRC and LVS runsets, implemented in particular languages or tools. Moreover, the information will be used also for the automatic generation of the corresponding test cases for the DRC and LVS runsets.

## IV. From Rule Definition to DRM and DRC

In fact, typically, every DR is constructed from the rule number, the rule parameter such as width, space, overlap, etc., and the layer name, followed by the description of the rule. The last thing is the size, which is typically maximum or minimum. Moreover, a rule may be exclusive for a specific voltage, devices, combination of layers or purpose.

In order to demonstrate how our general approach works, we decided to treat all width rules of a particular existing DRM of Tower-Jazz foundry. We collected all the width rules for all the layers. Then we transformed every rule to a set of short expressions. We proved that an integrator, who writes DRM, may compose any width rule as detailed as she/he wants by composing the expressions without having to add anything manually.

We had a lot of meetings with the target audience of the tool that implements our approach: the integrators. We wanted to understand what is the best way to build the user interface and where we may encounter difficulties. After summing these meetings, we understood that our Achilles heel of the traditionally used practice is the inconsistency of the rule writing. In fact, adding a rule without considering the previous rules or the way that they were written may cause inconsistency in DRM. Moreover, they mostly used to patch new phrase to the old rule, which describes the new need, without changing all the rule from scratch. In order to overcome the obstacle, we analyzed every width rule and divided it into its components in one long table, taking in account what is the purpose of each one as well as what are the corresponding constraints.

For example: if we use nMOS transistors and the gate layer with 3.3V voltage then we approve one value of minimum width. Unlikely, if we use pMOS transistors for the same gate layer with 5V voltage then we approve an absolutely different value of minimum width. We concluded with the help of Tower-Jazz's experts that we may map all the additions to the width DRs into six main categories:

1) Rules for special layers like marking layers;
2) Rules for layer under other layers;
3) Device dependent rules;
4) Voltage dependent rules;
5) Area despondent rules; For example, two layers are used to define thick gate oxide 5V for mask generation and device recognition. **AREA2** defines area with thick oxide either 3.3V. **AREA6** marks thick oxide as 5V for DRC, LVS and MDP purposes.
6) Purpose dependent rules.

In order to translate all these short sentences into one rule, we got help from Mentor Graphics experts with profound knowledge how *Calibre* works. For example: The most comment and basic example to write a width rule will be coded as follows:

```
XP.W.1 {
    @XP.W.1: XP width, min. 0.XX (XP.W.1)
    internal XP< 0.8 region singular abut> 0 < 90
}
```

Let us consider a more complicated example. A metal width rule **MI.W.2** for I=2,.,6 is formulated as follows:

**MI.W.2**

Minimal width of MI line, connected to a *wide* MI.

In order to better understand the above, we look at the rule's layout in Fig. 1. Now, we see that layer M2 is connected to a *wide* M2. The metal is *wide* if it dimensions are equal or bigger then 35um. Note, that the definition unfortunately does not appear at all in the original formulation in the rule and it is expected to be *known* from the *common knowledge* of the integrators' team. However, the narrow metal, according to the DRs, is approved to be minimum 1um. Otherwise, if it is smaller, our runset must report the violation. In this case, these details are hidden in the original formulation of the rule and must be extracted from other sources of knowledge.

The main problem in the maintenance of DRMs and the corresponding runsets is that, as a rule, the well defined, consistent and well supported source of the knowledge does not exist at all and it is replaced by some common local folklore, transferred verbally in the integrators' community. Our approach starts from precise definitions of all such shortcuts, which are reviewed by the corresponding experts and supported in a uniform way.

In our particular case, we have, for example, **M2NRW** shortcut that actually means in *Calibre* coding:

M2NRW = ((M2MS or (M2slits interact M2MS)) interact M2WIDE) not M2WIDE.

Now, let us code the rule in *Calibre* for M2.

- The first thing, to be written in the runset file, is the rule name, followed by {. In our specific example, it should be:
  **M2.W.2** {
  In this way, we know where this rule begins.
- Next, usually, we want to write comments for this rule to make it easier maintained. We start the comment with sign @. That leads us to the next line in the runset:
  @M2.W.2: Width of Narrow Metal, Connecting to Wide Metal min. **0.YY** ( M2.W.2 )
- Now we put the body of the rule for constraints, which are interpreted as violations for this specific layer:
  X2=not outside edge M2NRW M2WIDE
  EX2=expand edge X2 by 0.01
  area EX2 < 0.02
- Sign } finishes the composition of the rule, so that we determine where it ends.

As the result of our coding, we receive the following automatically generated piece of the runset:

```
M2.W.2 {
    @M2.W.2: Width of Narrow Metal, Connecting to
    Wide Metal min. 1 ( M2.W.2 ).
    X2=not outside edge M2NRW M2WIDE
    EX2=expand edge X2 by 0.01
    area EX2 < 0.02

}
```

The considered example represents a single rule of dozens of rules, while each such a rule has dozens of layers. Eventually, each rule must be translated into DRC statements. We have shown how the coding may be automatized.

## V. IMPLEMENTATION DETAILS

In this section, we show in great details, how our general approach is implemented in a particular toy-tool. We start from a complete snapshot of the GUI, see Fig. 2, then, we explain each step.

### A. *Let us start*

The user(integrator) is expected to provide her/his password, when starting the tool, see Fig. 2 step 1.

### B. *What about the process?*

Using the tool, the user may add a new process, remove an existing process or use a stored process, see Fig. 2 step 2.

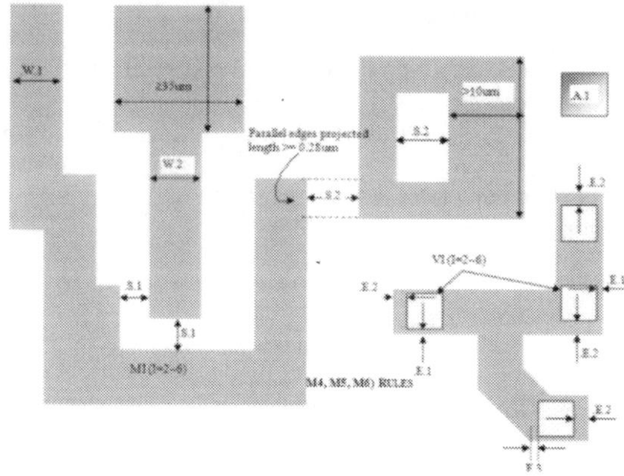

Figure 1. **M2.W.2** rule

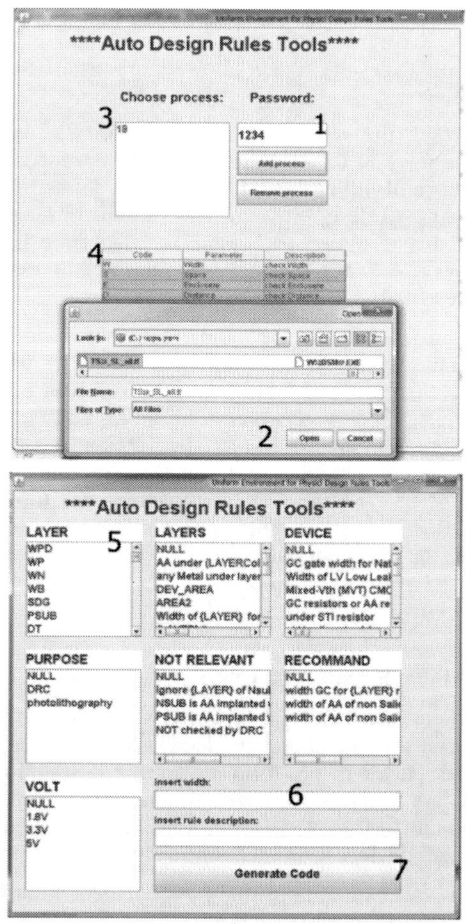


Figure 2. Complete snapshot of the GUI

### C. Which layer?

When the process is chosen, see Fig. 2 step 3. The techfile of the chosen process is used in order to access the list of the available layers.

### D. Composing a rule

When the layer is chosen, the user gets the list of all available categories of the rule. By double-clicking on the desired category, the user gets all the pre-defined sub-categories, available in order to compose the new rule, see Fig. 2 step 4. The sub-categories include in our particular case (but not limited in the general case to):

- the list of all layers from the techfile as well as special layers, like marking layers;
- the list of purposes and recommended options;
- the list of not relevant cases and available devices;
- the list of voltages.

The user may choose any allowed combination of the sub-categories for the new rule, see Fig. 2 step 5. If some combination of the sub-categories is not allowed then the fact is checked automatically by the tool and the user is updated accordingly.

Now, the user should insert the value of the rule: width in our particular case, as well as a free style comment, see Fig. 2 step 6. These are the only values, which are inserted and not chosen from pre-defined options. Then, the corresponding DR is put to its place in the DRM.

### E. Generating the code of the rule

It remains to choose the corresponding tool: Calibre in our example, see Fig. 2 step 7. The corresponding code is generated automatically by the tool.

### F. Testing the generated code of the rule

In order to test the generated code, we composed a layout with the corresponding DRC violation. The violation was found and reported by the automatically generated runset.

## VI. Method of Automatic Generation of Test Cases for Verifying DRC/LVS Runsets, Using Process Independent Pre-Defined Generic Set of Parametrized Templates

In general, dozens of test cases per a design rule should be provided in order to guarantee correctness and completeness of all DRC runsets implemented in all tools and all languages. Moreover, different test cases should be created for failing and passing conditions per each design rule. In addition, all the test cases must be maintained and modified according to any relevant change in DR. As for now, both code of DRC runsets and test cases are manually created and maintained. All the above justifies that automated methodology and system should be proposed for these tasks.

We propose a new approach to the automated test cases generation for DRC runsets again based on the fact that there exists a finite fixed set of categories, which may be defined at once, such that the categories cover all (or most) design rules for any given process or technology. The set again contains such categories as width rules, spacing rules, enclosure rules etc. Then we propose to re-use the parametrized patterns,

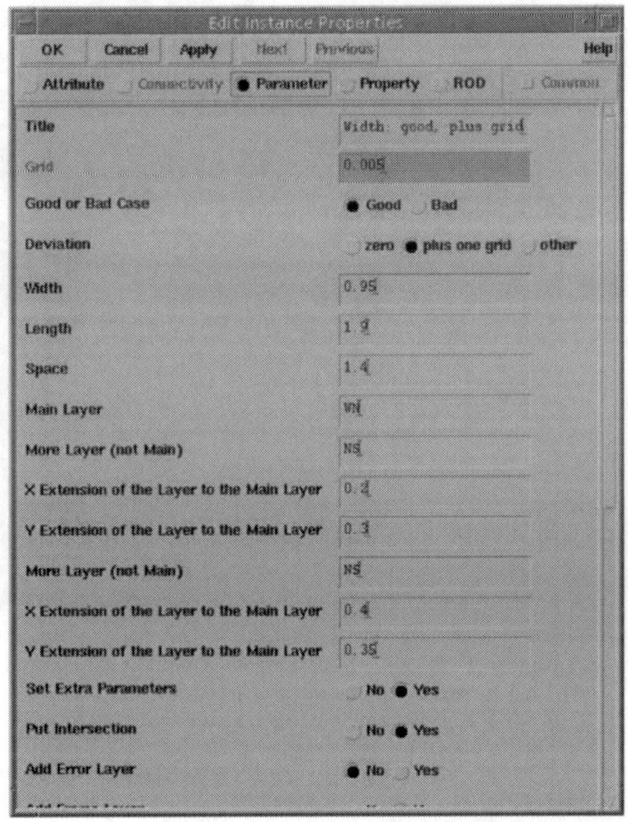


Figure 3. Menu to generate test cases

defined for DRM generator, for each category such that, the pattern may be calibrated to the particular testing purposes by assignment of the corresponding parameters.

Fig. 3 illustrates the concept. The example shows some part of the technology parameters such as the layout layers and purposes as they are defined in the technology file, different values taken from DRM, as well as parameters, related to the testing purpose such that the failing or passing case and its particular version.

In addition, the corresponding report format may be defined using, for example, error layers and so on. All the parameters (or any part of them) may be assigned either manually or in some automated way. The assignment procedure leads to creation of a particular instance of the template that corresponds to the chosen pattern, testing purpose, etc.

Fig. 4 illustrates one of the possible implementation of such instantiation. The particular test case generator was written in SKILL and it is included as an integrated part in the proposed tool.

This approach may be extended to the case of automatically created testcases for LVS checking as well. In fact, the list of legal devices of the process as well as their detailed description is available in DRM. DRM may contain dozens of legal devices such that their final list for the process may be combined from different sub-sets, according to additional options or limitations. LVS runsets are implemented, using different tools

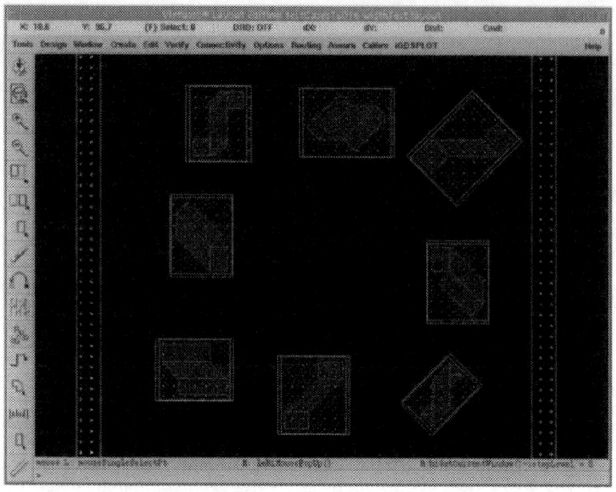

Figure 4. Automatically generated test cases

and program languages, each one with its own algorithms and particular implementations of checking procedures for different features.

Hundreds of test cases per a legal device should be provided in order to guarantee correctness and completeness of all LVS runsets, implemented in all tools and languages. Moreover, different test cases should be created for failing and passing conditions per each legal device and/or their combination. In addition, all the test cases must be maintained and modified according to any relevant change in DRM.

Our method comprises first of all creating of a data structure (say, a table) with a device identifier, its description (including involved layers and connectivity), and the corresponding values from DRM. The data structure contains all legal devices for the process. Any design specific options or limitations, which affect the recognition process, may be added.

Then, the device descriptions and design specific options are implemented into a set of test cases. The implementation is expected to be automatic for both failing and passing conditions. Next, the testcases are organized in a data structure (say, a library) that is suitable for the further run of LVS checkers. Finally, the LVS runset is run against the testcases to determine if the LVS runset is correct and complete. The LVS test case generator is still not included in the implemented tool.

## VII. Conclusion and Outlooks

In this paper, we propose a general approach that allows automatized generation of a design rule manuscript, based on a final set of pre-defined patterns. The particular instantiations of the patterns in the DRM generator are then used for automatic generation of DRC and LVS runsets as well as the corresponding test cases.

The approach is based on the fact that usually almost all design rules may be divided into relatively small set of categories: width, space/distance, enclosure, extension, coverage, etc. Moreover, the set of legal devices for any process or technology may be divided into final set of independent categories: transistors, capacitors, resistors, diodes and so on.

The environment that partially implements the approach is provided.

We restricted ourselves to the case of automatic generation of a DRM and a DRC runset, which defines and verifies limitations, related to width of different layers, as well as the automatic generation of the corresponding set of test cases. The complete tool would produce automatically the DRM, the DRC/LVS runsets and the testcases to test them in a uniform way for all layers and all legal devices.

The approach may be extended to automatic generation of other runsets, say, antenna runsets and the corresponding test cases. In general, the approach may be applied in a uniform way to all steps of the of masks' generation and verification.

*Acknowledgments*

We are would like to thank T. Estrugo (Tower-Jazz) for valuable discussions, general support and his many suggestions. We are would like to thank U. Krispil (Mentor Graphics) for his technical assistance. We also appreciate the effort of our students M. Ankonina and N. Mazuz, who implemented the tool.

## References

[1] E. Ünver, Implementation of a Design Rule Checker for Silicon Wafer Fabrication, ser. MTL memo. Massachusetts Institute of Technology, Department of Electrical Engineering and Computer Science, 1994.

[2] L. Seiler, A Hardware Assisted Methodology for VLSI Design Rule Checking, ser. MIT/LCS/TR-. Mass. Inst. of Technology, Laboratory for Computer Science, 1985.

[3] T. Blank, M. Stefik, and W. vanCleemput, "A parallel bit map processor architecture for DA algorithms," in Proceedings of the 18th Design Automation Conference, ser. DAC '81. Piscataway, NJ, USA: IEEE Press, 1981, pp. 837–845.

[4] R. M. Lougheed and D. L. McCubbrey, "The Cytocomputer: A practical pipelined image processor," in ISCA, J. Lenfant, B. R. Borgerson, D. E. Atkins, K. B. Irani, D. Kinniment, and H. Aiso, Eds. ACM, 1980, pp. 271–277.

[5] D. Wittenmyer, Offline Design Rule Checking for VLSI Circuits. University of Toledo., 1992.

[6] K. Bowden, "Method for generating test patterns," Apr. 18 2000, uS Patent 6,052,809.

[7] G. Richardson and D. Rigg, "Method and system for automatic generation of DRC rules with just in time definition of derived layers," Aug. 26 2003, US Patent 6,611,946.

[8] D. Shei and J. Cheng, "Configuration management and automated test system ASIC design software," Dec. 30 1997, US Patent 5,703,788.

[9] S. O'Brien, "Methods and systems for performing design checking using a template," Aug. 4 2009, US Patent 7,571,419.

[10] P. Selvam, "Method for generating integrated functional testcases for multiple boolean algorithms from a single generic testcase template," Feb. 24 2009, US Patent 7,496,876.

[11] T. Youngman and J. Nordman, "Language and templates for use in the design of semiconductor products," Oct. 11 2011, US Patent 8,037,448.

[12] K. Okuaki, "Automatic LVS rule file generation apparatus, template for automatic LVS rule file generation, and method for automatic lvs rule file generation," Oct. 6 2005, US Patent App. 11/093,100.

[13] D. Shei and J. Cheng, "Configuration management and automated test system ASIC design software," Dec. 30 1997, US Patent 5,703,788.

[14] J. Crouse, T. Lowe, L. Miao, J. Montstream, N. Vogl, and C. Wyckoff, "Method for comprehensively verifying design rule checking runsets," May 4 2004, US Patent 6,732,338.

[15] W. DeCamp, L. Earl, J. Minahan, J. Montstream, D. Nickel, J. Oler, and R. Williams, "Method for verifying design rule checking software," May 16 2000, US Patent 6,063,132.

[16] J. Lawrence, "Techniques for verifying error detection of a design rule checking runset," Jul. 23 2009, US Patent App. 12/017,524.

This page intentionally left blank.

# Incremental Reasoning on Strongly Distributed Fuzzy Systems

Elena V. Ravve and Zeev Volkovich
Software Engineering Department
Ort Braude College
Karmiel, Israel
Email: {cselena,vlvolkov}@braude.ac.il

***Abstract*—We introduce the notion of strongly distributed *fuzzy* systems and present a uniform approach to incremental problem solving on them. The approach is based on the systematic use of two logical reduction techniques: Feferman-Vaught reductions and syntactically defined translation schemes. The fuzzy systems are presented as logical structures $\mathcal{A}$'s. The problems are presented as fuzzy formulae on them. We propose a uniform template for methods, which allow (for a certain cost) evaluation of formulae of fuzzy logic $\mathcal{L}$ over $\mathcal{A}$ from values of formulae over its components and values of formulae over the index structure $\mathcal{I}$.**

***Keywords*–*Fuzzy systems; Incremental reasoning; Reduction sequences; Syntactically defined translation schemes; Translations; Transductions.***

## I. Introduction

Decomposition and incremental reasoning on switch systems comes back to early 60's [1] [2]. Since Zadeh introduced the fuzzy set theory in [3], by exploiting the concept of membership grade, numerous attempts to investigate fuzzy systems and their properties have been applied. In this context, the theory of disjunctive decompositions of [1] [2] and others, was shown to be insufficient. From the pioneering works, investigating the problem, we mention only [4], where an approach for obtaining simple disjunctive decompositions of fuzzy functions is described. However, the approach is not scalable to large functions and hardly implemented. The summary of the first results may be found in [5]. See [6] for the next contributions in the field.

Jumping to the 90's, we mention [7], which deals with the problem of general max-min decomposition of binary fuzzy relations defined in the Cartesian product of finite spaces. In [8], a new method to derive the membership functions and reference rules of a fuzzy system was developed. Using this method, a complicated Multiple Input Single Output system can be obtained from combination of several Single Input Single Output systems with a special coupling method. Moreover, it was shown how the decomposition and coupling method reduces complexity of the network, used to represent the fuzzy system. Theoretical results on structural decomposition of general Multiple Input Multiple Output fuzzy systems are presented in [9]. Some recent results on a decomposition technique for complex systems into hierarchical and multi-layered fuzzy logic sub-systems may be found in [10].

For $\alpha$-decomposition of [11], originated from $max - min$ composition of [12], in [13], it was shown that every fuzzy relation $R$ is always generally effectively $\alpha$-decomposable. Moreover, calculating of $\rho(R) = min\{|Z| : R = Q\alpha T, Q \in F(X \times Z), T \in F(Z \times Y)\}$ is an NP-complete problem. A new concept for the decomposition of fuzzy numbers into a finite number of $\alpha$-cuts provided in [14].

In this paper, we propose a *generalized* purely theoretical approach to incremental reasoning on fuzzy distributed systems. This approach allows us to give the precise definition of locality. Moreover, we propose a template, such that if one follows it successfully then it is possible to reduce evaluation of a fuzzy formula on the composed structure to evaluation of *effectively algorithmically* derived formulae on components with a final post-processing. We show two cases, when the template may be successfully applied to two the most popular semantics of fuzzy logic. Finally, we give some complexity analysis of the method.

We consider fuzzy logic as a infinite-valued (infinitely-many valued) logic, in which the law of excluded middle does not hold. In fact, the truth function for an extension of a First Order Logic ($FOL$) relation $R$ with a fuzzy relation is a mapping in the interval $[0, 1]$. History of many-valued logics (a propositional calculus, in which there are more than two truth values) comes back to early 20's of the previous century [15][16]. One of the first formalizations of such a view may be found in [17]. The approach leads to the following definition of a fuzzy truth-value lattice [18]: *A fuzzy truth-value lattice* is a lattice of fuzzy sets on $[0, 1]$ that includes two complete sublattices $\mathbf{T}$ and $\mathbf{F}$ such that:

1) $\forall v_1 \in \mathbf{T}\ \forall v_2 \in \mathbf{F} :$ $v_1$ and $v_2$ incomparable, and
2) $\forall S \in \mathbf{T} :$ $lub(S) \in \mathbf{T}$ and $glb(S) \in \mathbf{T}$, moreover $\forall S \in \mathbf{F} :$ $lub(S) \in \mathbf{F}$ and $glb(S) \in \mathbf{F}$, and
3) $\forall v \in \mathbf{T}\ \forall \epsilon \in [0, 1]$ : if $\exists v^* \in \mathbf{T} :$ $v^* \leq_l v + \epsilon$ then $v + \epsilon \in \mathbf{T}$, moreover $\forall v \in \mathbf{F}\ \forall \epsilon \in [0, 1]$ : if $\exists v^* \in \mathbf{F} :$ $v^* \leq_l v + \epsilon$ then $v + \epsilon \in \mathbf{F}$, where

$\mathbf{T}$ and $\mathbf{F}$ respectively denote the set of all **TRUE**-characteristic truth-values and the set of all **FALSE**-characteristic false-values in the lattice; $lub$ and $glb$ are the labels of the *least upper bound* and the *greatest lower bound*.

In a particular definition of a truth-value lattice, $lub$ and $glb$ are interpreted by specific operations. There exists a variety of fuzzy set intersection and union definitions [19], and $lub$ and $glb$ can be defined to be any corresponding ones of them. Moreover, systems based on real numbers in $[0, 1]$ having truth-characteristics distinguished [17], commonly use $0.5$ as the splitting point between **FALSE**- and **TRUE**-characteristic regions, where $0.5$ is considered an **UNKNOWN**- characteristic truth-value. In such a case, $lub$ corresponds to $max$, $glb$ corresponds to $min$ and $\leq$ is the usual real number less-than-or-equal-to relation. For a possible connection of fuzzy logic and graph grammars, see [20].

In this paper, we generalize and extend the coupling method of [8] by systematic application of two logical reduction techniques to the field of reasoning on fuzzy distributed systems. The distributed systems are presented as logical structures $\mathcal{A}$'s. We propose a uniform template for methods, which allow for certain cost evaluation of formulae of fuzzy logic $\mathcal{L}$ (with a particular choice of $lub$ and $glb$) over $\mathcal{A}$ from values of formulae over its components and values of formulae over the index structure $\mathcal{I}$. In this paper, we consider only relational structures. We assume that the reader has general logical background as may be found in [21], [22].

The logical reduction techniques are:

**Feferman-Vaught reduction sequences** (or simply, reductions) were introduced in [23]. Given logical structure $\mathcal{A}$ as a composition of structures $\mathcal{A}_i, i \in I$ and index structure $\mathcal{I}$. Reduction sequence is a set of formulae such that each such a formula can be evaluated locally in some site or index set. Next, from the local answers, received from the sites, and possibly some additional information about the sites, we compute the result for the given global formula. In the logical context, the reductions are applied to a relational structure $\mathcal{A}$ distributed over different sites with structures $\mathcal{A}_i, i \in I$. The reductions allow the formulae over $\mathcal{A}$ to be computed from formulae over the $\mathcal{A}_i$'s and formulae over index structure $\mathcal{I}$.

**Translation schemes** are the logical analogue to coordinate transformations in geometry. The fundamental property of translation schemes describes how to compute transformed formulae in the same way Leibniz' Theorem describes how to compute transformed integrals. The fundamental property has a long history, but was first properly stated by Rabin [24].

General complexity analysis of incremental computations in the proposed framework may be found in [25].

The paper is organized as follows. In Section II, we discuss different ways of obtaining structures from components. Section III introduces the notion of abstract translation schemes. Section IV is the main section of the paper, where we state and prove our main Theorem 4. Section VI summarizes the paper.

## II. Disjoint Union and Shuffling of Structures

The first reduction technique that we use is *Feferman-Vaught reductions* [23]. In this section, we start to discuss different ways of obtaining structures from components. We mostly follow [26][27]. The *Disjoint Union* of a family of structures is the simplest example of juxtaposing structures over an index structure $\mathcal{I}$ with universe $I$, where none of the components are linked to each other. In such a case the index structure $\mathcal{I}$ may be replaced by an index set $I$.

We start our considerations from First Order Logic ($FOL$). Second Order Logic ($SOL$) is like $FOL$ but allows quantification over relations. If the arity of the relation restricted to 1 then we deal with Monadic Second Order Logic ($MSOL$). We recall the following definitions:

*Definition 1 (Quantifier Rank of Formulae):* Quantifier rank of formula $\varphi$ ($qr(\varphi)$) is defined as follows:

- for $\varphi$ without quantifiers $qr(\varphi) = 0$;
- if $\varphi = \neg\varphi_1$ and $qr(\varphi_1) = n_1$, then $qr(\varphi) = n_1$;
- if $\varphi = \varphi_1 \cdot \varphi_2$, where $\cdot \in \{\vee, \wedge, \rightarrow\}$, and $qr(\varphi_1) = n_1$, $qr(\varphi_2) = n_2$, then $qr(\varphi) = max\{n_1, n_2\}$;
- if $\varphi = Q\varphi_1$, where $Q$ is a quantifier, and $qr(\varphi_1) = n_1$, then $qr(\varphi) = n_1 + 1$.

*Definition 2 (Disjoint Union):*
Let $\tau_i = \langle R_1^i, \ldots, R_{j^i}^i \rangle$ be a vocabulary of structure $\mathcal{A}_i$. In the general case, the resulting structure is $\mathcal{A} = \dot{\bigsqcup}_{i\in I}\mathcal{A}_i = \langle I \cup \dot{\bigcup}_{i\in I} A_i, P(i,v), Index(x), R_j^I (1 \leq j \leq j^I), R_{j^i}^i, (i \in I, 1 \leq j^i \leq j^i), \rangle$ for all $i \in I$, where $P(i,v)$ is true iff element $a$ came from $A_i$, $Index(x)$ is true iff $x$ came from $I$.

*Definition 3 (Partitioned Index Structure):*
Let $\mathcal{I}$ be an index structure over $\tau_{ind}$. $\mathcal{I}$ is called *finitely partitioned* into $\ell$ parts if there are unary predicates $I_\alpha$, $\alpha < \ell$, in the vocabulary $\tau_{ind}$ of $\mathcal{I}$ such that their interpretation forms a partition of the universe of $\mathcal{I}$.

The following classical theorem holds:

*Theorem 1:*
Let $\mathcal{I}$ be a finitely partitioned index structure. Let $\mathcal{A} = \dot{\bigsqcup}_{i\in I}\mathcal{A}_i$ be a $\tau$–structure, where each $\mathcal{A}_i$ is isomorphic to some $\mathcal{B}_1, \ldots, \mathcal{B}_\ell$ over the vocabularies $\tau_1, \ldots, \tau_\ell$, in accordance to the partition ($\ell$ is the number of the classes). For every $\phi \in MSOL(\tau)$ there are:

- a boolean function $F_\phi(b_{1,1}, \ldots, b_{1,j_1}, \ldots, b_{\ell,1}, \ldots, b_{\ell,j_\ell}, b_{I,1}, \ldots, b_{I,j_I})$
- $MSOL$–formulae $\psi_{1,1}, \ldots, \psi_{1,j_1}, \ldots, \psi_{\ell,1}, \ldots, \psi_{\ell,j_\ell}$
- $MSOL$–formulae $\psi_{I,1}, \ldots, \psi_{I,j_I}$

such that for every $\mathcal{A}$, $\mathcal{I}$ and $\mathcal{B}_i$ as above with $\mathcal{B}_i \models \psi_{i,j}$ iff $b_{i,j} = 1$ and $\mathcal{B}_I \models \psi_{I,j}$ iff $b_{I,j} = 1$ we have

$$\mathcal{A} \models \phi \text{ iff } F_\phi(b_{1,1}, \ldots, b_{1,j_1}, \ldots, b_{I,1}, \ldots, b_{I,j_I}) = 1.$$

Moreover, $F_\phi$ and the $\psi_{i,j}$ are computable from $\phi$, $\ell$ and vocabularies alone, but are tower exponential in the quantifier rank of $\phi$.

Note that in most real applications, $F_\phi$ and the $\psi_{\alpha,j}$ are single exponential in the quantifier rank of $\phi$.

**Proof:** The proof is classical, see in particular [28].

Now, we introduce an abstract preservation property of $XX$-combination of logics $\mathcal{L}_1, \mathcal{L}_2$, denoted by $XX - PP(\mathcal{L}_1, \mathcal{L}_2)$. $XX$ may mean, for example, Disjoint Union. The property says roughly that if two $XX$-combinations of structures $\mathcal{A}_1, \mathcal{A}_2$ and $\mathcal{B}_1, \mathcal{B}_2$ satisfy the same sentences of $\mathcal{L}_1$ then the disjoint unions $\mathcal{A}_1 \sqcup \mathcal{A}_2$ and $\mathcal{B}_1 \sqcup \mathcal{B}_2$ satisfy the same sentences of $\mathcal{L}_2$. The reason we look at this abstract property is that the property $XX - PP(\mathcal{L}_1, \mathcal{L}_2)$ and its variants play an important role in our development of the Feferman-Vaught style theorems. This abstract approach was initiated by [23] and further developed in [29][30]. Now, we spell out various ways in which the theory of a disjoint union depends on the theory of the components. First, we look at the case, where the index structure is fixed.

*Definition 4 (Preservation Property with Fixed Index Set):*

For two logics $\mathcal{L}_1$ and $\mathcal{L}_2$ we define
*Disjoint Pair*
**Input of operation:** Two structures;
**Preservation Property:** if two pairs of structures $\mathcal{A}_1, \mathcal{A}_2$ and $\mathcal{B}_1, \mathcal{B}_2$ satisfy the same sentences of $\mathcal{L}_1$ then the disjoint unions $\mathcal{A}_1 \sqcup \mathcal{A}_2$ and $\mathcal{B}_1 \sqcup \mathcal{B}_2$ satisfy the same sentences of $\mathcal{L}_2$.
**Notation:** $P - PP(\mathcal{L}_1, \mathcal{L}_2)$
*Disjoint Union*
**Input of operation:** Indexed set of structures;
**Preservation Property:** if for each $i \in I$ (index set) $\mathcal{A}_i$ and $\mathcal{B}_i$ satisfy the same sentences of $\mathcal{L}_1$ then the disjoint unions $\bigsqcup_{i\in I} \mathcal{A}_i$ and $\bigsqcup_{i\in I} \mathcal{B}_i$ satisfy the same sentences of $\mathcal{L}_2$.
**Notation:** $DJ - PP(\mathcal{L}_1, \mathcal{L}_2)$

The *Disjoint Union* of a family of structures is the simplest example of juxtaposing structures where none of the components are linked to each other. Another way of producing a new structure from several given structures is by mixing (shuffling) structures according to a (definable) prescribed way along the index structure.

*Definition 5 (Shuffle over Partitioned Index Structure):*
Let $\mathcal{I}$ be a partitioned index structure into $\beta$ parts, using unary predicates $I_\alpha, \alpha < \beta$. Let $\mathcal{A}_i, i \in I$ be a family of structures such that for each $i \in I_\alpha$ $\mathcal{A}_i \cong \mathcal{B}_\alpha$, according to the partition. In this case, we say that $\bigsqcup_{i\in I} \mathcal{A}_i$ is the *shuffle of $\mathcal{B}_\alpha$ along the partitioned index structure $\mathcal{I}$*, and denote it by $\biguplus^{\mathcal{I}}_{\alpha<\beta} \mathcal{B}_\alpha$.

Note that the shuffle operation, as defined here, is a special case of the disjoint union, and that the disjoint pair is a special case of the finite shuffle.

In the case of variable index structures and of $FOL$, Feferman and Vaught observed that it is not enough to look at the $FOL$-theory of the index structures, but one has to look at the $FOL$-theories of expansions of the Boolean algebras $PS(\mathcal{I})$ and $PS(\mathcal{J})$ respectively. $PS$ is used for *Power Set*.

Gurevich suggested another approach, by looking at the $MSOL$ theories of structures $\mathcal{I}$ and $\mathcal{J}$. This is really the same, but more in the spirit of the problem, as the passage from $I$ to an expansion of $PS(\mathcal{I})$ remains on the semantic level, whereas the comparison of theories is syntactic. There is not much freedom in choosing the logic in which to compare the index structures, so we assume it always to be $MSOL$.

*Definition 6 (PP with Variable Index Structures):*
For two logics $\mathcal{L}_1$ and $\mathcal{L}_2$ we define
*Disjoint Multiples*
**Input of operation:** Structure and Index structure;
**Preservation Property:** Given two pairs of structures $\mathcal{A}, \mathcal{B}$ and $\mathcal{I}, \mathcal{J}$ such that $\mathcal{A}, \mathcal{B}$ satisfy the same sentences of $\mathcal{L}_1$ and $\mathcal{I}, \mathcal{J}$ satisfy the same $MSOL$-sentences. Then the disjoint unions $\bigsqcup_{i\in I} \mathcal{A}$ and $\bigsqcup_{j\in J} \mathcal{B}$ satisfy the same sentences of $\mathcal{L}_2$.
**Notation:** $Mult - PP(\mathcal{L}_1, \mathcal{L}_2)$
*Shuffles*
**Input of operation:** A family of structures $\mathcal{B}_\alpha : \alpha < \beta$ and a (finitely) partitioned index structure $\mathcal{I}$ with $I_\alpha$ a partition.
**Preservation Property:** Assume that for each $\alpha < \beta$ the pair of structures $\mathcal{A}_\alpha, \mathcal{B}_\alpha$ satisfy the same sentences of $\mathcal{L}_1$, and $\mathcal{I}, \mathcal{J}$ satisfy the same $MSOL$-sentences. Then the schuffles $\biguplus^{\mathcal{I}}_{\alpha<\beta} \mathcal{A}_\alpha$ and $\biguplus^{\mathcal{J}}_{\alpha<\beta} \mathcal{B}_\alpha$ satisfy the same sentences of $\mathcal{L}_2$.
**Notation:** $Shu - PP(\mathcal{L}_1, \mathcal{L}_2)$ or for finite shuffles: $FShu - PP(\mathcal{L}_1, \mathcal{L}_2)$.

*Observation 1:*
Assume that for two logics $\mathcal{L}_1$, $\mathcal{L}_2$ we have the preservation property $XX - PP(\mathcal{L}_1, \mathcal{L}_2)$ and $\mathcal{L}'_1$ is an extension of $\mathcal{L}_1$, $\mathcal{L}'_2$ is a sub-logic of $\mathcal{L}_2$, then $XX - PP(\mathcal{L}'_1, \mathcal{L}'_2)$ holds as well.

*Observation 2:*
For two logics $\mathcal{L}_1$, $\mathcal{L}_2$ the following implications between preservation properties hold: $DJ - PP(\mathcal{L}_1, \mathcal{L}_2)$ implies $P - PP(\mathcal{L}_1, \mathcal{L}_2)$ and, for fixed index structures, $Mult - PP(\mathcal{L}_1, \mathcal{L}_2)$, $Shu - PP(\mathcal{L}_1, \mathcal{L}_2)$ and $FShu - PP(\mathcal{L}_1, \mathcal{L}_2)$. Moreover, for variable index structures we have $Shu - PP(\mathcal{L}_1, \mathcal{L}_2)$ implies $FShu - PP(\mathcal{L}_1, \mathcal{L}_2)$ and $Mult - PP(\mathcal{L}_1, \mathcal{L}_2)$.

*Definition 7 (Reduction Sequence for Shuffling):*
Let $\mathcal{I}$ be a finitely partitioned $\tau_{ind}$-index structure and $\mathcal{L}$ be logic. Let $\mathcal{A} = \biguplus^{\mathcal{I}}_{\alpha<\beta} \mathcal{B}_\alpha$ be the $\tau$–structure which is the finite shuffle of the $\tau_\alpha$-structures $\mathcal{B}_\alpha$ over $\mathcal{I}$. A *$\mathcal{L}_1$-reduction sequence for shuffling* for $\phi \in \mathcal{L}_2(\tau_{shuffle})$ is given by

1) a boolean function $F_\phi(b_{1,1}, \ldots, b_{1,j_1}, \ldots, b_{I,j_I})$
2) set $\Upsilon$ of $\mathcal{L}_1$–formulae $\Upsilon = \{\psi_{1,1}, \ldots, \psi_{\beta,j_\beta}\}$
3) $MSOL$–formulae $\psi_{I,1}, \ldots, \psi_{I,j_I}$

and has the property that for every $\mathcal{A}$, $\mathcal{I}$ and $\mathcal{B}_\alpha$ as above with $\mathcal{B}_\alpha \models \psi_{\alpha,j}$ iff $b_{\alpha,j} = 1$ and $\mathcal{B}_I \models \psi_{I,j}$ iff $b_{I,j} = 1$ we have

$$\mathcal{A} \models \phi \text{ iff } F_\phi(b_{1,1}, \ldots, b_{1,j_1}, \ldots, b_{\beta,1}, b_{I,j_I}) = 1.$$

Note that we require that $F_\phi$ and the $\psi_{\alpha,j}$'s depend only on $\phi$,$\beta$ and $\tau_1, \ldots, \tau_\beta$ but not on the structures involved.

Now, we list which Preservation Properties hold for which fuzzy logics.

*Theorem 2:*
Let $\mathcal{I}$ be an index structure and $\mathcal{L}$ be a fuzzy logic with either $lub$ and $glb$, defined as set intersection and union [19], or $lub$ corresponds to $max$, $glb$ corresponds to $min$ [20].
Then $DJ - PP(\mathcal{L}, \mathcal{L})$ and $FShu - PP(\mathcal{L}, \mathcal{L})$ hold.
**Proof:**
$\cap, \cup$: *The proof by analyzing and extension of the proof in [23], [31].*
$max, min$: *The proof by analyzing and extension of the proof in [31], [32].*

## III. Syntactically Defined Translation Schemes

The second logical reduction technique that we use is *the syntactically defined translation schemes*, which describe transformations of logical structures. The notion of abstract translation schemes comes back to Rabin [24]. They give rise to two induced maps, translations and transductions. Transductions describe the induced transformation of logical structures and the translations describe the induced transformations of logical formulae.

*Definition 8 (Translation Schemes $\Phi$):*
Let $\tau_1$ and $\tau_2$ be two vocabularies and $\mathcal{L}$ be a logic. Let $\tau_2 = \{R_1, \ldots, R_m\}$ and let $\rho(R_i)$ be the arity of $R_i$. Let $\Phi = \langle \varphi, \psi_1, \ldots, \psi_m \rangle$ be formulae of $\mathcal{L}(\tau_1)$. $\Phi$ is *$\kappa$-feasible for $\tau_2$ over $\tau_1$* if $\varphi$ has exactly $\kappa$ distinct free variables and each $\psi_i$ has $\kappa\rho(R_i)$ distinct free variables. Such a $\Phi = \langle \varphi, \psi_1, \ldots, \psi_m \rangle$ is also called a *$\kappa$–$\tau_1$–$\tau_2$–translation scheme*

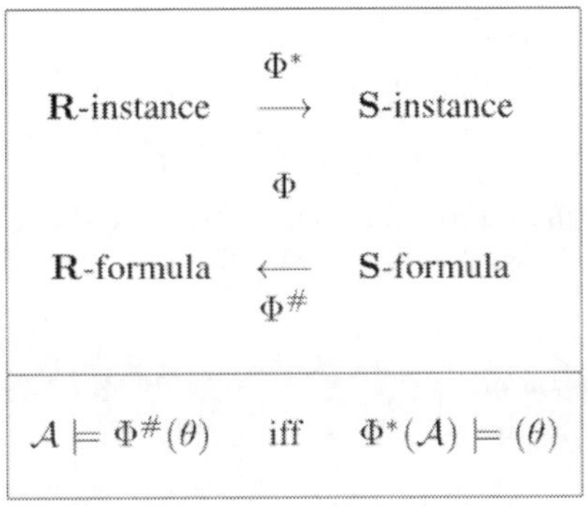


Figure 1. Components of translation schemes and the fundamental property

or, shortly, a *translation scheme*, if the parameters are clear in the context.

In general, Definition 8 must be adopted to the given fuzzy logic $\mathcal{L}$, if it is not straightforward. For a fuzzy logic $\mathcal{L}$ with a translation scheme $\Phi$ we can *naturally* associate a (partial) function $\Phi^*$ from $\tau_1$–structures to $\tau_2$–structures.

*Definition 9 (The induced map $\Phi^*$):*
Let $\mathcal{A}$ be a $\tau_1$–structure with universe $A$ and $\Phi$ be $\kappa$–feasible for $\tau_2$ over $\tau_1$. The structure $\mathcal{A}_\Phi$ is defined as follows:

1) The universe of $\mathcal{A}_\Phi$ is the set $A_\Phi = \{\bar{a} \in A^\kappa : \mathcal{A} \models \varphi(\bar{a})\}$.
2) The interpretation of $R_i$ in $\mathcal{A}_\Phi$ is the set
$$A_\Phi(R_i) = \{\bar{a} \in {A_\Phi}^{\rho(R_i)\cdot\kappa} : \mathcal{A} \models \psi_i(\bar{a})\}.$$
Note that $\mathcal{A}_\Phi$ is a $\tau_2$–structure of cardinality at most $\mid A \mid^\kappa$.
3) The partial function $\Phi^* : Str(\tau_1) \to Str(\tau_2)$ is defined by $\Phi^*(\mathcal{A}) = \mathcal{A}_\Phi$. Note that $\Phi^*(\mathcal{A})$ is defined iff $\mathcal{A} \models \exists\bar{x}\varphi$.

For fuzzy logic $\mathcal{L}$ with a translation scheme $\Phi$ we can also *naturally* associate a function $\Phi^\#$ from $\mathcal{L}(\tau_2)$–formulae to $\mathcal{L}(\tau_1)$–formulae.

*Definition 10 (The induced map $\Phi^\#$):*
Let $\theta$ be a $\tau_2$–formula and $\Phi$ be $\kappa$–feasible for $\tau_2$ over $\tau_1$. The formula $\theta_\Phi$ is defined inductively as follows:

1) For $R_i \in \tau_2$ and $\theta = R(x_1, \ldots, x_m)$ let $x_{j,h}$ be new variables with $i \leq m$ and $h \leq \kappa$ and denote by $\bar{x}_i = \langle x_{i,1}, \ldots, x_{i,\kappa}\rangle$. We put $\theta_\Phi = \psi_i(\bar{x}_1, \ldots, \bar{x}_m)$.
2) For the boolean connectives the translation distributes, i.e. if $\theta = (\theta_1 \vee \theta_2)$ then $\theta_\Phi = (\theta_{1\Phi} \vee \theta_{1\Phi})$ and if $\theta = \neg\theta_1$ then $\theta_\Phi = \neg\theta_{1\Phi}$, and similarly for $\wedge$.
3) For the existential quantifier, we use relativization, i.e. if $\theta = \exists y\theta_1$, let $\bar{y} = \langle y_1, \ldots, y_\kappa\rangle$ be new variables. We put $\theta_\Phi = \exists\bar{y}(\varphi(\bar{y}) \wedge \theta_{1\Phi})$.
4) For (monadic) second order variables $U$ of arity $\ell$ ($\ell = 1$ for $MSOL$) and $\bar{v}$ a vector of length $\ell$ of first order variables or constants we translate $U(\bar{v})$ by treating $U$ like a relation symbol above and put
$$\theta_\Phi = \exists V(\forall\bar{v}(V(\bar{v}) \to (\phi(\bar{v_1}) \wedge \ldots \phi(\bar{v_\ell}) \wedge (\theta_1)_\Phi))).$$
5) The function $\Phi^\# : \mathcal{L}(\tau_2) \to \mathcal{L}(\tau_1)$ is defined by $\Phi^\#(\theta) = \theta_\Phi$.

*Observation 1:* If we use $MSOL$ and $\Phi^*$ is over $MSOL$ too, and it is vectorized, then we do not obtain $MSOL$ for $\mathcal{A}_\Phi$. In most of feasible applications, we have that $\Phi^*$ is not vectorized, but not necessarily.

*Observation 2:*

1) $\Phi^\#(\theta) \in$ fuzzy $FOL$ ($FFOL$) provided $\theta \in FFOL$, even for vectorized $\Phi$.
2) $\Phi^\#(\theta) \in MSOL$ provided $\theta \in MSOL$, but only for scalar (non–vectorized) $\Phi$.

The following fundamental theorem is easily verified for correctly defined $\mathcal{L}$ translation schemes, see Figure 1. Its origins go back at least to the early years of modern logic [33, page 277 ff]. See also [21].

*Theorem 3:*
Let $\Phi = \langle\varphi, \psi_1, \ldots, \psi_m\rangle$ be a $\kappa$–$\tau_1$–$\tau_2$–translation scheme, $\mathcal{A}$ a $\tau_1$-structure and $\theta$ a $\mathcal{L}(\tau_2)$–formula. Then
$$\mathcal{A} \models \Phi^\#(\theta) \text{ iff } \Phi^*(\mathcal{A}) \models \theta.$$

## IV. Strongly Distributed Fuzzy Structures

The disjoint union and shuffles as such are not very interesting. However, combining them with translation schemes gives as a rich repertoire of composition techniques. Now, we generalize the disjoint union or shuffling of fuzzy structures to *Strongly Distributed Fuzzy Structures* in the following way:

*Definition 11 (Strongly Distributed Fuzzy Structures):*
Let $\mathcal{I}$ be a finitely partitioned index structure and $\mathcal{L}$ be $FFOL$. Let $\mathcal{A} = \bigsqcup_{i\in I}\mathcal{A}_i$ be a $\tau$–structure, where each $\mathcal{A}_i$ is isomorphic to some $\mathcal{B}_1, \ldots, \mathcal{B}_\beta$ over the vocabularies $\tau_1, \ldots, \tau_\beta$, in accordance with the partition. For a $\Phi$ be a $\tau_1$–$\tau_2$ $\mathcal{L}$–translation scheme, the *$\Phi$–Strongly Distributed Fuzzy Structure*, composed from $\mathcal{B}_1, \ldots, \mathcal{B}_\beta$ over $\mathcal{I}$ is the structure $\Phi^*(\mathcal{A})$, or rather any structure isomorphic to it.

Now, our main Theorem 4 can be formulated as follows:

*Theorem 4:*
Let $\mathcal{I}$ be a finitely partitioned index structure, $\mathcal{L}$ be $FFOL$ such that Theorem 2 holds for it. Let $\mathcal{S}$ be a $\Phi$–Strongly Distributed Fuzzy Structure, composed from $\mathcal{B}_1, \ldots, \mathcal{B}_\beta$ over $\mathcal{I}$, as above. For every $\phi \in \mathcal{L}(\tau)$ there are

1) a boolean function $F_{\Phi,\phi}(b_{1,1}, \ldots, b_{1,j_1}, \ldots, b_{I,j_I})$,
2) $\mathcal{L}$–formulae $\psi_{1,1}, \ldots, \psi_{1,j_1}, \ldots, \psi_{\beta,1}, \ldots, \psi_{\beta,j_\beta}$ and
3) $MSOL$–formulae $\psi_{I,1}, \ldots, \psi_{I,j_I}$

such that for every $\mathcal{S}$, $\mathcal{I}$ and $\mathcal{B}_i$ as above with $\mathcal{B}_i \models \psi_{i,j}$ iff $b_{i,j} = 1$ and $\mathcal{I} \models \psi_{I,j}$ iff $b_{I,j} = 1$ we have
$$\mathcal{S} \models \phi \text{ iff } F_{\Phi,\phi}(b_{1,1}, \ldots, b_{1,j_1}, \ldots, b_{I,j_I}) = 1.$$

Moreover, $F_{\Phi,\phi}$ and $\psi_{i,j}$ are computable from $\Phi^\#$ and $\phi$, but are tower exponential in the quantifier rank of $\phi$.

**Proof:** *By analyzing the proof of Theorem 2 with Theorem 3.*

Now, we provide an example of the applicability of our approach. Let us consider the following composition of two input graphs $H$ and $G$. $G$ can be viewed as a display graph, where on each node we want to have a copy of $H$, such that certain additional edges between the copies are added. In practice, this is an extended model on massage passing. The nodes marked with $L^j$ are the communication ports.

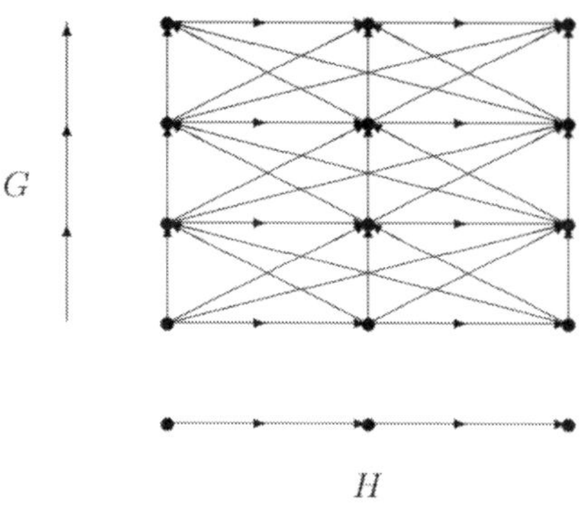


Figure 2. Uniform graph substitution.

Let $G = \langle V_G, R\rangle$ and $H = \langle V_H, S, L^j(j \in J)\rangle$ be two relational structures ($J$ is finite), then their composition

$$\mathcal{S} = \langle V_{\mathcal{S}}, L^1_{\mathcal{S}}, ..., L^{|J|}_{\mathcal{S}}, S_{\mathcal{S}}, R^j_{\mathcal{S}}(j \in J)\rangle$$

is defined as follows, see Figure 2:

- $V_{\mathcal{S}} = \dot{\bigcup}_{g\in G} V^g_H$, where each $V^g_H$ is isomorphic to $V_H$;
- $L^j_{\mathcal{S}}(w)$ is true if $w$ belongs to $L^j$;
- $S_{\mathcal{S}} = \{(w, v) : w \in V^g_H, v \in V^g_H, S(w, v)\}$;
- $R^j_{\mathcal{S}} = \{(w, v) : L^j(w), L^j(v), P(i, w), P(i', v), R(i, i')\}$.

It is easy to see (Figure 2) that this construction can be obtained from the Cartesian product $G \times H$ by a $FOL$ translation scheme without vectorization. However, the Cartesian product cannot be obtained from $\dot{\bigsqcup}_{g\in G} H$ without vectorization. $\mathcal{S}$ can be obtained from the disjoint union $\dot{\bigsqcup}_{g\in G} H$ by a $FOL$ translation scheme. The following proposition makes it precise.

*Proposition 1:*
$\mathcal{S}$ is isomorphic to $\Phi^*(\dot{\bigsqcup}_{g\in G} H)$ with

$$\Phi = \langle \phi, \psi_{L^1_{\mathcal{S}}}, \ldots, \psi_{L^J_{\mathcal{S}}}, \psi_S, \psi_{R^1_{\mathcal{S}}}, \ldots, \psi_{R^J_{\mathcal{S}}}\rangle, \text{ and}$$

$\phi = \exists i(P(i, x) \wedge Index(i))$,
$\psi_{L^j_{\mathcal{S}}} = \exists i((P(i, x) \wedge Index(i)) \wedge L^j(x))$,
$\psi_S = \exists i((Index(i) \wedge (P(i, w) \wedge P(i, v))) \wedge S(w, v))$,
$\psi_{R^j_{\mathcal{S}}} = \exists i \exists i'((((Index(i) \wedge Index(i')) \wedge R(i, i')) \wedge (L^j(w) \wedge L^j(v))) \wedge (P(i, w) \wedge P(i', v)))$.

In this example, depending on the choice of the interpretation of the $L^j$'s, more sophisticated parallel data communication systems can be modeled, but not all.

## V. Outline of the Method

Our general scenario is as follows: given a strongly distributed fuzzy structure $\mathcal{A}$ with index structure $\mathcal{I}$. Formula $\phi$ of fuzzy logic must be evaluated on $\mathcal{A}$.
**The question is**: *What is the reduction sequence of $\phi$ if any?*

Here, we propose a general approach to answer the question and to compute the reduction sequences algorithmically. The general template is defined as follows:

### A. Prove preservation theorems

Given fuzzy logic $\mathcal{L}$.

*1) Define disjoint union of $\mathcal{L}$-structures:* In the general case, we use Definition 2 of *Disjoint Union (DJ)* of the components: $\mathcal{A} = \dot{\bigsqcup}_{i\in I} \mathcal{A}_i$.

*2) Define a preservation property $XX - PP$ for $\mathcal{L}$:* After we introduced the appropriate disjoint union of structures, we define the notion of a *Preservation Property (PP)* for the fuzzy logic.

*3) Prove the $XX - PP$ for $\mathcal{L}$:* Results like Theorem 2 are not always true as it was shown in [26].

### B. Define Translation Schemes

Given fuzzy logic $\mathcal{L}$. Definition 8 introduces the classical *syntactically defined translation schemes* [24]. Definitions 8 gives rise to two induced maps: translations and transductions. Transduction $\Phi^*$ describes the induced transformation of $\mathcal{L}$-structures and the translation $\Phi^{\#}$ describes the induced the induced transformations of logical formulae. The fundamental Theorem 3 should hold for correctly defined $\mathcal{L}$ translation schemes.

### C. Strongly Distributed Fuzzy Structures

Given a $\mathcal{L}$-structure $\mathcal{A}$. At this step, we have defined disjoint unions (and shuffles) of $\mathcal{L}$-structures. Using translation scheme $\Phi$, we introduce the notion of *Strongly Distributed Fuzzy Structures* in Definition 11. Now, the proof of theorems like Theorem 4 should pretty straightforward and provides the desired reduction sequence. In fact, $F_{\Phi,\phi}$ and the $\psi_{i,j}$ of Theorem 4 are computable from $\Phi^{\#}$ and $\phi$. However, we note that they are tower exponential in the quantifier rank of $\phi$.

### D. Incremental Reasoning on Strongly Distributed Fuzzy Systems

Finally, we derive a method for evaluating $\mathcal{L}$-formula $\phi$ on $\mathcal{A}$, which is a $\Phi$-strongly distributed fuzzy composition of its components. The method proceeds as follows:
**Preprocessing:** Given $\phi$ and $\Phi$, but not a $\mathcal{A}$, we algorithmically construct a sequence of formulae $\psi_{i,j}$ and an evaluation function $F_{\Phi,\phi}$ as in Theorem 4.
**Incremental Computation:** We compute the local values $b_{i,j}$ for each component of the $\mathcal{A}$.
**Final Solution:** Now, Theorem 4 states that $\phi$, expressible in the corresponding fuzzy logic $\mathcal{L}$, on $\mathcal{A}$ may be effectively computed from $b_{i,j}$, using $F_{\Phi,\phi}$.

## VI. Conclusion and Outlook

In this work, we introduced the notion of strongly distributed fuzzy systems and presented a uniform approach to incremental automated reasoning on such systems. The approach is based on systematic use of two logical reduction techniques: Feferman-Vaught reductions and the syntactically defined translation schemes.

Our general scenario is as follows: Given a fuzzy structure $\mathcal{A}$ that is composed from structures $\mathcal{A}_i$ ($i \in I$) and index structure $\mathcal{I}$. A formula $\phi$ of fuzzy logic $\mathcal{L}$ describes a property to be checked on $\mathcal{A}$. The question is: What is the reduction sequence for $\phi$, if any such a sequence exists?

We showed that if we can prove preservation theorems for $\mathcal{L}$ as well as if $\mathcal{A}$ is a strongly distributed composition of its components, then the corresponding reduction sequence for $\mathcal{A}$ can be effectively computed algorithmically. In such a case, we derive a method for evaluating an $\mathcal{L}$-formula $\phi$ on $\mathcal{A}$, which is a $\Phi$-strongly distributed composition of its components.

First, given $\phi$ and $\Phi$, but not a $\mathcal{A}$, we algorithmically construct a sequence of formulae $\psi_{i,j}$ and an evaluation function $F_{\Phi,\phi}$. Next, we compute the local values $b_{i,j}$ for each component of the $\mathcal{A}$. Finally, our main theorems state that $\phi$, expressible in the corresponding logic $\mathcal{L}$ on $\mathcal{A}$, is effectively computed from $b_{i,j}$, using $F_{\Phi,\phi}$.

We plan to apply the proposed methodology to the incremental reasoning, based on the promising variations of $WMSOL$ as introduced recently in [34] [35] [36] (see also [37]).

## REFERENCES

[1] R. Ashenhurst, "The decomposition of switching functions," Annals Computation Lab., Harvard Univ., vol. 29, 1959, pp. 74–116.

[2] H. Curtis, A new approach to the design of switching circuits. Van Nostrand, 1962.

[3] L. Zadeh, "Fuzzy sets," Information and Control, vol. 8, no. 3, 1965, pp. 338 – 353.

[4] A. Kandel, "On the decomposition of fuzzy functions," IEEE Trans. Computers, vol. 25, no. 11, 1976, pp. 1124–1130.

[5] A. Kandel and H. Davis, The First Fuzzy Decade: (bibliography on Fuzzy Sets and Their Applications), ser. Computer science report. New Mexico Inst. of Mining and Techn., 1976.

[6] A. Nola, E. Sanchez, W. Pedrycz, and S. Sessa, Fuzzy Relation Equations and Their Applications to Knowledge Engineering. Norwell, MA, USA: Kluwer Academic Publishers, 1989.

[7] J. Vrba, "General decomposition problem of fuzzy relations," Fuzzy Sets and Systems, vol. 54, no. 1, 1993, pp. 69 – 79.

[8] C. Zhong, "A new approach to generate Fuzzy system," in Proceeding of the IEEE Singapore International Symposium on Control Theory and Application, 1997, pp. 250–254.

[9] H. Ying, "Structural decomposition of the general MIMO fuzzy systems," International Journal of Intelligent Control and Systems, vol. 1, no. 3, 1996, pp. 327–337.

[10] M. Mohammadian, "Supervised learning of fuzzy logic systems." Encyclopedia of Artificial Intelligence, 1510-1517(2009), 2009.

[11] Y. Yang and X. Wang, "On the convergence exponent of decomposable relations," Fuzzy Sets and Systems, vol. 151, no. 2, 2005, pp. 403 – 419.

[12] E. Sanchez, "Resolution of composite fuzzy relation equations," Information and Control, vol. 30, no. 1, 1976, pp. 38 – 48.

[13] Y. Yang and X. Wang, "The general $\alpha$-decomposition problem of fuzzy relations," Information Sciences, vol. 177, no. 22, 2007, pp. 4922 – 4933.

[14] A. Seibel and J. Schlattmann, "A generalized $\alpha$-level decomposition concept for numerical fuzzy calculus," in Proceedings of the 16th World Congress of the International Fuzzy Systems Association (IFSA), 2015.

[15] J. Łukasiewicz, "O logice trójwartoćiowej," Ruch Filozoficzny, vol. 5, 1920, pp. 170 – 171.

[16] E. Post, Introduction to a General Theory of Elementary Propositions. Columbia University, 1920.

[17] P. Doherty and D. Driankov, "Nonmonotonicity, fuzziness, and multi-values," in Fuzzy Logic, R. Lowen and M. Roubens, Eds. Dordrecht: Kluwer Academic Publishers, 1993, pp. 3–15.

[18] T. Cao and P. Creasy, "Fuzzy types: a framework for handling uncertainty about types of objects," International Journal of Approximate Reasoning, vol. 25, no. 3, 2000, pp. 217 – 253.

[19] G. Klir and B. Yuan, Fuzzy Sets and Fuzzy Logic: Theory and Applications. Upper Saddle River, NJ, USA: Prentice-Hall, Inc., 1995.

[20] J.-M. Hasemann, "Planning, behaviours, decomposition, and monitoring using graph grammars and fuzzy logic," in Proceedings of the Second International Conference on Artificial Intelligence Planning Systems, University of Chicago, Chicago, Illinois, USA, June 13-15, 1994, 1994, pp. 275–280.

[21] H. Ebbinghaus, J. Flum, and W. Thomas, Mathematical Logic, 2nd edition, ser. Undergraduate Texts in Mathematics. Springer-Verlag, 1994.

[22] H. Ebbinghaus and J. Flum, Finite Model Theory, ser. Perspectives in Mathematical Logic. Springer, 1995.

[23] S. Feferman and R. Vaught, "The first order properties of products of algebraic systems," Fundamenta Mathematicae, vol. 47, 1959, pp. 57–103.

[24] M. Rabin, "A simple method for undecidability proofs and some applications," in Logic, Methodology and Philosophy of Science II, ser. Studies in Logic, Y. B. Hillel, Ed. North Holland, 1965, pp. 58–68.

[25] E. Ravve and Z. Volkovich, "Four scenarios of effective computations on sum-like graphs," in Proc. of the The 9th Intern. Multi-Conference on Computing in the Global Informationin Technology, 2014, pp. 1–8.

[26] E. V. Ravve, Z. Volkovich, and G.-W. Weber, "A uniform approach to incremental automated reasoning on strongly distributed structures," in GCAI 2015. Global Conference on Artificial Intelligence, ser. EasyChair Proceedings in Computing, G. Gottlob, G. Sutcliffe, and A. Voronkov, Eds., vol. 36. EasyChair, 2015, pp. 229–251.

[27] E. Ravve, Z. Volkovich, and G.-W. Weber, "Reasoning on strongly distributed multi-agent systems," in Proceedings of the 17th International Symposium on Symbolic and Numeric Algorithms for Scientific Computing, 2015, pp. 251–256.

[28] C. Chang and H. Keisler, Model Theory, 3rd ed., ser. Studies in Logic, vol 73. North–Holland, 1990.

[29] J. Makowsky, "Compactness, embeddings and definability," in Model-Theoretic Logics, ser. Perspectives in Mathematical Logic, J. Barwise and S. Feferman, Eds. Springer Verlag, 1985, ch. 18.

[30] ——, "Some observations on uniform reduction for properties invariant on the range of definable relations," Fundamenta Mathematicae, vol. 99, 1978, pp. 199–203.

[31] J. Makowsky and E. Ravve, "Incremental model checking for decomposable structures," in Mathematical Foundations of Computer Science (MFCS'95), ser. Lecture Notes in Computer Science, vol. 969. Springer Verlag, 1995, pp. 540–551.

[32] E. Ravve, Z. Volkovich, and G.-W. Weber, "Effective optimization with weighted automata on decomposable trees," Optimization Journal, Special Issue on Recent Advances in Continuous Optimization on the Occasion of the 25th European Conference on Operational Research (EURO XXV 2012), vol. 63, 2014, pp. 109–127.

[33] D. Hilbert and P. Bernays, Grundlagen der Mathematik, I, 2nd ed., ser. Die Grundleheren der mathematischen Wissenschaften in Einzeldarstellungn. Springer Verlag, Heidelberg, 1970, vol. 40.

[34] S. Kreutzer and C. Riveros, "Quantitative monadic second-order logic," in 28th Annual ACM/IEEE Symposium on Logic in Computer Science, LICS 2013, New Orleans, LA, USA, June 25-28, 2013, 2013, pp. 113–122.

[35] N. Labai and J. Makowsky, "Weighted automata and monadic second order logic," in Proceedings Fourth International Symposium on Games, Automata, Logics and Formal Verification, GandALF 2013, Borca di Cadore, Dolomites, Italy, 29-31th August 2013., 2013, pp. 122–135.

[36] B. Monmege, "Spécification et vérification de propriétés quantitatives: Expressions, logiques et automates," Ph.D. dissertation, Laboratoire Spécification et Vérification, École Normale Supérieure de Cachan, Cedex, France, 2013.

[37] N. Labai and J. Makowsky, "Logics of finite Hankel rank," in Fields of Logic and Computation II - Essays Dedicated to Yuri Gurevich on the Occasion of His 75th Birthday, 2015, pp. 237–252.

# Modelling Behavior Patterns in Cellular Networks

T. Couronne
Orange Labs
France Telecom R&D,
Paris, France
Email:Thomas.Couronne@orange-ftgroup.com

V. Kirzner
Institute of Evolution
University of Haifa
Haifa, Israel
Email:valery@research.haifa.ac.il

K. Korenblat, E.V. Ravve, Z. Volkovich
Software Engineering Department
Ort Braude College
Karmiel, Israel
Email:{katerina,cselena,vlvolkov}@braude.ac.il

*Abstract*—**In this paper, we explore customer behavior in cellular networks. We develop a novel model of the fundamental user profiles. The study is based on investigation of activities of millions of customers of Orange, France. We propose a way of decomposition of the observed distributions according to certain external criteria. We analyze distribution of customers having the same number of calls during a fixed period. A segmentation of the population is provided by an approximation of the considered distribution by means of a mixture of several more "basic" distributions presenting the "granularity" of the user's activity. In order to examine the meaning of the found approximation, a clustering of the customers is provided using their daily activity, and a new clustering procedure is constructed. The optimal number of clusters turned out to be three. The approximation is the reduced in the optimal partition to a single-exponential one in one of the clusters and to two double-exponential in others. This fact confirms that the proposed partition corresponds to reliable consequential social groups.**

***Keywords–Consumer behavior pattern; Market segmentation; Probability distribution; Mixture distribution model; Machine learning; Unsupervised classification; Clustering.***

## I. INTRODUCTION

General view of consumer behavior is a study how people, groups and companies purchase, work with and organize goods, services, ideas and knowledge in order to meet their needs and desires [1][2]. Such a multidisciplinary study strives to understand the decision-making processes of customers and serves as a basis for market segmentation. Through market segmentation, large mixed markets are partitioned into smaller sufficiently homogeneous sectors having similar needs, wants, or demand characteristics.

In the cellular networks context, the mentioned products and services can be expressed in spending of the networks resources such as the number of calls, SMS and bandwidth. In fact, market segmentation in this area is able to characterize behavior usage or preferences for each customers' sector; in other words, to typify the customers' profiles, aiming to use this pattern to intimately adopt specific products and services to the clients in each market segment.

The research, presented in this paper, is devoted to developing of a novel model of the fundamental user behavior patterns (user profiles) in the cellular networks. We base our study on analyzing of the underlying distribution of customers having the same number of calls during a fixed period, say a day. A segmentation of the population is provided by an approximation of the considered distribution by means of a mixture of several more "basic" distributions, which present the "granularity" of the user's activity. Actually, the mixture distribution models have come to be conventional in machine learning due to their fruitful applications in unsupervised classification (clustering), where the underling probability distribution is decomposed into a mixture of several simple ones, which correspond to subgroups (clusters) with high inner homogeneity.

Hypothetically, each one of these sets corresponds to a social group of users having its own dynamics of calls depending upon the individual group social parameters. As it will be demonstrated in this contribution, an empirical densities of the studied underlying distributions are monotone decreasing and do not exhibit multi-modality. These properties characterize mixtures of the exponential distribution [3][4]. Hence, in this research, an exponential distribution mixture model is applied, and a three-exponential distribution well-fits the needed target.

In fact, the common applications, for instance in clustering, of the known *Expectation Maximization algorithm*, which estimates parameters of mixture models, suggests the *Gaussian Mixture Model* of the data. However, many studies are recently devoted to analysis of non-Gaussian processes, which are often related to the power law distributions. Nevertheless, the very existence of such a law does not depend on the particular model, but rather it is a result of the process being non-Gaussian in its own nature. Such models arise in some fields of human endeavor. In fact, the Zipf's law declares that the words occurrences in a text collection is inversely proportional to its position in the sorted frequency list.

In order to explore the meaning of the found approximation, a clustering of the customers is provided using daily activity of the customers. Moreover, a new clustering procedure is constructed in the spirit of the bi-clustering methodology. The estimated optimal number of clusters turned out to be three; in addition, the mentioned approximation is the reduced in the optimal partition to a single-exponential one in one of the clusters and to two double-exponential in others. This fact confirms that the proposed partition corresponds to reliable consequential social groups. Here, we emphasize the fact that the similarity measure, applied in the clustering process, is formed without any reference to the previously discussed mixture model.

The results, reported in the paper, are obtained by means of a study of the daily activity of a real group of users during the period from March 31, 2009 through April 11, 2009. For each considered day, several million users in this group are active (making one or more calls), and the time location of each input or output call is known. The sets of active users on different days vary significantly.

The remainder of this paper is structured as follows. Section II is devoted to a distribution model of the user activity and its decomposition. Section III describes the customer clustering procedure and its evaluations. Section IV summarizes the paper.

## II. Distribution Model of User Activity

In this section, we consider a mixture model approximation of the underlying distribution of users having the same number of calls during a day ($DSN$ distribution). We distinguish two types of user activity: input calls (Activity 1) and output calls (Activity 2). All users (about five millions) are divided into groups according to their number of calls per day. The $i$-th group contains all customers having exactly $i$ calls per a day. The size of the $i$-th group is denoted by $N_i$.

Obviously, the groups' content and sizes are, generally speaking, not the same for different days. The amount groups with $i > 100$ is very small in the dataset. They are most likely containing "non-standard" users: sales agents, call centers and so on. We discard such groups together with users, who do not call at all in a given day. Actually, this lack of activity could be explained by factors, which are not directly related to the user activity on the network.

De facto, for all collected days, the curves are of almost the same monotonically decreasing form. On the other hand, it is naturally to assume that the underlying population is actually a mix of several different sub-populations. Practically, a mixture distribution model with exponential components appears to be an appropriate approximation to $DSN$. Mixture distribution models appear in many applications such as an inherent and straightforward tool in order to pattern the population heterogeneity. The assumption about exponential distributed mixture components commonly invokes in the study of lifetime or more universal duration data. We give the following simple $k$-finite exponential mixture model, having density function of the form

$$f(x) = \sum_{j=1}^{k} A_j exp(-t_j x), \tag{1}$$

where $A_j$ and $t_j$, $j = 1, ...k$ are non-negative numbers, and $\sum_{j=1}^{k} A_j = 1$.

For a given number of components $k$, the *Expectation–Maximization algorithm* is a traditional method for maximum likelihood estimates for finite mixtures. This well understandable technique is much admired because it satisfies a monotonic convergence property and can be easily implemented. Nevertheless, there are several known drawbacks of the method. In fact, if there are multiple maxima, the algorithm may discover a local maximum, which is not a global one. Moreover, the obtained solution strongly depends on the initial values selection (see, e.g. [5]).

In this contribution, another approach in the spirit of the linear regression methodology is applied without any prior suggestion about the components number $k$. For this purpose, we initially form the explanatory variable $X = (1, 2, ..., 100)$ and the response $Y$, which for each value $x \in X$ is composed of the logarithm values of the normalized frequencies of $DSN$ in a day: $ln\left(f(x)\right)$.

Using the standard simple regression methodology (see, e.g. [6]), a linear regression model is identified: $Y = a + bX$ and the first estimation of the density $f(x)$ in (1) is constructed $f^{(1)}(x) = A_1 \exp(-t_1 x)$, for $A_1 = \exp(a)$ and $t_1 = -b$. In the next step, a new response is built $Y = ln\left(f(x) - f^{(1)}(x) + C\right)$, where $C$ is a sufficiently positive number, insuring that $f(x) - f^{(1)}(x) + C > 0$ for all $x$ and $j$; then, the described procedure is repeated and so on. In each step, $p$-value coefficient of significance:

$$F = \frac{R^2(X,Y)}{1 - R^2(X,Y)}(100 - 1) \tag{2}$$

is calculated. The process is stopped if the actual $p$-value is greater than the traditional level of significance 0.05. Here, $R(X, Y)$ is the *Pearson correlation coefficient* between $X$ and $Y$. For all cases of daily activity, the method has been stopped after three components were extracted.

TABLE I. $p$-VALUES

| component number | 1 | 2 | 3 | 4 |
|---|---|---|---|---|
| $p$-value | 0 | 8.6e-06 | 0.025 | 0.282 |

The parameters of model (1), calculated for each of the 13 studied days, demonstrate high stability of the exponent indexes $(t_1, t_2, t_3)$, which are practically independent on time but are rather somewhat different on the weekends, i.e. Saturday (4.04 and 11.04) and Sunday (5.04). Amplitudes $A_1, A_2, A_3$ differ to a greater degree (in percentage terms). Thus, the absolute number of active users varies from day to day to a greater extent than the distribution pattern, which actually corresponds to a set of exponent indexes. The $p$-values, calculated for the first of the considered days, are presented in Table I.

In the case of input calls, the ratio of the exponent indexes is: $3 \cdot t_1 \approx t_2, 3 \cdot t_2 \approx t_3$. In the case of output calls, this ratio is somewhat different: $2 \cdot t_1 \approx t_2, 3.5 \cdot t_2 \approx t_3$. The decay value, $x_0$, of each component in (1) is chosen to normalize the component value at this point to 1. The components are not equivalent in the sense of their decay value. Thereby, the exponent with index $t_3 = 1.0$ and amplitude $A_3 = 500,000$ (these parameter values are typical of one of the three exponents, which constitute the daily activity) already decays at $x_0 = 13$. For the second typical pair of parameter values ($t_2 = 0.33$ and $A_2 = 400,000$), the decay occurs at $x_0 = 39$. The exponent with $t_1 = 0.12$ and $A_1 = 90,000$ has the longest effect on $DSN$ ($x_0 = 95$).

Accordingly, two of the three components that describe user activity disappear in the middle of the considered interval of calls. Only the third exponent continues, and its values can be considered to represent the "asymptotic behavior" of the distribution. The relatively complex nature of the obtained empirical distribution model of user activity may be indicative of the heterogeneity of the entire set of users. This set is conceivably composed of a few groups such that the total user activity in a group is described by a certain simpler distribution.

Obviously, the social status, gender and age of the users affect their activity on telephone networks; however such type of personal data is not available for us. Therefore, in the following section we divide the users into groups based merely on the features of their individual activity during a given day.

## III. User classification

As it was justified in the previous section, we proceeded from the assumption that the obtained three-component exponential mixture model reflects the inner customers' behavior patterns, demonstrated by the data. In order to identify these patterns, all the users under investigation are divided into groups according to a comparable daily performance.

A straightforward clustering of the original data is hardly expected to deliver a robust and meaningful partition. Actually, such a situation is a common place in the current practice. Moreover, in many applications, the aim is to reveal not merely potential clusters, but also a quite small number of variables, which adequately settle that partition. For instance, the sparse $K$-means, proposed in [7], at once discovers the clusters and the key clustering variables.

A procedure in the spirit of such a bi-clustering methodology, where features and items are simultaneously clustered, is applied in this paper. First of all, 24 hours inside a day (the features) are clustered according to the corresponding users' activity. In the next step, the users are divided in groups according to their occurrences in the hour's partition. As a result, a sufficiently robust clustering of users is obtained together with the clusters' description in terms of the call activity.

### A. Clustering of hours

In order to outline a similarity between hours in a day, we consider each hour as a distribution of users across the actual numbers of calls within this hour. It means: how many people did not call at all in this hour, how many people called just one time, two times and so on.

A dissimilarity between hours from the point of view of the users' behavior can be naturally characterized by a distance between the corresponding distributions. Generally speaking, any asymptotically distribution-free statistic is suitable for this purpose. In this study, we employ the well-known *Kolmogorov-Smirnov ($KS$) two sample test statistic* (see, e.g., [8][9]), which is actually the maximal distance between two empirical normalized cumulative distribution functions.

Calculating the $KS$-distance for each pair of hours, we get a $24 \times 24$ distance matrix. Now, the *Partitioning Around Medoids ($PAM$) clustering algorithm* (see, e.g., [10]) is applied in order to cluster the data. This algorithm operates merely with a distance matrix, but not with the items themselves; it is feasible for small data sets (such as considered one composed from 24 hours) and a small number of clusters. In order to divide a data set into $k$ clusters using $PAM$, firstly, $k$ objects from the data are chosen as initial cluster centers (medoids) with the intention to attain the minimal total scattering around them (to reduce the loss function value). Then, the process iteratively replaces each one of these center points by non-center ones with the same purpose. If any further change cannot improve the value of the loss function then the procedure ends.

Except of the clustered data, $PAM$ includes as an input parameter the number of clusters $k$. Hence, the first step of our procedure is devoted to estimation of the optimal number of hour's clusters. For this purpose, the well-known *Silhouette coefficient* of [11] is employed. Here, ideas of both cohesion and separation are combined, but for individual points, as well as for partitions. For each point, the Silhouette index takes values in $[-1, 1]$ interval, such that the Silhouette mean value, calculated across the whole data, close to one specifies "well clustered" data, and value -1 characterizes a very "poor" clustering solution. Therefore, the Silhouette mean value, found for several different numbers of clusters, can indicate the most appropriate number of clusters by its maximal value. The number of clusters was checked in the interval of $[2-10]$, and the optimal one was found to be 3 for all the considered data sets (i.e., for all considered days). An example of Silhouette plots (for 05.04 and 10.04) is shown in Fig. 1.

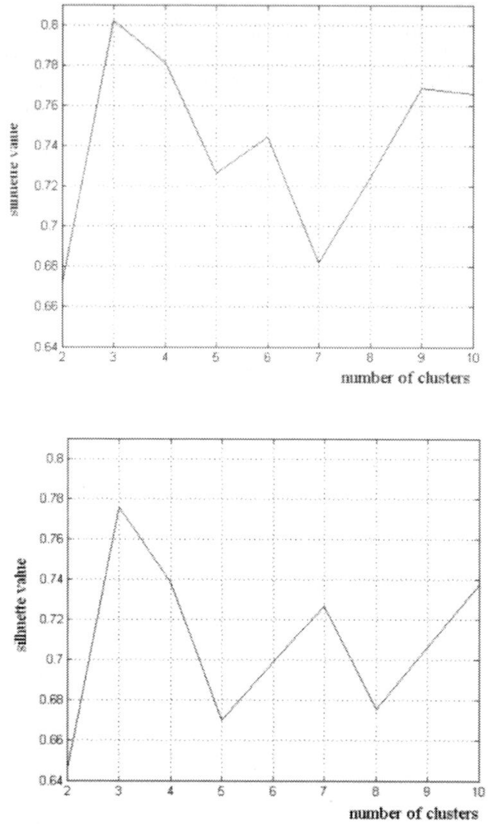


Figure 1. Silhouette plots for 05.04 (upper) and 10.04 (lower)

From the observed partition of 24 hours into 3 hour clusters, it can be concluded that although the partitions slightly depend on the particular data set (date), the overall structure of the clusters is preserved. Namely, there is a silent 'night' cluster, an active 'day' cluster, and a 'morning/evening' cluster.

*1) Clusterization procedure:* Now, every user is represented by means of a three dimensional vector $(r_1, r_2, r_3)$, where $r_i$ is the ratio of a user's activity during a cluster of hours number $i$. More precisely, it is a fraction of a user's calls during the cluster $i$ in the total number of calls during a day. The proposed resampling clustering procedure is based on the well-known $K$*-means* (see, e.g., [12]) algorithm, implementing de-facto the idea, proposed in [13].

The $K$-means algorithm has two input parameters: the

number of clusters $k$ and the data set to be clustered $X$. It strives to find a partition $\pi(X) = \{\pi_1(X), \ldots, \pi_k(X)\}$ minimizing the following loss function

$$\rho_{\{c_1,\ldots c_k\}}(\pi(X)) = \frac{1}{N}\sum_{j=1}^{k}\sum_{x\in\pi_j(X)} \|x - c_j\|^2, \qquad (3)$$

where $c_j$, $j = 1, \ldots, k$ is the mean position (the cluster centroid) of the objects belonging to cluster $\pi_j(X)$, and $N$ is the size of $X$. Initially, the centroid set can be predefined or chosen randomly. Using the current centroid set, the $K$-means algorithm assigns each point to the nearest centroid, aiming to form the current clusters, and, then, recalculates centroids as the clusters means.

The process is reiterated until the centroids are stabilized. In the general case, as a result of this procedure, the objective function (3) reaches its local minimum. As a matter of fact, in the $K$-means algorithm, a partition is unambiguously defined by the centroid set and vise versa. Moreover, in the general case, the loss function (3) can be used for assessing the quality of arbitrary partition $\widehat{\pi}(X)$ with respect to the given set of centroids $\{c_1, \ldots c_k\}$.

The resampling procedure allows partitioning a large data set, based upon partitioning its parts. The algorithm is presented below:

*Algorithm 1:* **Input:**

- $X$ - dataset to be clustered;
- $k$ - the number of clusters;
- $N$ - the number of samples;
- $m$ - the sample size.
- $\varepsilon$ - the threshold value.

**Procedure:**

1) Randomly draw $N$ samples of size $m$ from $X$ without replacement.
2) For each sample $S_i$
   a) In the first iteration, the centroid set $C$ is chosen randomly.
   b) Clustering $S_i$ by $K$-means algorithm with starting from the given centroid set $C$.
   c) Clustering $\pi(X)$ of the whole data set by assignment to the nearest centroid using centroids obtained in the previous step.
   d) Calculate the object function value of $\pi(X)$ according to (3).
3) Choose from a set $\{S_1, \ldots, S_N\}$ a sample $S_0$ with the minimal object function value.
4) If the first iteration is being processed or if the absolute difference between two minimal object function values calculated for two sequential iterations is greater than $\varepsilon$, replace $C$ with the set of centroids of $\pi(S_0)$, and return to step 2; otherwise stop.

*2) Choosing number of users' clusters:* In order to evaluate the optimal number of clusters, it is natural to compare stability of the obtained partition for different cluster numbers. To this end, we repeat the user clustering procedure ten times on the same data set and evaluate the Rand index value between all obtained partitions. The *Rand index* [14], represents the measure of similarity between two partitions. It is calculated by counting the pairs of samples, which are assigned to the same or to different clusters in these partitions. The closeness of the Rand index value to 1 indicates similarity of the considered partitions.

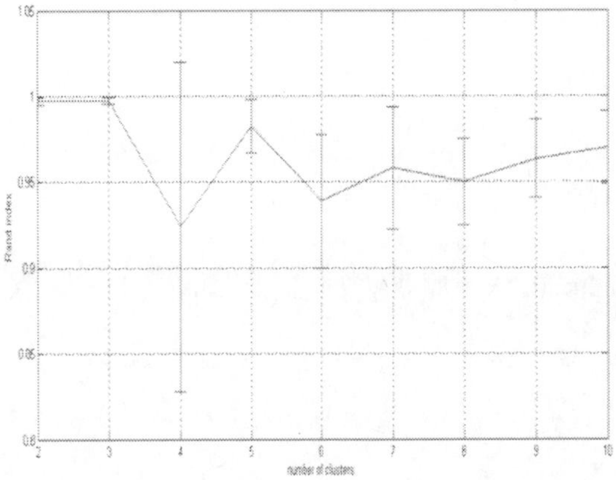


Figure 2. Rand index plot for the dataset 01.04

TABLE II. MINIMUM OF AVERAGE DISTANCES TO THE NEAREST CENTROID FOR THE FIRST 5 ITERATIONS OF RESAMPLING PROCEDURE

| iteration num | 1 | 2 | 3 | 4 | 5 |
|---|---|---|---|---|---|
| min avg of dist | 0.014487 | 0.013302 | 0.013295 | 0.013309 | 0.0132901 |

For the same purpose also *Adjusted Rand index* [15], which is the corrected-for-chance version of Rand index, can be used. However, in our consideration, it is suitable to use the regular one because it well reflects partitions' closeness. The mean value of the obtained Rand indexes naturally characterizes partition stability by its maximal value. Thereby, the 'true' number of clusters corresponds to the most stable partition.

### *B. Experimental study*

*1) 'True' number of clusters estimation:* In order to estimate the optimal number of clusters in the users' clusterization procedure, we repeat the clustering stability evaluation procedure, described in Section III-A2, for each of the possible numbers of clusters in the interval $[2, 10]$. The results for all dates are very similar. Fig. 2 demonstrates an example of Rand-index curve for 01.04. It is easy to see that the maximal stability attitudes appear for $N = 2$ and $N = 3$.

Recall that the purpose of the user clustering is to recognize behavior patterns, which represent the general structure of the user population. Let us consider two possible estimators for 'true' number of clusters from this point of view. We describe a behavior pattern via an average level of the users' activity within each of 3 hour clusters, defined in Section III-A. In this way, we take a three-dimensional representation of users and calculate the mean as well as standard deviation of each coordinate in each user cluster.

The user activity patterns, found for 01.04, are shown in Fig. 3 by means of the error bar plot of values in each hour cluster. Recall that for the given data we obtained a 'night'

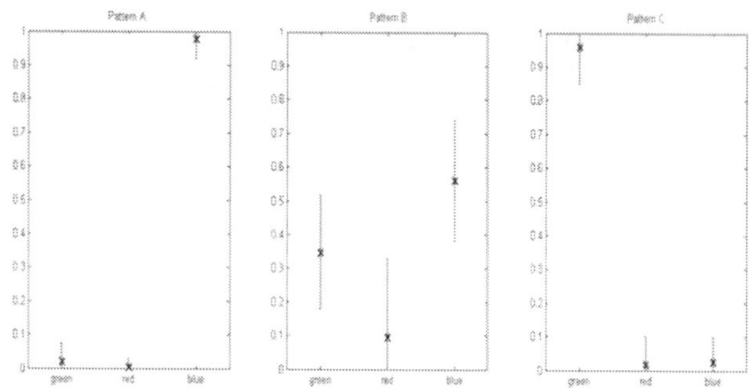

Figure 3. Profiles of 3 customer clusters for work day (01.04; Activity 1)

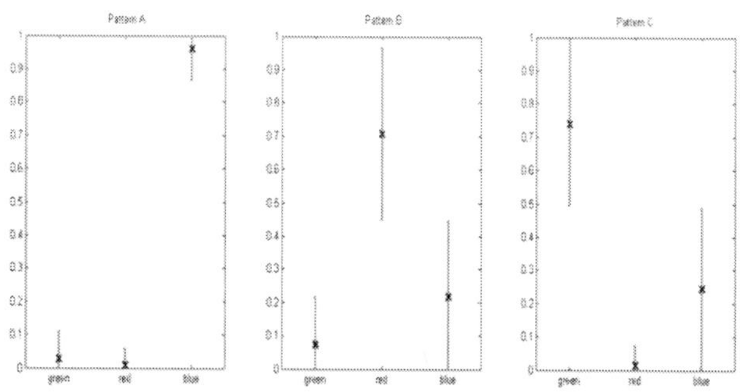

Figure 4. Profiles of 3 customer clusters for off day (05.04; Activity 1)

cluster with hours 1-8; a 'day' cluster with hours 11-21; and a 'morning/evening' cluster containing hours 9-10 and 22-24. For example, pattern A (the left panel in the picture) is characterized by the prevalence of the day activity since the average activity value is 0.84 for the 'day' hour cluster, in comparison with the values of 0.09 and 0.06 for the other hour clusters. Similarly, the behavior pattern B (the middle panel) describes users with significant activity in all hour clusters, while the pattern C (the right panel) is characterized by high activity in the morning-evening hours.

The obtained result shows that we have a "clear" partition into 2 clusters and that one of them is well divided into 2 more sub-clusters. In fact, the two-clusters partitions contain the cluster corresponding to Pattern B and the united cluster for Patterns A and C. For our purposes, therefore, it is natural to choose 3 as the "true" number of clusters. Actually, it is a common situation in cluster analysis, where the "ill-pose" number of clusters determination task can have several solutions depending on the model resolution.

*2) Procedure convergence:* Now, we demonstrate that the resampling clustering procedure converges very fast. Table II shows the minimal objective function values for the first five iterations of the resampling procedure, conducted on 100 samples for $k = 3$ (for others $k$ the situation is similar). The results show that even in the second iteration the minimal average of the distances does not change significantly as compared to the first iteration. In the subsequent iterations, this value remains constant to within 0.0001.

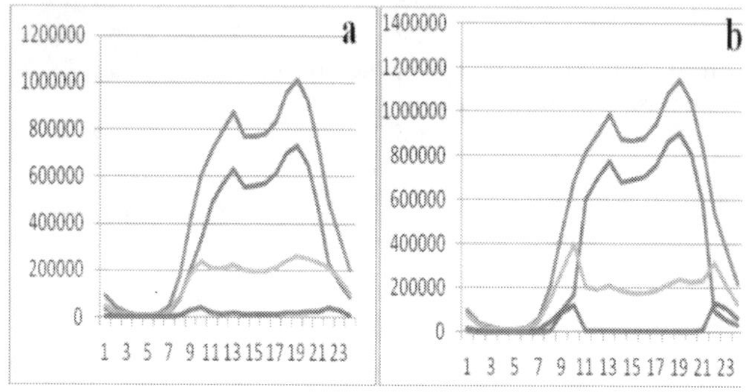


Figure 5. (a) Distribution of Activity 1 for the clusters obtained for Activity 2. (b) Distribution of Activity 1 for the clusters obtained for Activity 1. Date: 08.04.

*3) Profile stability:* Further, we use the behavior patterns for comparison of the results of our procedure on different datasets. The obtained results show that they are stable both for work days and off days. However, the difference between work and off days is significant (see Fig. 3 and 4 for comparison).

Although, qualitative descriptions of profiles are very similar in both cases: pattern A with prevalent "day" activity; pattern B with significant activity throughout 24 hours and pattern C with prevalent "morning-evening" activity; in off days higher "night" activity is detected.

### C. Call activity, associated within patterns

Let us consider the call activity of users, located in each one of the found clusters. The total activity of all the users within a day has a density with two peaks. One of them is placed in the workday middle, and the second one, the higher peak, is located in the period after 7 p.m such that a local activity minimum is observed immediately after. The shape of the corresponding density in the first cluster (A) is actually the same. However, the user's activity almost does not vary in the second cluster (B), i.e. the density curve has several insignificant peaks, and the activity decreases at 10 p.m. The total activity of the users belonging to cluster three (C) has two peaks located in the morning and in the evening of a day.

Furthermore, we observe that the distribution of calls during a day for all three clusters is almost independent on the activity type, see Fig. 5. Here, the blue curves corresponds to the total activity densities of all the users; the red, green and brown ones give the total activity densities for clusters 1, 2 and 3, respectively. Note that both activity types have the same distribution shapes.

*1) Features of the cluster model parameters:* The model, which we use, reveals major differences between the $DSN$ of the entire set of users and the $DSN$'s for the individual clusters. For Activity 1, the $DSN$ for Cluster 1 is almost always best fitted by a single exponent. However, in more than half of the cases, the $DSN$ for Cluster 2 is fitted by two exponents. Moreover, during the weekend period, the curve is fitted by three exponents. The $DSN$ for Cluster 3 is usually fitted by two exponents, while the three-exponent fit sometimes arises without regard for the day of the week. For Activity 2, the above regularities are more pronounced for Clusters 1 and 2, since all the best fits for Cluster 3 are two-exponential.

Our results demonstrate an obvious simplification of the $DSN$s for Clusters 1-3 as compared to the $DSN$ for the total set of users. Nevertheless, joining any two of these clusters results in a three-component $DSN$. At the same time, random partition into three clusters (with the same number of users as in the calculation of Clusters 1, 2, 3 as mentioned above) yields the same three exponent indexes, $t_1 = 0.11$, $t_2 = 0.31$ and $t_3 = 1.01$ for all three clusters. The results coincide with those calculated for the total set of users on the same day.

Thus, simplification of the cluster model shows that the partition into Clusters 1-3 actually reflects different activity characteristics for different groups of users. There are some differences on the weekends, but on the whole the parameters of a particular $DSN$ are the same for each day. Note also that the $DSN$'s of Clusters 2 and 3 are not in the least close to the second or third component (exponent) of the total set $DSN$. Indeed, in our model, the $DSN$ of Cluster 2 consists mainly of two exponents, with one exponent disappearing at the decay value of 30, while the other as a rule not decaying up to the value of 70. The $DSN$ of Cluster 3 also has long-lasting components (up to 100 and more).

## IV. CONCLUSION

In the present study, we are interested in the mechanisms, which generate non-Gaussian distributions. We investigate the reason that non-Gaussian distributions occur in the social sciences. Internet activity and, in particular user activity on social networks, appears to be an appropriate area for such analysis. Numerous studies suggest different models of social networks and try to link particular network characteristics to some measure of the user activity. These characteristics often obey the hyperbolic law in one form or another.

Although, the social activity distribution of a population takes a specific and constant form, it can be assumed that the observed distribution is in some sense an averaged one. Obviously, it is composed of various types of distributions, generated by different social layers. We have in mind not only the groups, arising from the simplest types of differences such as age and gender, but also the more complex features of the population under consideration. It can be assumed that the demonstration of the hyperbolic law or, in contrast, the combination of distribution laws for various social groups, depends on the nature of the user joint activity. In some cases, each user's action is in some sense sequential, so that their average behavior can be considered in the framework of a single law.

An example of parallel user activity is the number of records in an email address book, cf. [16]. In cases, where users' actions occur in parallel, each user group, which is uniform with respect to some criterion, can generate its own law of activity distribution. Since telephone calls are also more likely to be a parallel user's activity in the sense.

In this research, we expected to find that the observed distribution of calls is the sum of several distribution functions, corresponding to different social groups of users. The limited number of these groups is an important prerequisite for such differentiation because averaging over the groups is absent in this case. In [17], we introduced the notion of user strategy (with respect to alternating different types of telephone activity) and showed that the number of different strategies is small.

Therefore, we expected to obtain a small number of groups with equivalent user activity. Having no real-life socio-relevant parameters, we assumed that the peculiarities of a user's activity during a day may correlate with the user's social status. Finally, we partitioned the results into three clusters, with 70, 21, and 9 user percentages in these clusters. We showed that these clusters have simpler distribution functions than those for the total population.

## REFERENCES


[1] I. Simonson, Z. Carmon, R. Dhar, A. Drolet, and S. Nowlis, "Consumer research: in search of identity," Annual Review of Psychology, vol. 52, 2001, pp. 249–275.

[2] P. Kotler and K. Keller, Marketing Management, ser. MARKETING MANAGEMENT. Pearson Prentice Hall, 2006.

[3] N. Jewell, "Mixtures of exponential distributions," The Annals of Statistics, vol. 10, no. 2, 1982, pp. 479–848.

[4] J. Heckman, R. Robb, and J. Walker, "Testing the mixture of exponentials hypothesis and estimating the mixing distribution by the method of moments," Journal of the American Statistical Association, vol. 85, no. 410, 1990, pp. 582–589.

[5] A. Dempster, N. Laird, and D. Rubin, "Maximum likelihood from incomplete data via the EM algorithm," Journal of the Royal Statistical Society, vol. 39, no. 1, 1977, pp. 1–38.

[6] J. Kenney and E. Keeping, "Linear regression and correlation," in Mathematics of Statistics: Part 1, 3rd ed. NJ: Princeton, Van Nostrand, 1962, ch. 15, pp. 252–285.

[7] D. Witten and R. Tibshirani, "A framework for feature selection in clustering," Journal of the American Statistical Association, vol. 105, no. 490, 2010, pp. 713–726.

[8] R. Lopes, P. Hobson, and I. Reid, "The two-dimensional Kolmogorov-Smirnov test," in Proceeding of the XI International Workshop on Advanced Computing and Analysis Techniques in Physics Research, Nikhef, Amsterdam, the Netherlands, April 23-27, 2007. Proceedings of Science, 2007.

[9] ——, "Computationally efficient algorithms for the two-dimensional Kolmogorov-Smirnov test," Journal of Physics: Conference Series, vol. 119, no. 4, 2008, p. 042019.

[10] L. Kaufman and P. Rousseeuw, Finding groups in data: an introduction to cluster analysis, ser. Wiley series in probability and mathematical statistics. New York: Wiley, 1990, a Wiley-Interscience publication.

[11] P. Rousseeuw, "Silhouettes: A graphical aid to the interpretation and validation of cluster analysis," Journal of Computational and Applied Mathematics, vol. 20, 1987, pp. 53 – 65.

[12] D. MacKay, Information Theory, Inference & Learning Algorithms. New York, NY, USA: Cambridge University Press, 2002.

[13] J. Kogan, C. Nicholas, and M. Teboulle, Grouping Multidimensional Data: Recent Advances in Clustering, 1st ed. Springer Publishing Company, Incorporated, 2010.

[14] N. Vinh, J. Epps, and J. Bailey, "Information theoretic measures for clusterings comparison: Is a correction for chance necessary?" in Proceedings of the 26th Annual International Conference on Machine Learning, ser. ICML '09. New York, NY, USA: ACM, 2009, pp. 1073–1080.

[15] S. Wagner and D. Wagner, "Comparing Clusterings – An Overview," Universität Karlsruhe (TH), Tech. Rep. 2006-04, 2007.

[16] M. Newman, S. Forrest, and J. Balthrop, "Email networks and the spread of computer viruses," Physical Review E, vol. 66, Sep 2002, p. 035101.

[17] T. Couronné, V. Kirzhner, K. Korenblat, and Z. Volkovich, "Some features of the users activities in the mobile telephone network," Journal of Pattern Recognition Research, vol. 1, 2013, pp. 59–65.

**International Academy, Research,**
**and Industry Association (IARIA)**
412 Derby Way
Wilmington, DE 19810

CURRAN ASSOCIATES INC.
proceedings.com

ISBN 978-1-5108-3370-8

9 781510 833708